APPLICATION OF INFORMATION TECHNOLOGIES TO THE MARITIME INDUSTRY

Edited by
C. Guedes Soares
Instituto Superior Técnico

J. Brodda
BALance Technology Consulting

© Copyright 1997 – 1999 MAREXPO Consortium

MAREXPO is funded by the EU ESPRIT programme for information technology. The contents of this publication does not necessarily reflect the official opinions of the European Commission. All individual presentations are courtesy of the particular projects and their respective partners and companies. It may not be copied, reproduced or modified in whole or in part for any purpose without written permission. In addition to such written permission, acknowledgement of the authors of the source and all applicable portions of the copyright notice must be clearly referenced. All rights reserved.

Cover: Marta Figueiredo

Printed by:
PUBLISAN – Publicidade e Serviços, Lda. – Santarém
June, 1999

ISBN: 972-689-157-4
Depósito Legal: 140 686/99

Portuguese Publisher:
EDIÇÕES SALAMANDRA, LDA
Campo Pequeno, 50-2º esq.
1000-081 Lisboa

Distribution: Sodilivros, Lda.
Rua de Campolide, 183-B – 1070 Lisboa
Telefones: 387 89 02/3 – Fax: 387 62 81

FOREWORD

It is an actual challenge for the industry, the European Member States and the European Union to maintain and improve the position of its maritime industries. In order to retain technological leadership and to fully utilise productivity and improvement potentials, efforts must be concentrated on human resources, research and development and the exploitation of information technology.

An efficient maritime industry can guarantee that Europe will be in a position to participate adequately and successfully in international trade, and benefit from the exploitation of the oceans. Therefore, the current situation in the different maritime industries and their adjustment and development processes, as well as their willingness to co-operate, are of importance to Europe's future.

In this respect "information" as a vital resource has a significant impact on the maritime future. For those maritime players able to exploit and further develop this resource, a maritime information society will be a liberating experience, giving more individual choices, business and employment opportunities and cultural enrichment.

The European maritime industry is a high tech industry with a strong economic potential. Ships and offshore devices are complex and large multifunctional systems combining different technologies, like materials, propulsion systems, electronics and navigation technologies, which have to be integrated into a system in close co-operation with the supplier industry. The production of modern cruise ships, high speed ferries, advanced merchant ships and sophisticated naval vessels places increasing demands from the technological and logistical point of view. Advanced tools for engineering allow the ultimate optimisation of material, travelling speed and any kind of resource consumption, for example fluid dynamics calculation, structural analysis including finite element calculations using high performance computing.

In this sense, the project MAREXPO, in which context this book has been edited, is committed to the dissemination of knowledge on maritime research, technology and development, especially to results achieved in projects running under the European Union's information technology programme Esprit in close connection to the G7 project on the Maritime Information Society (MARIS). Results from European R&D programmes supported the transition of traditional shipbuilding towards a high technology industry during the last decade. MAREXPO increases awareness of Information and Communication Technologies and shows its potential to improve the industry's competitiveness in different maritime business processes. MAREXPO supports the Commission's R&D programmes and stimulates the rapid take-up and implementation of R&D results in industry, by disseminating knowledge on best practice implementation.

For the target group of small and medium sized enterprises from all maritime sectors MAREXPO prepared a set of show material which introduces the maritime industry as a high tech industry, gives an overview of the European research and development mechanisms and provides easy access to research and development results achieved within the information technology programme Esprit. The show material comprises a set of posters, a brochure, a multimedia CD-ROM and a presentation in the world wide web. MAREXPO presented European maritime research on 21 major fairs, conferences and workshops world-wide within the period from August 1997 to June 1999. Furthermore, MAREXPO successfully contributed to the European Pavilion at the EXPO 98 in Portugal with three demonstrators illustrating high technology in the life cycles of ships for ship design, automated manufacturing, and survey.

A consortium of eight European companies comprising Odense Steel Shipyard (DK), Kockums Computer Systems (S), Det Norske Veritas (N), Instituto Superior Técnico (P), Bremen Institute of Industrial Technology and Applied Work Science (D), TNO (NL) and ArchiMedia (GR) was working on MAREXPO under co-ordination of BALance Technology Consulting (D). It was a great pleasure to work with this group of advanced and experienced scientists and it is our personal feeling that we have succeeded in a contribution towards a European integration. We would like to take this opportunity to thank the consortium for their co-operative way of working, valuable contributions and their friendship.

The MAREXPO book is a final activity of the project. It provides you as an interested reader with valuable background information about results of maritime research projects with respect to information and communication technology. Beyond results from European projects you will also find contributions from authors around the world. This shows that co-operation in this field is becoming even more international and global. We are convinced that the information contained in this book will help the industry to better understand and apply the state-of-the-art of the technology. This will also lead to an increasing awareness about European supporting measures for co-operative R&D and will lead to an extended participation of the industry in the new R&D schemas offered by the 5th Framework Programme. The consortium is convinced that MAREXPO has supported this development by a sustainable contribution to increase knowledge and awareness in the industry about maritime research in the area of information and communication technology.

We hope you enjoy reading the book.

Carlos Guedes Soares   Joachim Brodda
Instituto Superior Técnico   BALance Technology Consulting

The MAREXPO Consortium is made up of eight leading companies and institutions from the most relevant sectors in maritime industry with significant experience from more than 30 successful European research projects.

INDEX

1. The Concept of Virtual Enterprises and its Relevance for the Maritime Domain — *11*
   C. Odendahl and A.-W. Scheer

2. MARIFlow: A Workflow Management System for Maritime Industry — *33*
   A. Dogac, C. Beeri, A. Tumer, M. Ezbiderli, N. Tatbul, C. Icdem, G. Erus, O. Cetinkaya and N. Hamali

3. Interorganizational Workflow Based on Electronic Data Interchange in Maritime Industry — *53*
   T. Kuhlmann, R. Lampig, C. Massow and J. Schumacher

4. Advanced Supply Chain Management Strategies for the Maritime Industry — *61*
   R. Ahlers and J. Brodda

5. IT Application for Ship Management and Ship Operation — *87*
   E. Rensvik

6. STEP: its rationale, its development and its structure — *105*
   J. Owen

7. The EXPRESS Data Specification Language — *125*
   J. Rangnes

8. Ship Hull Product Model — *147*
   M. Ventura, J. Victoria and C. Guedes Soares

9. MariSTEP – A Prototype of STEP for Shipbuilding — *163*
   B. Gischner, J. Howell, B. Kassel, P. Lazo, C. Sabatini and R. Wood

10. Sharing Structural Design Models using STEP — *177*
    S-H. Han

11. Modelling Shipboard Piping — *195*
    R. Schuler

12. The Use of CAD in the Development of an Engine Room Arrangement Model — *217*
    B. Kassel

13. New ICT Tools in Shipbuilding 233
    M. Cremon and A. Favretto

14. Planning and Scheduling of Shipyard Processes 255
    G. Chryssolouris, N. Papakostas, S. Makris and D. Mourtzis

15. Improving the Competitiveness of SMEs in the European Shiprepair 275
    Sector by the Use of Information Technology
    G. Bruce and A. McDowall

16. Impact of Information Technologies on Ship Classification Procedure 295
    M. Huther and M. F. Renard

17. Multiple Criteria Genetic Algorithms: A Catamaran Design Study 313
    P. Sen, and D. Todd

18. Automatic Fairing and Shape-preserving Methodologies 331
    P. Kaklis and H. Nowacki

19. Variational Principles for Surface Generation and Modification with the 349
    Functional of the Clamped Plate
    A. Nawotki

THE CONCEPT OF VIRTUAL ENTERPRISES AND ITS RELEVANCE FOR THE MARITIME DOMAIN

C. Odendahl[1] and A.-W. Scheer[2]

Institute for Information Systems (IWi), University of Saarland
Im Stadtwald, Geb. 14.1, D-66123 Saarbrücken, Germany
[1]odendahl@iwi.uni-sb.de, [2]scheer@iwi.uni-sb.de

Abstract

Co-operations between enterprises become more and more important. As a possible arrangement of entrepreneurial co-operation Virtual Enterprises are discussed in science and practice. Hereby a virtualisation of the production of goods and services is carried out in the way that goods and services are not being produced by an actually existing enterprise, but via a loose and temporary combination of partner companies. Each partner company of a Virtual Enterprise implements only a special part of the value chain, namely the part, which it can execute best due to its core competencies. The potentials of this co-operation form are a high flexibility in acting and the ability to react quickly to market demands.

In the following chapter the concept of Virtual Enterprises is described at first. Based on this description potentials, tasks and problems of this new co-operation form are mentioned. Furthermore the applicability of Virtual Enterprises in the maritime domain is sketched The section terminates with a summary of the research work which is to be done in the MARVIN project. The MARVIN project aims at supporting a Virtual Enterprise in the maritime domain via the so-called *Maritime Enterprise Integration Tool*.

1 The concept of Virtual Enterprises

1.1 Theoretical Background

The roots of the term "virtual" derive from the Latin word "virtus"(Scholz, 1997). Virtus represents such qualities as "efficiency", "bravery" and "perfection". In our contemporary language the term "virtual" generally represents:

- not real,
- but apparently existing,
- representing a reality,
- capable of having an effect.(Scholz, 1997, Krystek, 1997)

In this respect the representation of a reality is of great importance. Therefore a virtuality exists only if a specific object is represented in that way. According to Scholz (1997) a virtual object is defined by the following four characteristics

1. Constituting characteristics, which show the original as well as the virtualised object.
2. Physical attributes which are normally associated with the original object but which do not exist within the virtualised object.
3. Special additional features which are necessary for the virtualisation of the object.
4. Benefits as advantage which result from the falling away of the physical attributes.

The characteristics can be identified with the help of the concept of the virtual memory of a computer:

1. Constituting characterisation: Ability to store information.
2. Non-existent physical attributes: Non-existent memory chips.
3. Special additional features: hard disc; ability of the computer to process data on the hard disc like in the main memory.
4. Benefits: Ability to process tasks (programs) without having the necessary main memory capacity; cutting down expenses, because hard disc memory is cheaper than main memory.

By this characterisation the virtual object is attached to the quality of being advantageous. But if in the example of the virtual memory the benefit falls away because of a possible reversal of the storage media price relation, it will still be virtual. Therefore this characteristic is further completed to an expected benefit.

The adjective "virtual" describes the quality of an object not to exist in reality but to have the possibility to be available (Hermann, 1996). As far as an enterprise is concerned this is to say that the enterprise does not exist in reality but for the client it seems to be available. From the perceptive and theoretical point of view a virtual enterprise appears to the clients as a "second level reality"(Scholz, 1997). The virtuality is achieved by the co-operation of independent enterprises producing a common service. A single partner enterprise is only active in a defined part of the value-added chain. In this connection Davidow and Malone talk about a *"... shapeless structure with porous and continuously changing boundaries between enterprises, suppliers and clients*"(Davidow and Melone, 1993), which from inside also seems to be formless.

Within the scope of the constitutive characteristics of the virtualised objects the Virtual Enterprise is described as follows (Scholz, 1997):

1. Constituting characteristics: Provision of goods and services, appearance as one enterprise.
2. Non-existent (physical) attributes: e.g. legal framework, eventually previous locations, buildings, contracts, co-ordination forms.
3. Special additional features: Informational technology, new competencies, new concepts of co-ordination.
4. Expected benefits: Higher flexibility, access to new markets.

A management point of view is provided by the understanding of a Virtual Enterprise of Byrne, Brand and Port as "*a temporary network of independent companies - suppliers, customers, even erstwhile rivals - linked by information technology to share skills, costs, and access to one another's market. It will have neither a central office nor organization chart. It will have no hierarchy, no vertical integration.*" (Byrne, Brandt and Port, 1993). In addition to these features a loose union of different enterprises without a common legal basis is demanded (Scholz, 1996).

The definition of a Virtual Enterprise of Mertens and Faisst (1997) provides a completing modification of the definition of Arnold and Härtling (1995) respectively the working definition of Arnold, et al (1995), which tries to derive a consensus from the existing interpretations of the term Virtual Enterprise.

Definition „Virtual Enterprise":

A virtual enterprise is a co-operation form of legally independent enterprises, institutions and/or individuals, that produce a service on the basis of a common business understanding. The co-operating units participate in the horizontal and/or the vertical collaboration major with their core competencies and appear to third parties as a homogeneous enterprise. Furthermore the institutionalisation of central management functions for design, management and development of the Virtual Enterprise are extensively abandoned and the necessary demand for co-ordination and harmonisation is covered by appropriate information and communication systems. The Virtual Enterprise is connected to a mission and ends with this mission.

So they agree with Sydow (1996) and Behme (1995) whereby the latter explicitly emphasises that Virtual Enterprises are in reality an "organisational collective", i.e. it is not *one* enterprise respectively one organisation.

Virtual enterprise partners are better positioned to use emerging market opportunities to their advantage. They stay in a virtual arrangement just as long as they achieve a higher profitability than in their own business or in another co-operative arrangement (Goldman, Nagel and Preiss, 1995). The goal of the co-operation in a Virtual Enterprise is to achieve a market potential that could not be reached by a single enterprise on its own (Dangelmaier, 1996). In order to achieve the primary goal of using the synergy in a Virtual Enterprise, a maximal flexibility of the Virtual Enterprises as well as of the partner enterprises must be guaranteed. The advantages of the Virtual enterprises are founded in the following aspects:

- The collection of complementary core competencies enables the implementation of projects as well as producing outputs which none of the partners could realise as a single entity.
- The entrepreneurial risks and resource costs, in particular for personnel and technology, are distributed among the partners.
- Through the partners' joint and/or complementary business processes, and the diminishing of costs for production, infrastructure, and knowledge it is possible to reduce the time span between product development and commercialisation drastically.
- By participating in Virtual Enterprises the market entry barriers for new enterprises are decreased. Moreover, the virtual arrangement allows for better market coverage as well as the opportunity to leverage the name of a well-known partner.

Basically there are two directions of virtualisation in building up a Virtual Enterprise. The origin of the first possibility is a single enterprise that has so far realised all production processes on its own. By consistent outsourcing enterprise internal process elements and thereby the organisational units that work in these elements are separated from the enterprise. The term outsourcing comes from "**Out**side **Re**source **Using**"(Friedrich, 1996). The goal of outsourcing is to obtain unprofitable resources and competencies from the external market at lower costs and with better quality. Consistently the enterprise concentrates on its core competencies (Prahalad and Hamel, 1991). The enterprises, which are thereby integrated in the production process, are legally and economically independent from the initial enterprise as well as from other organisational units acquired in the same way. Such associations of enterprises are in economical competition according to which the strategy of concentration on an enterprises core competencies is generally considered very positive (Eversheim et. al., 1996, Friedrich, 1995, Markus and Young, 1996). However, because of the concentration on a core competence, when the enterprises form a co-operation, there is the danger of devolving the corresponding know-how upon the partners. In this way a core competence can be weakened (Krüger, Buchholz and Rohm, 1996). Furthermore, in the case of a unilateral concentration, there is the danger of dependency on the corresponding co-operations. Because of this an enterprise would lose a part of its autonomy because it cannot exist without the co-operation. Therefore in the following a competence is demanded for participating in a Virtual Enterprise. The term competence describes the ability to produce a defined output efficiently. The provision of any competence not only core competencies seems to be sufficient if the partners of a Virtual Enterprise can achieve in this way a common goal that could not have been achieved economically by a single enterprise or if the partners would have been competitors (Dangelmaier, 1996).

Because of the improved ability of the externalised enterprises to produce goods and services and the resulting connections from the previous collaboration, the emergence of a new alliance among the partner enterprises is possible. In an extreme case such a co-operation can be considered as a Virtual Enterprise (cf. Figure 1). When focussing the consideration to the industry, this direction of virtualisation, that leads to a Virtual Factory, is characterised by the term Top-Down-Virtualisation (Schuh, 1997). Another term for such a development of a Virtual Enterprise is Quasi-Externalisation (Faisst, 1998).

The origin of the opposite direction of virtualisation is a number of economically and legally independent enterprises. On the basis of the assumption that by co-operation the possibility emerge to produce goods and services in a better way, or to produce a specific output at all, organisation forms are build up such as e.g. Strategic Alliances or Strategic Networks (cf. Figure 1). These co-operation forms are normally long-term oriented and based on the involvement of capital as well as guarantees by contract. But if the corporations are inclined to be short-term oriented and to have a particular flexibility, Virtual Enterprises will be suggested (Ott, 1996). Other terms of this direction of virtualisation are Quasi-Internalisation (Faisst, 1998) and in case of an industrial enterprise Bottom-up-Virtualisation (Schuh, 1997).

The discussion about Virtual enterprises becomes more and more the initiator for the development of new approaches for the solution of specific economic problems (Benjamin and Wigand, 1995). However, the analysis on the topic clearly shows that some problem areas have not yet been satisfactorily addressed:

- The common basis of trust as a foundation for co-operation depends on a profound "culture of trust" (Scholz, 1996). Trust-based relationships can only be developed over a longer period of time, which is contradictory to the temporary structure of virtual enterprises.
- Virtual enterprises rely on loose forms of contracts, which can be quickly realised, e.g. electronic contracts (Byrne, Brandt and Port, 1993). Up to now there are few legal possibilities for such contractual forms.

Thus, questions of legal liability and the granting of warranties have not yet been considered satisfactorily (Szyperski and Klein, 1993).
- The Virtual Enterprise concept also implies that one enterprise may participate in multiple Virtual Enterprises. This increases the possibilities for conflict-of-interest situations, which may have a degrading impact on other trust-based relationships.
- The costs associated with co-ordinating the partners cannot be precisely estimated. Hence, there are no definitive research results on the scope and magnitude of the transactions costs associated with co-ordinating virtual organisations.

Procedures for searching for partners are another area, which merits additional consideration. If there is a lengthy search for partners, it not only causes high costs, but also the time-to-market for new and innovative products is prolonged.

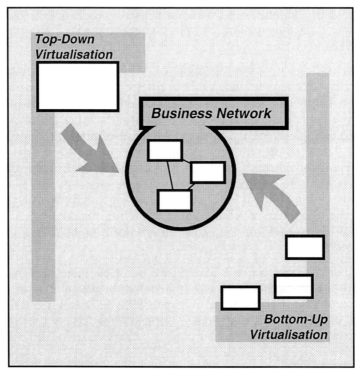

Figure 1: Directions of Virtualisation (in support of Schuh, 1997)

1.2 IT systems for Virtual Enterprises

The business processes emerging in the context of Virtual Enterprises are not only the disassemble of traditional processes along the value-added chain. The processes in a Virtual Enterprise can even be spread over several levels.

For example one level covers entities which are involved in task of preparing the actual process. In this way the construction describes the Virtual Enterprise from a special point of view. Without this specification it is not possible to establish an adequate co-operative arrangement for corresponding order. Thus, on an abstract level the construction has a constituting effect on the Virtual Enterprise. If it is necessary to demand the services of a broker in order to generate the Virtual Enterprise, then this broker will neither be assigned to the actual production. A further level can be built by a sales and distribution department, which is independent of the Virtual Enterprise. In this case the co-operation arrangement has produced for an anonymous market and sold the produced output to the distributor. Then the distributor takes the role of the customer. Taking into account all these aspects one can describe the business processes of a Virtual Enterprise as a two-dimensional structure of competencies (cf. Figure 2). One dimension of the structure is time. The other dimension describes levels of content in the sense of the dependence of one level on the one lying above. The tasks of each level can be performed by a Virtual Enterprise so that it leads to recursive application of the concept.

From the characteristics of Virtual Enterprises, for instance being a temporary arrangement of autonomous entities, specific demands of a support by an information system are derived. The introduction of such information systems has to be performed quickly and easily. Moreover the existence of such an information may not obstruct the dissolution of the co-operation after the successful operation. That means that there should not be any entanglement of capital of the partner companies concerning an information system, which is not used anymore after the termination of the co-operation.

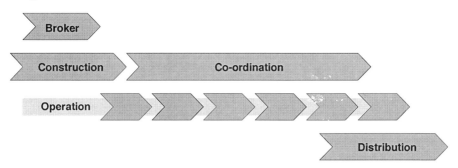

Figure 2: Value-added Chain of Virtual Enterprises

These demands allow a comparison with the demands of an enterprise or a private person concerning the presentation in the World Wide Web (WWW). For building up a web presence it is normally too expensive to operate one's own web server, to integrate the web server into the internet and to let it be administrated by qualified personnel. Instead of this the business of the internet provider has established in this field. The internet provider offers the possibility to rent space on the providers web server. By this means the above mentioned tasks are executed by the provider.

In analogy to the concept of an internet provider a system provider could provide the information system for Virtual Enterprises. By this means the purchase of own soft- and hardware is cut for the participating companies. Of course it is not sufficient only to provide access to a traditional information system in order to support a Virtual Enterprise. The software itself has to be adapted to such a provider concept. For instance the customising has to depict in a way that this process could be carried out quickly and easily. Otherwise the installation of the information system would obstruct the temporality of the Virtual Enterprise.

Because the system provider supports the business processes of the particular Virtual Enterprises and hereby builds up the platform for their operation, he serves different networks simultaneously and still exists after a specific Virtual Enterprise is dissolved, so a three-dimensional structure results, like it is shown in Figure 3.

The provision of an information system by a system provider has to be done via an electronic medium which is accessible for all participants of a Virtual Enterprise and which not only enables the communication but also the interaction between the partner companies. As the most suitable communication platform satisfying those demands the internet, especially the WWW, is currently considered. With about 163,5 million users worldwide (URL Focus, 1999) and over 5 million servers (URL Netcraft, 1999) in nearly 200 countries (URL ISOC, 1998) the WWW is the widest propagated medium for the above mentioned purpose. Further reasons for the adequacy of the WWW are the provision of a graphical user interface, the application of multimedia elements as well as the platform independent usage, which enables the operating system overlapping use of the internet services. The usage by the most popular operating systems (UNIX, MS Windows, Mac OS) is realised by programs for query and presentation of information of the internet, so called browsers.

In the third chapter the research work of the MARVIN project is described. The goal of the MARVIN project is an information system, which supports a Virtual Enterprise in the maritime domain via an integration tool. The integration tool will fit the demands of a system provider. The interaction between the user and the integration tool will be realised via the WWW. The system itself will follow the inherent distribution of the problem domain and will be implemented as a multi-agent-system.

For a better understanding of the concept of Virtual Enterprises in the following chapter the life-cycle of a Virtual Enterprise is described. The description declares the function and task, which have to be managed in a Virtual Enterprise.

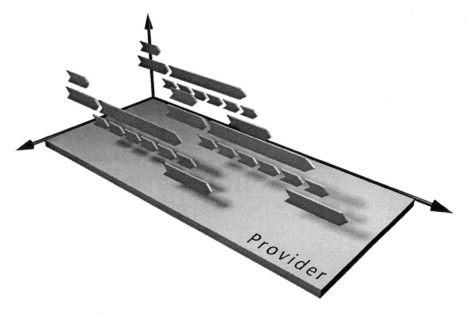

Figure 3: Concept of a system provider

2 Life-cycle of Virtual Enterprises

In this section a life-cycle model for Virtual Enterprises is presented. With the help of this model the functions should be described which have to be supported for the continuous design of Virtual Enterprises.

For the determination of the different phases to be managed during a co-operation one could use the phase model of the project management (Grochla, 1959, Schuber and Küting, 1981, Küting and Zink, 1983). On an abstract level there is a differentiation between planning and operation phases. A more detailed view shows the phases requirement determination, goal definition, partner search, partner selection, co-operation configuration, operation and completion.

For Virtual Enterprises as a possible co-operation form with characteristics described in the first section, these phases can be identified in special. By this means a typical life-cycle for Virtual Enterprises can be derived, because the co-operation is connected to a mission and terminated after cycling the phases.

Figure 4 shows the life-cycle model, which is the basis for the following consideration. The division into the phases identification, partner search, conclusion, operation and dissolution follows the description of Mertens and Faisst (1997).

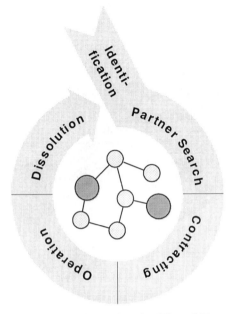

Figure 4: Life-cycle of a Virtual Enterprise

2.1 Identification

In general the identification phase has the task to determine the need to co-operate, the definition of the goal to be gained by co-operation and the definition of the co-operation project. On the one hand there are customers, who are looking for a Virtual Enterprise for special product and on the other hand there are companies that wish to participate in a Virtual Enterprise. So both user groups have to be considered in the continuous design of a Virtual Enterprise.

For a company the reason to think about co-operation could be an innovative business idea with consequence to co-operate, a decision of the management to use co-operation as a future strategy, a query of other companies to co-operate or the determination that special parts of the company have to be outsourced. It is important that for a company the benefit of the co-operation is at least as high as if the company would produce on its own or would not produce the according output (Grochla, 1959). By this means there are two possible starting situations for a company to become a partner of a Virtual Enterprise. In the first case a company is willing to co-operate without a specific product idea. If there is a set of companies without a product idea, a customer can trigger a Virtual Enterprise. That means, the customer is also part of the business. In the second case a company with a specific product idea is looking for partners to produce the concerning output in co-operation. This can happen for instance when the output is produced for an anonymous market. In this case the triggering partner company takes partly the role of the customer.

For an information system which should support a Virtual Enterprise both groups, partner companies and customers, have to be supported in the sense of a company respectively a customer management. In the identification phase the information system has to collect elementary data of the participants. This data builds up the basis for the future support. Because most data is company respectively customer specific, aspects of data security have to be regarded. As a heuristic only data which is necessary should be collected at the time when it is needed. This is also important to avoid a multiple collection of data which are dynamic. An example for such dynamic data is capacity information of a company. The identification of their core competencies is of relevance for companies which want to participate in a Virtual Enterprise. For the customer respectively the company taking the role of the customer the goods and service to be produced by a Virtual Enterprise have to be specified.

2.2 Partner Search

Based on the specification of goods and services during the partner search the corresponding Virtual Enterprise is configured. This process is a selection of the partner companies out of a pool of potential offerers for the different core competencies needed in the Virtual Enterprise.

The description of mechanism to select the most suitable partner companies should clarify the process of partner search. The mechanism is part of the prototype system DEVICE of a co-operation exchange for Virtual Enterprises. The partner search is implemented as a five-layer filtering mechanism (cf. **Figure 5**) (Odendahl, Reimer and Marzen, 1998):

The first filter (competence) selects all companies which have one or more competencies needed for the Virtual Enterprise. The second filter (parameter) determines if the selected companies satisfy the requirements to participate in the Virtual Enterprise. These requirements concern for instance the existence of the communication channels needed for interaction with the information system as well as with the other partner companies. Furthermore the customer can specify requirements which are audited through this filter. An example for a customer demand is the location of the partner companies in a special area or country. This requirement will be relevant if the exchange of material and intermediate products shall be minimized.

The third filter (capacity) is an example for the above mentioned dynamic data. Because this information can only be evaluated depending on the actual workload it is senseless to collect this information in advance. Thus the relevant companies will be asked for this information if this filter is applied. Only companies with sufficient capacity to produce the corresponding part of the value-added chain in the given deadlines are taken into consideration. The evaluation of capacity is important for a frictionless co-ordination of the co-operation arrangement.

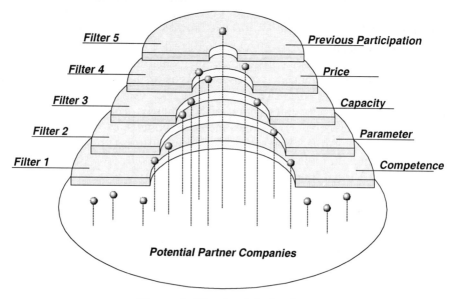

Figure 5: Filtering Mechanism

The fourth filter (price) operates on the cost calculation of the partner companies. Each company which has passed the first three filters is called to prepare a tender for the goods and services, it should bring into the Virtual Enterprise. For each part of the value-added chain only the most attractive companies are taken into further account. In combination with the other filters and the liability of the tender this filter audits the existence of core competencies. Only companies which concentrate on a demanded competence can be more attractive than the competitors if this competence is part of the core business.

If there is still indifference between different candidates for a specific part of the value-added chain, the participation in other co-operations is considered by the fifth filtering. The basis for this filter is the assessment of the participants of a Virtual Enterprise by the customer and the partner companies among themselves. The assessment is performed in the dissolution phase.

2.3 Conclusion

After selecting the most suitable partners the modalities of the co-operation have to be determined. The determination is to be done under consideration of the actual situation of the partners and the market. The modalities concern the common target and the conditions of the co-operation.

The concept of Virtual Enterprises is based on trust by definition, where trust has an integration function for the more temporary arrangement (Bohr and Sieber, 1996, Härtling, 1996, Scholz, 1996). With this background a legal framework could be let out of consideration. But the application of such a culture of trust in practice has proved to be a problem (Odendahl, Reimer and Marzen, 1998). Moreover the culture of trust opposes against the temporary character of a Virtual Enterprise, because trust can only arise over a certain period of time.

By this means Virtual Enterprises depend on loose legal frameworks, which are e.g. implemented by electronic contracts (Byrne, Brandt and Port, 1993). But up to now there are no juridical possibilities or approaches according to the legal protection of such company arrangements. For instance questions about liability and warranty as well as the usage of benefit as a juridical state of facts are not yet sufficiently clarified (Scholz, 1997).

2.4 Operation

After having focussed on planning processes in the preceding phases the performance of the co-operation constitutes the operative phase. To guarantee an efficient execution of the co-operation and to identify misleading developments as well as improvement potentials of the processes, a suitable control instrument should be used. During the execution it is also possible that there is feedback to the preceding phases. This can be the case, if a position within the arrangement has to be filled anew because of a failure of one partner company. Further tasks of this phase are described in chapter 3 in the context of the MARVIN project.

2.5 Dissolution

The main tasks of this phase are the control of the dissolution and storage of relevant information gathered during the co-operation.

The control of the dissolution includes the initiation of the contracted dissolution procedures and the valuation of the vacant positions (Faisst, 1998). The storage of information about the co-operation serves mainly the customer service. This will especially be of relevance if the Virtual Enterprise produces an output its period of use ends after the dissolution of the co-operation. In this case it must be clear how in the case of warranty this claim is served.

3 Virtual Enterprises in the maritime domain

3.1 Domain description

First the question whether Virtual Enterprises exist in practice should be clarified. It is certain, that some products can not be better produced by an Virtual Enterprise than by a traditional enterprise. This will be the case if the cost for transportation of intermediate products from one partner to the other is very high. Another aspect is the existence of a brand. For these reasons in practice it will be easier to establish "top-down-virtualized" enterprises (cf. chapter 1) and most examples mentioned in literature are of this type.

First example is taken from the textile industry. The sport item manufacturer PUMA is a traditional enterprise of the textile industry, which was restructured to overcome a company crises (Faisst, 1998). The resulting company concentrates on its core competencies development, design and marketing. Manufacturing and world-wide logistics are outsource (Figure 6).

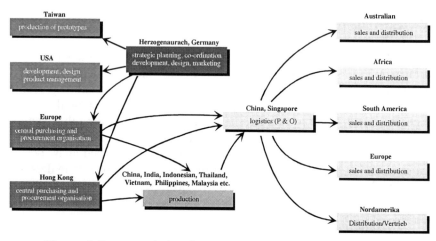

Figure 6: Process-chain of PUMA (Metens and Faisst, 1997)

Further examples can be found in the automotive industry. For instance Micro Compact Car AG (MCC) produces the Smart car in an arrangement between different partners each concentrating on its core competence.

Another interesting example of the automotive industry is Porsche. Because of capacity problems in the production of the Boxster Porsche the final assembly was outsourced to the Finnish automotive constructor Valmet

Automotive Inc. (Kranke, 1998). Valmet does not only produce for Porsche but also for Saab and Opel. In consequence network structures like it is shown in **Figure 7** arise.

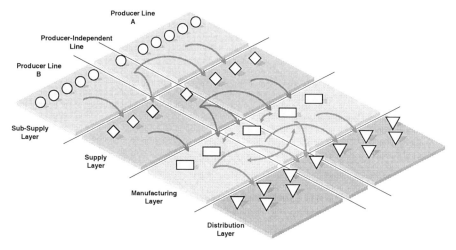

Figure 7: Network structure in the automotive industry

In the maritime domain virtual structures can also be identified and this is the focus of the MARVIN project. MARVIN stands for *Maritime Virtual Enterprise Network* and is sponsored by the European Commission (EP 29049). Business objectives of MARVIN are:

- To increase the competitiveness of ship management, ship classification, and ship repair in Europe.
- To reduce the out-of-service time of ships in operation.
- To reduce the risk of casualties and environmental pollution due to accidents at sea.
- To provide guidance on legal issues of running a virtual operation on the internet.

To clarify, in which way MARVIN supports a Virtual Enterprise in the maritime domain, one has to determine,

- who is taking the role of the customer,
- who are the partner companies building the Virtual Enterprise
- and what is the output of the Virtual Enterprise.

The object of consideration is the grounding of a ship. In this case the ship is not able to navigate anymore. If the ship is damaged, it also has to be repaired in a ship yard. Both services have to be provided by third parties. In this sense the Ship Crew respectively the Ship Owner takes the role of the customer demanding for these services.

The services are not offered by one provider but by a set of actors (Jaramillo, Makris and Mourtzis, 1999):

- **ER Company:** Emergency Response Company contracted by the owner to technically assist the vessel in case of accidents.
- **Ship Yard:** Company which provides the infrastructure and facilities to repair the vessel after the accident. This includes suppliers and subcontractors.
- **Tug Company:** Company which is contracted by either the Owner or the Yard to provide the necessary tugs for re-floating the vessel and towing it to the shipyard.
- **Class Society:** Classification Society from which the vessel obtained the class certificates and which is responsible for the necessary surveys and inspections of the vessel after the accident.
- **Insurance Company:** Organization with which the Owner of the vessel has arranged an Insurance Contract (Policy) to cover costs of damage, loss or liability caused by any perils of the sea.

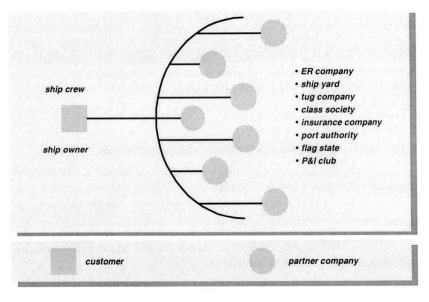

Figure 8: Virtual Enterprise in the maritime domain

Further actors are Port Authority, Costal Authority, Flag State and P&I Club. The total service can only be provided by the co-operation of the different actors. But for the Ship Crew respectively the Ship Owner it would be desirable to get the services by one entity. To satisfy this requirement the actors should build up a Virtual Enterprise with *one face to the customer* (cf. Figure 8). Advantages of such a Virtual Enterprise are:

- A speed up of the processes, because the customer (Ship Crew/Ship Owner) does not have to contact all the actors but only one defined contact point.

- A multiple collection of information about the ship and the actions, which have to be done, are cut. The relevant data will be exchanged within the Virtual Enterprise. This will also speed up the processes.

- The total costs of providing the corresponding services will be reduced because of a better co-ordination of the actors within the Virtual Enterprise.

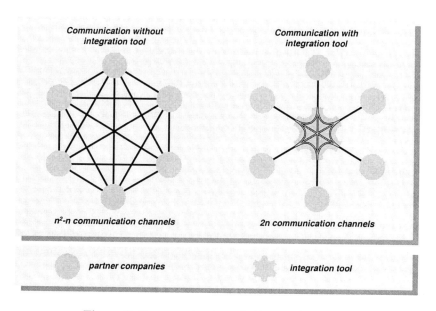

Figure 9: Communication via Integration tool

3.2 Goals of the MARVIN project

In order to establish a Virtual Enterprise in the maritime the following technical objectives are traced in the MARVIN project:

- To define a standard-based infrastructure for the management of maritime processes that integrates state-of-the-art information and communication technology. The focus will be on the usage and enhancement of standards for products and process data exchange The scope of integration includes applications to workflow management, maintenance planning, ship design and construction, and approval and certification.

- To develop an integration tool that facilitates and co-ordinates the interaction between actors forming a Virtual Enterprise in the maritime industry.
- To validate the proposed infrastructure and tools within two separate scenarios, one for emergency repair and one for planned maintenance.
- To recommend legal precautions and means for running a maritime virtual organisation within the current legal framework. The role of actual legal documents, such as those used in emergency situations, will be investigated. Issues concerning data protection and security, intellectual property and confidentiality are in scope of MARVIN, as well as studies within the areas of jurisdiction and choice of law.

Figure 9 shows the communication via the integration tool. The integration tool links the partner companies together. By this means there is a reduction of the communication channels between them as well as the interfaces between the partners` software systems. Detailed information about the content as well as the progress of the MARVIN project can be found via the WWW (URL: http://research.dnv.no/marvin).

References

ARNOLD, O., FAISST, W., HÄRTLING, M. and SIEBER, P., "Virtuelle Unternehmen als Unternehmenstyp der Zukunft?", Ehrenberg, D.; Griese, J.; Mertens, P. (Hrsg.), Arbeitspapier der Reihe „Informations- und Kommunikationssysteme als Gestaltungselement Virtueller Unternehmen" Nr. 2/1995.

ARNOLD, O. and HÄRTLING, M., "Virtuelle Unternehmen: Begriffsbildung und diskussion", Ehrenberg, D., Griese, J., Mertens, P. (Hrsg.), Arbeitspapier der Reihe, Informations und Kommunikationssysteme als Gestaltungselement Virtueller Unternehmen" Nr. 3/1995.

ASHKENAS, R. et al., "The Boundaryless Organization", Breaking the Chains of Organizational Structure. San Francisco 1995, pp. 195-197

BEHME, W., "ZP-Stichwort: Virtuelle Unternehmen", ZP, 6 (1995) Nr. 6.

BENJAMIN R. I. and WIGAND R., "Electronic Markets and Virtual Value Chains on the Informations Superhighway", Sloan Management Review, 36(1995)2.

BOHR, D. and SIEBER, P., "Informatik-Unternehmen im Internet - Eine empirische Studie in der Schweiz und in Deutschland", Ehrenberg, D.,

Griese, J., Mertens, P. (Hrsg.), Arbeitspapier der Reihe „Informations- und Kommunikationssysteme als Gestaltungselement Virtueller Unternehmen" Nr. 5/1996.

BYRNE, J. A., BRANDT, R. and PORT, O., "The Virtual Corporation", Business Week, February 8th 1993, pp. 36-40.

DANGELMAIER, W., "Wie Partner miteinander reden", Logistik Heute, Nr.3 (1996), pp. 60-62.

DAVIDOW, W. H. and MALONE, M. S., "Das virtuelle Unternehmen, der Kunde als Co-Produzent", Frankfurt/Main-New York 1993.

EVERSHEIM, W., et. al., "Konzentration auf das Kerngeschäft: Ein systematisches Vorgehen für den Werkzeugbau", IO Management, 65 (1996) Nr. 9, pp. 75-79.

FAISST, W., "Die Unterstützung Virtueller Unternehmen durch Informations und Kommunikaitonssysteme - eine lebenszyklusorientierte Analyse", Diss., Erlangen-Nürnberg 1998.

FRIEDRICH, S. A., "Mit Kernkompetenzen den Wettbewerb gewinnen", IO Management, 64 (1995) Nr.4, pp. 87-91.

FRIEDRICH, S. A., "Outsourcing: Wie strategische Fehler vermieden werden können", IO Management, 65 (1996) Nr. 9, p. 70.

GOLDMAN, S. L.; NAGEL, R. N. and PREISS, K., "Agile Competitors and Virtual Organizations – Strategies for Enriching the Customer", New York et al 1995.

GROCHLA, E., "Betriebsverband und Verbandbetrieb. Wesen, Formen und Organisation der Verbände aus betriebswirtschaftlicher Sicht", Berlin 1959, pp. 31-37.

HAMEL, G. and PRAHALAD, C. K., "Competing for the Future", Boston Mass. 1994, pp. 205-213.

HÄRTLING, M., "Führungsinformationssysteme zur Unterstützung des Managements Vir-tueller Unternehmen", Ehrenberg, D., Griese, J., Mertens, P. (Hrsg.), Arbeitspapier der Reihe, Informations und Kommunikationssysteme als Gestaltungselement Virtueller Unternehmen" Nr. 5/1996.

HERMANN, U., "Die neue deutsche Rechtschreibung", Gütersloh 1996.

JARAMILLO, D., MAKRIS, S. and MOURTZIS, D., "Specification of the Emergency Repair Scenario", Internal report 1-00-W-1999-01-3, MARVIN project (EP 29049), 1999, pp. 3-4.

KRANKE, A., "Valmet fertigt Boxster - Vom Produzenten zum Zulieferer",

Logistik Heute, 7/8(1998)20, pp. 14-16.

KRÜGER, W., BUCHHOLZ, W. and ROHM, C., "Integration versus Desintegration", Das organisatorische Optimum in der Fertigung. Industrie Management 12 (1996) 3, pp. 6-10.

KRYSTEK, U., REDEL, W., and REPPEGATHER, pp., "Grundzüge virtueller Organisationen", Wiesbaden 1997.

KÜTING, K. and ZINK, K. J. (Hrsg.), "Unternehmerische Zusammenarbeit. Beiträge zu Grundsatzfragen bei Kooperation und Zusammenschluß", Berlin 1983.

LYNCH, R. P., "Business Alliances Guide", New York 1993, p. 7

Markus, A. and Young, D., "Strategic Outsourcing", LRP, 29 (1996) Nr. 1, pp. 116-119.

MERTENS, P. and FAISST, W., "Virtuelle Unternehmen - Idee, Informationsverarbeitung, Illusion", Scheer, A.-W. (Hrsg.), Organisationsstrukturen und Informationssysteme auf dem Prüfstand. 18. Saarbrücker Arbeitstagung 1997. Heidelberg 1997, pp. 101-135.

ODENDAHL, C., REIMER, S. and MARZEN, S., "Fallstudie zum Projekt Konzeption und Entwicklung einer Kooperationsbörse zur kontinuierlichen Gestaltung Virtueller Unternehmen. Bibliothek der Kooperationsbörse", URL: http://www.iwi.uni-sb.de/device, July 1998.

OTT, M. C., Virtuelle Unternehmensführung: Zukunftsweisender Ansatz im Wettlauf um künftige Markterfolge. OM, 44 (1996) Nr. 7-8.

PICOT A., REICHWALD, R. and WIGAND, R. T., "Die grenzenlose Unternehmung Information, Organisation und Management", 2. Aufl., Wiesbaden 1996, pp. 263f.

PRAHALAD, C. K. and HAMEL, G., "Nur Kernkompetenzen sichern das Überleben", HM, 13 (1991) Nr. 2, pp. 66-78.

SCHEER, A.-W., "Unternehmen 2000: Opfer von Reorganisationswellen oder Phönix aus der Asche?", Scheer, A.-W. (Hrsg.): Rechnungswesen und EDV. 15. Saarbrücker Arbeitstagung 1994. Heidelberg 1994, pp. 3-14.

SCHOLZ, C., "Strategische Organisation - Prinzipien zur Vitalisierung und Virtualisierung", Landsberg/Lech 1997.

SCHOLZ, C., "Virtuelle Unternehmen - Organisatorische Revolution mit strategischer Implikation", m&c – Management & Computer, 4(1996) 1, pp. 27-34.

SCHUBERT, W. and KÜTING, K., "Unternehmungszusammenschlüsse", München 1981, p. 118.

SCHUH, G., "Virtuelle Fabrik – Beschleuniger des Strukturwandels",

Schuh, G., Wiendahl, H.-P. (Hrsg.), Komplexität und Agilität. Berlin u.a. 1997.

SYDOW, J., "Virtuelle Unternehmung, Erfolg als Vertrauensorganisation?" OM, 7/8 (1996), pp. 10-13.

SZYPERSKI, N. and KLEIN, S., "Informationslogistik und virtuelle Organisationen", DBW, 53(1993)2, pp. 187-208.

URL FOCUS: http://focus.de/D/DD/DD36/DD36A/dd36a.htm, May 1999.

URL ISOC: http://www.isoc.org/infosvc/, October 1998.

URL NETCRAFT: http://www.netcraft.co.uk/Survey/, March 1999

MARIFlow
A Workflow Management System for Maritime Industry

Asuman Dogac, Catriel Beeri[*], Arif Tumer, Murat Ezbiderli, Nesime Tatbul, Cengiz Icdem, Guray Erus, Orhan Cetinkaya and Necip Hamali

Software Research and Development Center, Faculty of Engineering
Middle East Technical University (METU), 06531 Ankara Turkiye
asuman@srdc.metu.edu.tr

[*] Institute of Computer Science, Hebrew University
91904 Jerusalem Israel
beeri@cs.huji.ac.il

Abstract

The aim of MARIFlow Project is to provide a prototype of an architecture for automating and monitoring the flow of control and data over the Internet among different organisations. This "electronic medium", capable of delivering value-added services to the participants, encompasses many different technological areas: from communication to security, databases, transaction support and agents. The project will make use of these technologies to produce a workflow management system. In particular, the goal of the project is to develop an adaptable workflow engine through which the activities of the different participants in the maritime industry can be harmonised, combined, and expanded through better tracking of functional dependencies and documents, improved data access and handling, and lower administrative overheads.

The MARIFlow system is based on *data-centric* approach, that is, execution of activities on a host machine is triggered by arrival of data, and generates further data that is sent to participants in the process, where upon arrival may trigger further activities. Nevertheless, the important characteristic of such processes is distribution, not just in terms of geography, but also in terms of ownership, responsibility and autonomy. This paper also addresses the important issues such as security of the documents as well as the tracking of data and documents, for monitoring purposes.

1   Introduction

Workflow systems, in general, provide for declarative means for specifying the control flow among activities and extensive research and development, both in the academia and in the industry have contributed to various aspects of the workflow system in making a mature technology - Alonso (1995), Georgakopoulos (1995), Miller (1997), Ming Shan (1998), Dayal (1998), Muth (1998), Sheth (1998), Vossen (1998), Alonso (1998), Cichocki and Rusinkiewicz (1998), and Dogac (1998). However in most of the systems, data flow is restricted to the parameters of the involved activities often disconnected from the description of the flow itself. In other words, the workflow management systems as used by industry today, use a process centric approach. Thus, they lack a mechanism with which it is possible to define the source of data, control its flow over the net, and identify and possibly invoke the activities that make use of it. The workflow engine to be developed as part of this project will address these crucial issues with a special emphasis on the ease of use, maintenance, and customization to the needs of maritime industry.

In maritime industry, materials used in shipbuilding or repairs need to be certified by a classification society. In current practice, the material is checked while it is at the production plant and the "quality data", related to this material, is delivered to the classification society. If the quality data fulfills the requirements, a paper certificate is issued and delivered to the production plant as well as to the customer. Once issued the certificate follows the material to the main shipyard or to one of the subcontractors from where it is eventually added to the ship's documentation file. The certificate is checked at every production stage as well as at ship's handover and at each survey during ship's life cycle. In an industry involving the flow of large amount of paper documents among different organizations, this is a slow, expensive, tedious, error-prone and very limiting process, which in some cases can hinder the ability to improve the service quality. In this work we describe an architecture that provides for automating and monitoring the flow of control and data over the Internet among different organizations and companies with special attention to maritime industry.

In the MARIFlow system, the higher order process is defined through a graphical user interface, which is then mapped to a textual language called FlowDL. FlowDL allows indicating the source of the documents, their control flow and the activities that make use of these documents. A process definition in FlowDL is executed through co-operating agents, called MARCAs (MARIFlow Co-operating Agents), that are automatically initialized at each site that the process executes. The initiation of agents and monitoring facilities are managed through Java programs which can be used by authorized users through Web. The main Web page through which the tools can be started is shown in Figure 1.

MARCAs are responsible for handling the activities at their sites, routing the documents in electronic form, according to the process description among other MARCAs, keeping track of process information by logging activities, and providing for the security and authentication of documents during communication.

Figure 1. MARIFlow MARCA Tools Web Page

The overall system should be immune to failures, and the processing power should be distributed such that it will not generate a serious bottleneck built around a single machine, which is accessed extensively. The participants of the workflow system should decide and behave on their own rather than being invoked or commanded by other programs in a centralized fashion. These requirements necessitate an agent-based architecture for the workflow system, where independent entities capable of completing complex assignments without intervention are used rather than tools that must be manipulated by a user.

In the MARIFlow system, the responsibilities of MARCAs in order to support the requirements given above are defined as follows:

- A MARCA receives messages through a persistent queue and evaluates them to decide what action to take. The persistent queue is necessary so that the agent does not lose its state after a program crash, site failure etc.

- It persistently stores the documents it receives. If the organization that the MARCA resides on has a firewall mechanism, it is also MARCA's responsibility to pass the documents to the in-house system, get the

resulting documents from the system and forward them to the related agents as specified in the process definition.
- Process related information should be stored persistently for further monitoring purposes. Therefore it is MARCA's responsibility to direct related information to a database through its JDBC interface.
- A process definition is compiled at a host and through a special MARCA the information is distributed over the system to other MARCAs necessary for the given workflow definition at initialization phase. That special MARCA is also responsible for data warehousing for monitoring purposes.

This paper is organized as follows: In Section 2, the general architecture of the system is described. This section introduces the MARIFlow Cooperating Agents (MARCAs), the FlowDL workflow definition language, monitoring of the workflow processes along with an example definition for maritime industry to illustrate to details of the architecture. Section 3 describes how security and authentication of documents are handled in MARIFlow. The availability and scalability issues are discussed in Section 4. In Section 5, the work that remains to be done is described namely the persistency of the messages to recover from failures and compensation of activities. Finally, Section 6 concludes the paper.

2 The Architecture of the System

2.1 An Overview of the Architecture

Figure 2 gives an overview of the general architecture of the MARIFlow system. Each organization may have in-house applications inside a firewall protected from unauthorized access. MARCAs exist on a host machine outside the firewall relative to the site network. The MARIFlow agent informs in-house applications when necessary through internal process initiator and is responsible for sending and receiving documents and process related information through the firewall mechanism.

In MARIFlow an inter-enterprise workflow is defined graphically where the workflow designer specifies domains, tasks and process information which are used in building the process definition. The graphical representation of the process definition is mapped to FlowDL, the language used in MARIFlow, and from that definition the specifications for each MARCA is generated. The compilation of the process definition is done on the coordinating MARCA, which is installed in one of the sites. The behavioral structure, obtained from the process definition, for each MARCA is then transmitted to corresponding agent and MARCAs become available for distributed workflow management. It should be noted that this transmission along with the communication at instance level should be realized through persistent queues in order to survive through system crashes and other problems.

2.2 MARIFlow Cooperating Agents: MARCAs

A workflow instance in MARIFlow is executed by co-operating agents called MARCAs. There is exactly one MARCA at each site participating to the workflow execution and it handles all the activities running at its site. At initialization, once in their life time, the sites download the generic MARCA template from a given URL. At compilation time the guards of activities within the responsibility of a MARCA are determined according to the process definition. Guards are special mechanisms based on intertask dependencies - Attie (1993), Singh (1996). They are logical expressions for significant events of activities of a MARCA like "start" or "terminate". MARCAs evaluate these guards with the messages that they receive to decide on their actions. In other words, guards inform the MARCA when to execute a certain activity. A detailed formal description of obtaining guard expressions from a given workflow specification is given in Dogac (1998). All of the information about guard structures is obtained from the process definition at the initialization phase of the MARCA.

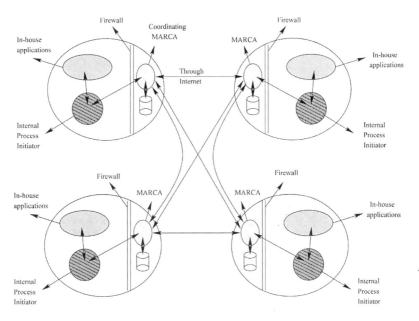

Figure 2. An Overview of the Architecture

There is a special MARCA in the workflow system called the coordinating MARCA. A workflow definition is realized through the coordinating

MARCA and compiled only once. During this compilation, guard structure for each MARCA participating the system along with the interactions with the other MARCAs are obtained and the MARCAs are initialized with this information by the coordinating MARCA. A single MARCA residing on a host is capable of handling multiple workflow definitions and multiple instances of a given workflow at a certain time. All messages are differentiated by unique workflow id obtained from the definition and instance ids that are automatically assigned by the system for each instance generated.

MARIFlow agents communicate with each other through TCP/IP over the Internet. Network concurrent accesses to a single port is handled by Java's Net Package by assigning dynamic ports for each request. Simple message buffering and queuing are also provided by this package. These queuing facilities have been extended to persistent queue implementation and transactional agent communication for safe and consistent transmission.

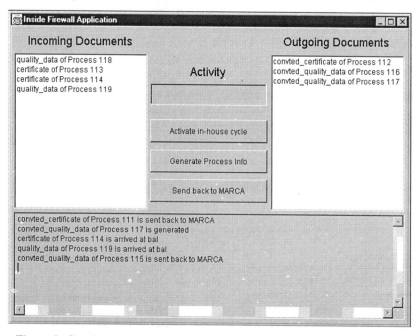

Figure 3. Graphical User Interface for Process Control inside the Firewall

MARCAs communicate with each other through an Agent Communication Language, which is specific to MARIFlow agents, hence they do not communicate with agents in the outside world. This is because communicating with outside world agents is not necessary within the scope of the work. During a session, each message is preceded by an activity identifier along with workflow and instance ids. This information is necessary to identify how a received document or message should be managed according to the activity identifier.

A MARCA sends a document and process related information inside the firewall through an e-mail. Since the content of the documents may be binary, they are encoded prior to the attachment by traditional mime base64 encoding used in e-mail messages.

A program inside the firewall processes the incoming mail and extracts the documents, process related information, workflow and instance ids, the activity that will use this document inside the firewall and displays this information through a GUI as shown in Figure 3. When a document arrives through an e-mail it is shown in the *Incoming Documents* list of the interface. When a document is highlighted (i.e. selected), the activity that will use this document appears in the *Activity* box. The *Activate in-house Cycle* button may be used to start the given activity provided that API of the activity is available. *Send back to MARCA* button is used to transfer the document selected in the *Outgoing Documents* list to the MARCA outside if the related information form of the document is filled via the interface displayed when *Generate Process Info* button is used.

We have chosen to send the response back to MARCA through e-mail mechanism to be system independent as much as possible, since some firewall architectures disallow packet transmission in both directions. The reader program for the mailbox is based upon POP3 and receives the messages through the POP3 server port. This choice is also an effort to be system independent in MARIFlow since POP3 is independent of the structure of the mailbox in different operating system implementations.

2.3 Workflow Definition Language: FlowDL

In MARIFlow system, a workflow process definition is given in FlowDL as a collection of blocks, tasks and other sub-processes as well as some explicit declarations and commands to specify Internet domain addresses, sources of documents, process specific information to be used for monitoring the document flow, and activities for further processing on the documents. The term *activity* is used to refer to a block, a task, or a (sub)process.

FlowDL contains several kinds of blocks, which are used to define different kinds of flow types in the process definition: the activities that run in parallel, in serial or under conditions etc. These blocks along with the declarations done in the process definition code define the whole workflow system. The blocks types encapsulate the workflow primitives defined in Hollingsworth (1996), which are sequential, AND-split, AND-join, OR-split, OR-join and repeatable task.

In MARIFlow, an inter enterprise workflow is defined graphically by using the tool as shown in Figure 4. This tool allows the workflow designer to make the declarations, specify domains, tasks and process information. Afterwards, different types of blocks can be generated and added to the workflow by using the declarations in order to preserve consistency. The workflow definition is mapped to the textual FlowDL language. When this definition is parsed, the guards of each MARCA participating the system are generated and the agents are initialized with this information. The guards provide for the behavioral definitions of the MARCAs.

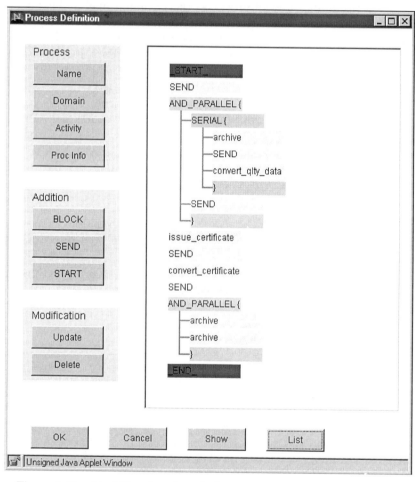

Figure 4. Graphical User Interface for Process Definition in MARIFlow

The advantages brought by block structured FlowDL language can be summarized as follows:
- The current workflow specification languages are unstructured and/or rule based, as noted in Sheth (1996). Unstructured languages make debugging/testing of a complex workflow difficult and rule based ones become inefficient when they are used for specification of large and

complex workflow processes due to the large number of rules and overhead associated with rule management. FlowDL avoids these disadvantages through its block-structured nature.

- A block structured language confines the inter-task dependencies to a well-formed structure that in turn proves extremely helpful in generating the guards of activities for distributed scheduling of a workflow.

- Blocks not only clearly define the data and control dependencies among tasks but also present a well-defined recovery semantics through compensation for a failed or aborted block.

In addition to activities, there are also assignment statements in FlowDL which access and update workflow relevant data. In this way the workflow designer has the ability to assign values to variables. Note that these variables are used in conditional and loop blocks.

2.4 Monitoring of Workflow Processes

Each MARCA stores all the messages it receives in a persistent log so that after a crash or a site failure the MARCA can be brought back to a consistent state by using the information in the log. The MARCAs also store additional process related information specified by the workflow designer through FlowDL inside the database system. Since Java is used in coding the MARIFlow system, a Java native JDBC interface is used for database connectivity. Consequently any database with a JDBC interface can be used by the MARCA.

Each MARCA sends a copy of the information it stores to the coordinating MARCA. Thus coordinating MARCA constitutes a data warehouse site for monitoring information. This site is available to any authorized user on the Internet through a Web interface and may further be replicated for availability purposes.

The authorized user can track the flow of a process instance through a graphical user interface as shown in Figure 5 by giving the process instance identifier and the workflow definition it belongs to. The Web interface reads the process definition of the selected workflow from the database, and produces a graphical representation from that information, with different colors for each block type and with lines connecting the blocks showing the flow of data and messages. Also the interface reads the instance information from the coordinating MARCA's database and reflects it on the graph so that the user can see the instant state of the process instance on the screen, along with the finished, on going and yet to be started activities.

The information kept in the database system of the coordinating MARCA can be queried through Java Applets directly from the Web.

The advantages of this monitoring architecture are as follows:

- It provides for high availability since the data is stored both in the MARCAs locally in a distributed manner and also in a data warehouse in a centralized manner.
- Authorized user can query the data warehouse from anywhere on the Internet by using a simple Web browser.
- Response to monitoring queries will be fast since data is obtained from a single store rather than performing distributed query processing.

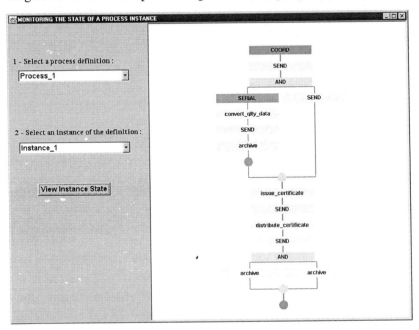

Figure 5. Graphical Monitoring Interface of the MARIFlow System

The databases of each MARCA can also be queried locally by authorized users.

2.5 The Certification Process Definition

The following is an example workflow defined in FlowDL reflecting a business scenario for a certification process in maritime industry:

PROCESS Certification ();

ACTIVITY archive (IN document arch_document);
ACTIVITY convert_qlty_data (IN document quality_data
        OUT document convted_q_d);

```
ACTIVITY convert_certificate(IN document certificate
        OUT document convted_cert);
ACTIVITY issue_certificate (IN document conv_quality_data
        IN document product_spec OUT document certificate);
ACTIVITY delete_from_archive();
ACTIVITY cancel_converted_data();
ACTIVITY cancel_certificate();

DOMAIN_DEFINITION {
        salzgitter_ag.de       szag;
        germanlloyd.org        gl;
        balance_bremen.de      bal;
        isisanisi.com          isisan;
}

struct process_info {
        string  order_no;
        string  material_no;
        string  customer_name;
        string  supplier_name;
        string  class_society_name;
        string  certificate_number;
}

DEFINE_PROCESS MARIFlow ()
{
        szag SENDS (quality_data) TO bal GENERATES (order_no
                material_no customer_name supplier_name
                class_society_name);
        AND_PARALLEL {
                SERIAL {
                        START convert_qlty_data (IN quality_data OUT
                                convted_q_d) AT bal COMPENSATED BY
                                cancel_converted_data();
                        bal SENDS (convted_q_d) TO gl AND isisan;
                        START archive (IN convted_q_d) AT isisan NON_VITAL
                                COMPENSATED BY delete_from_archive();
                }
                isisan SENDS  (prod_spec) TO gl;
        }
        START issue_certificate (IN convted_q_d IN prod_spec OUT
                certificate) AT gl GENERATES (certificate_number)
                COMPENSATED BY cancel_certificate();
        gl SENDS (certificate) TO bal;
        START convert_certificate (IN certificate OUT convted_cert)
                AT bal;
```

```
        bal SENDS (convted_cert) TO szag AND isisan;
        AND_PARALLEL {
                START archive (IN convted_cert) AT szag NON_VITAL
                        COMPENSATED BY delete_from_archive();
                START archive (IN convted_cert) AT isisan NON_VITAL
                        COMPENSATED BY delete_from_archive();
        }
}
```

Example 1. An Example Workflow Definition for the Maritime Industry

The process starts when the steel company (*szag*) sends the "quality data" to a service company (*bal*) to be transformed into EDIFACT (Electronic Data Interchange for Administration, Commerce and Transport) standard. Then within the scope of a block the following activities run in parallel:

- At *bal*, "quality_data" is converted into EDIFACT standard by invoking "convert_qlty_data" activity. The document produced, "convted_q_d", is sent to *gl* and *isisan*. At *isisan*, the arrived document is archived by invoking *archive* activity. Note that the block that comprises these activities is a SERIAL block where the items in the block are executed sequentially.

- The steel user (*isisan*) sends the product specification document to the classification society (*gl*).

Once *gl* receives the converted quality data, its system is notified to start the "issue_certificate" process. When the issued certificate, "certificate", is generated and delivered to the MARCA outside the firewall, it is transferred to *bal* again for conversion to EDIFACT standard and this document is sent to *szag* and *isisan*. Afterwards "archive" activities at *isisan* and *szag* are started and executed in parallel for converted certificate, "convted_cert". This completes the cycle of one instance in *Certification* process definition.

The guard structures for each MARCA is generated when the process definition is parsed and process tree is created as in Figure 6. The guards evaluate to true when the necessary messages and/or documents arrive at MARCAs either from the network or from the inside firewall application. Hence the necessary action is taken such as an activity is started or the execution through the blocks continues. In the running example, when "prod_spec" arrives at *gl* the guard still evaluates to false since for the guard to evaluate to true the arrival of document "convted_q_d" is also necessary. Therefore, only when both of the documents arrive at *gl* the guard evaluates to true and the necessary course of action is taken, that is, the "issue_certificate" task is invoked, to create the "certificate".

For monitoring purposes, each MARCA stores the following process related information persistently in a database system: order_no, material_no, customer_name, supplier_name, class_society_name and certificate_number. Note that the activity responsible for providing a specific piece of information, such as order_no, or certificate_number is obtained through the GENERATES statement of the activities. For example the activity "START issue_certificate (IN convted_q_d IN prod_spec OUT certificate) AT gl GENERATES (certificate_number);" declares that certificate_number will be produced by this activity.

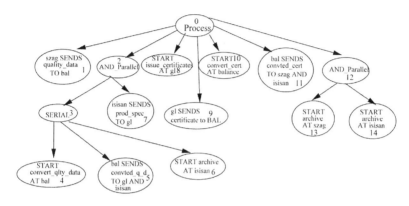

Figure 6. Process Tree of the Example Process Definition

Some example queries that can be readily answered by the database system include: Status of a certificate given its number, status of all certificates for a given steel order, number of certificates issued by the classification society etc. These queries can be executed through the User Interface specialized for this process definition, using any World Wide Web Browser capable of running Java Applets. Figure 7 depicts a customized GUI available for the MARIFlow project.

3 Authentication and Authorisation

Conducting business over a public network, like the Internet, requires mechanisms for authentication of messages, for authorization to access data and execute operations, and for privacy and security in general. We discuss briefly some of the requirements in our application domain, and how they relate to our software architecture.

Clearly, activities that are performed inside a company's firewall are irrelevant to our scenario; a company may use whatever mechanisms it chooses. Specific requirements arise with respect to company-to-company operation, to distributed intra-company operation, and to the overall operation of the MARCA network. We consider each in turn.

An example of a company-to-company operation is sending a quality document from a manufacturer to a classification company. In our scenario, this involves three companies, since a service company translates the document before being sent to the classification society. When a set of companies are involved in a well-defined business procedure, they naturally want the details to be protected from potential competitors. The obvious solution is to encrypt documents inside the firewall, using a scheme that is common to all involved parties. Such encryption also provides authentication of the sender of a message that can easily be verified by the receiver. Finally, an unauthorized receiver will not be able to read a message.

A common situation in our scenario is that representatives of the classification society are present in manufacturing sites, as part of the certification process. These representatives need access to documents of materials and parts, from their society's repository. Although this is an intra-company operation, it is similar in nature to the previous case. An intra-company scheme can be used to encrypt documents before they are passed outside the firewall. An encryption of the request for a document from a field agent can provide authentication, as well as privacy, since the message contents, namely the actual request, is then also not easily available to external entities.

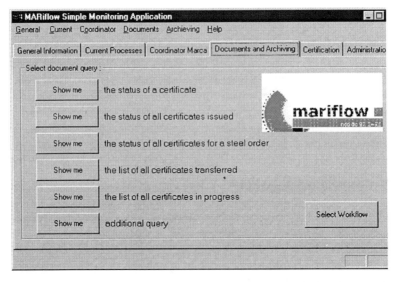

Figure 7. A monitoring Interface specific to the given Example Definition

In both situations above, as the MARCAs need to know the sources and destinations of messages, and the process to which they belong to, such details will have to be provided additionally to the encrypted message. As the MARCA system is outside the firewall, it cannot participate in the internal encryption scheme. To further increase the level of protection and of authentication, i.e., the certainly regarding the sources of received messages; the MARCAs use an independent encryption scheme. While this provides a reasonable degree of protection against casual listeners, clearly it does not provide the same level as the internal schemes, simply because the MARCAs are outside the firewalls, hence their code is open for analysis. Nevertheless, we believe that the solution is satisfactory, given the additional level of protection and authentication provided by the intra company systems. The alternative, namely the development of a trusted authority to manage protection and authentication schemes for all involved companies, requires both further research, such as development of virtual firewall for clusters of companies, as well as a rather drastic change in business procedures.

4   Availability and Scalability

When a site goes down, restarting the MARCA is under the responsibility of the Operating System's start up control. The site's start up control is to analyze the persistent logs of the MARCA and start a new instance using these stable logs created before the site crash. However, there is need for a further mechanism to prevent any Operating System related problem.

In MARIFlow, for each MARCA installed there is a background process at that site, called the "rescue process". The rescue process is responsible for monitoring the lifetime of the agent and checks the MARCA at specific time intervals through a predetermined socket. A thread of the MARCA listens to this socket and responds to the signals. If the MARCA does not respond to this process for a given period of time, the process starts sending signals more frequently. If the MARCA still does not respond, after sending a bunch of signals the process assumes that the MARCA is not functional. The two possibilities in this case are the MARCA could be blocked or it could be dead. When the rescue process is unable to find the OS process that belongs to this MARCA (i.e., it is dead), it instantiates a new MARCA by the help of the persistent logs related with the state of the agent.

Otherwise if the MARCA is blocked, it is necessary to kill the old instance prior to installation of a new instance. Since the logs are persistent it is possible to recover the state of the MARCA killed and hence the site does not suffer from any inconsistencies.

For the described mechanism to work correctly it is necessary to make sure that rescue process stays alive. Therefore, just as the rescue process checks to see that the MARCA stays alive, the MARCA also checks to ensure that the rescue process stays alive by signaling the rescue process at predefined time intervals. It is MARCA who re-instantiates the rescue process when it dies.

5   Future Work

The current prototype of the system does not yet include the mechanisms for the following issues:

5.1   Compensation

Compensation activities are used to logically undo the effects of the activities with which they are associated (Dayal, 1991). They are used when a failure occurs in the system and the system should be taken to a stable state before the failure. On the other hand, workflow processes are long-running activities consisting of many nested sub-activities. In an activity hierarchy, the failure of a sub-activity may cause its parent or higher level ancestors to abort. However, it is not acceptable to roll all the finished activities back in case of failures. A hierarchical approach to failure handling which allows for partially rolling back to the nearest point in process history tree where it is possible to restart execution is required. Moreover, failures should be handled in a timely and efficient fashion. Chen and Dayal (1996) provide such a mechanism that can be adapted into the MARIFlow system. It provides a failure handling mechanism consisting of two phases. When a sub-activity T fails, it is necessary to determine the impact of that failure on the ancestors of T by finding out the highest level ancestor that should be aborted. The root of the activity sub-tree to be logically undone upon T's failure is called the *Logical-Undo Root(LUR)* of T. Every activity in an activity hierarchy has a corresponding *LUR*, which may be one of the following:

- the closest non-vital ancestor since its failure can be ignored by its parent,
- the closest ancestor with a contingency activity (children of a contingency block),
- the closest ancestor without a parent, which may be the top-level process or a compensation activity.

Bottom-up searching for *LUR* in the process tree constitutes the first phase of the approach. After the *LUR* is found, the effects of the activities in the sub-tree with *LUR* as the root are removed in a top-down fashion. Applying the undo operation top-down provides a timely reaction to a failure by halting the activities in scope of *LUR* promptly. In this second phase, starting from the *LUR*, the finished activities are compensated (if they have compensation activities) taking the semantics of the blocks that enclose them into consideration. The approach also allows compensations to be made as high level as possible since compensating a high-level activity is more general than compensating a lower-level activity. After this two-phased algorithm is applied to the activity hierarchy, the execution restarts and rolls forward from the next activity after *LUR*.

5.2 Exception Handling

Hagen and Alonso (1998) propose a flexible approach to exception handling. In this approach, the business logic is separated from exception handling logic, which makes it easier to keep track of each. Exception handling code is separated from the normal code, which also provides reusability of components in addition to simplicity.

In Hagen and Alonso (1998), exceptions are treated as separate objects. Each has a name and parameters. Each exception type should be registered with the system giving its name and interface. Also, each one has a category that indicates the behavior of the handler with which it is associated. An exception handler is a special process that is started when an exception has been signaled. At the beginning, workflow components (activities), exceptions and handlers each handling an associated exception are defined in the system. Then, a workflow process is composed using these components. This component architecture approach provides both reusability and flexibility where different components can be used in different combinations in different workflow definitions. However, the approach does not have a solution for handling unpredictable events that may occur at execution time. All the exception cases and their handlers are given at the beginning.

6 Conclusions

In this paper we described an architecture for a workflow system for document flow over the Internet realized through cooperating agents. The architecture provides for the declarative specification and automatic generation of the application rather than producing large amounts of application specific code by the help of block structured nature of the workflow definition language.

The system attempted to bring solutions to user interaction through the Java based Web interfaces, reliable and automated document and data transfers through a distributed agent based architecture and it is more resistant to localized failures than that of centralized systems. The block structured nature of the language avoids unreachable states in the workflow execution and also the deadlocks (Alonso, 1995). The system also proposes an adaptable design and implementation so that the engine will run in different platforms ranging from a small set of personal computers to high end workstations and mainframes by the universal programming language Java.

The architecture is general enough to be applied to any domain however the example application is provided for maritime industry and therefore some of the user interfaces are customized accordingly. Nevertheless the core of the system, workflow specification, communication details and database activities are suitable for any kind of domain definition thanks to the layered architecture.

The first prototype of the system including the details that are worked around in this paper is available. The issues like compensation and exception handling are yet to be tackled.

References

G. ALONSO, R. GUNTHOR, M. KAMATH, D. AGRAWAL, A. El ABBADI, C. MOHAN, (1995), "Exotica/FDMC: A Workflow Management System for Mobile and Disconnected Clients", *Parallel and Distributed Databases*, The Netherlands.

G. ALONSO, C. HAGEN, H. SCHEK, M. TRESCH, (1998), "Towards a Platform for Distributed Application Development", in *Workflow Management Systems and Interoperability*, NATO ASI Series, A. Dogac, L. Kalinichenko, T. Ozsu, A. Sheth (Eds), Springer-Verlag pp. 195-221.

P. C. ATTIE, M. P. SINGH, A. SHETH, M. RUSINKIEWICZ, (1993), "Specifying and Enforcing Intertask Dependencies", *Proceedings of the 19th VLBD*, Dublin, Ireland

Q. CHEN, U. DAYAL, (1996), "A Transactional Nested Process Management System", in *Proceedings of 12th International Conference on Data Engineering*, New Orleans, LA.

A. CICHOCKI, M. RUSINKIEWICZ, (1998), "Migrating Workflows", in *Workflow Management Systems and Interoperability*, NATO ASI Series, A. Dogac, L. Kalinichenko, T. Ozsu, A. Sheth (Eds), Springer-Verlag pp. 339-355.

U. DAYAL, M. HSU, R. LADIN, (1991), "A Transactional Model for Long-Running Activities", *Proceedings of the 17th International Conference on Very Large Data Bases*, Barcelona

U. DAYAL, Q. CHEN, TAK W. YAN, (1998), "Workflow Technologies Meet the Internet", in *Workflow Management Systems and Interoperability*, NATO ASI Series, A. Dogac, L. Kalinichenko, T. Ozsu, A. Sheth (Eds), Springer-Verlag pp. 423-438.

A. DOGAC, E. GOKKOCA, S. ARPINAR, P. KOKSAL, I. CINGIL, B. ARPINAR, N. TATBUL, P. KARAGOZ, U. HALICI, M. ALTINEL, (1998), "Design and Implementation of a Distributed Workflow Management System: METUFlow", in *Workflow Management Systems and Interoperability*, NATO ASI Series, A. Dogac, L. Kalinichenko, T. Ozsu, A. Sheth (Eds), Springer-Verlag pp. 61-91.

D. GEORGAKOPOULOS, M. HORNICK, A. SHETH, (1995), "An Overview of Workflow Management: From Process Modeling to Workflow Automation Infrastructure", *Distributed and Parallel Databases*, Ahmed K. Elmagarmid (Ed-in-chief), Volume 3, Number 2, pp. 119-153.

C. HAGEN, G. ALONSO, (1998), "Flexible Exception Handling in the OPERA Process Support System", *18th International Conference on Distributed Computing Systems (ICDCS 98)*, Amsterdam, The Netherlands.

D. HOLLINGSWORTH, (1996), "The Workflow Reference Model", *Technical Report TC00-1003, Workflow Management Coalition*, Accessible via: http://www.aiai.ed.ac.uk/WfMC/

J. MILLER, D. PALANISWAMI, A. SHETH, K. KOCHUT, H. SINGH, (1997), "WebWork: METEOR$_2$'s Web-based Workflow Management System", *Journal of Intelligent Information Systems*, The Netherlands

P. MUTH, D. WODTKE, J. WEISSENFELS, G. WEIKUM, A. DITTRICH, (1998), "Enterprise-Wide Workflow Management Based on State and Activity Charts", in *Workflow Management Systems and Interoperability*, NATO ASI Series, A. Dogac, L. Kalinichenko, T. Ozsu, A. Sheth (Eds), Springer-Verlag pp. 281-303.

MING-CHIEN SHAN, J. DAVIS, W. DU, Y. HUANG, (1998), "HP Workflow Research: Past, Present, and Future", in *Workflow Management Systems and Interoperability*, NATO ASI Series, A. Dogac, L. Kalinichenko, T. Ozsu, A. Sheth (Eds), Springer-Verlag pp. 92-106.

A. SHETH, D. GEORGAKOPOULOS, S. JOOSTEN, M. RUSINKIEWICZ, W. SCACCHI, J. WILEDEN, A. WOLF, (1996), "Report from the NSF Workshop on Workflow and Process Automation in Information Systems", *SIGMOD Record*, 25(4):55-67

A. SHETH, K. KOCHUT, (1998), "Workflow Applications to Research Agenda: Scalable and Dynamic Work Coordination and Collaboration Systems", in *Workflow Management Systems and Interoperability*, NATO ASI Series, A. Dogac, L. Kalinichenko, T. Ozsu, A. Sheth (Eds), Springer-Verlag pp. 35-60.

M. SINGH, (1996), "Synthesizing Distributed Constrained Events from Transactional Workflow Specifications", *in Proceedings of the 12th International Conference on Data Engineering (ICDE'96)*, New Orleans

G. VOSSEN, M. WESKE, (1998), "The WASA Approach to Workflow Management for Scientific Applications", in *Workflow Management Systems and Interoperability*, NATO ASI Series, A. Dogac, L. Kalinichenko, T. Ozsu, A. Sheth (Eds), Springer-Verlag pp. 145-164.

INTERORGANISATIONAL WORKFLOW BASED ON ELECTRONIC DATA INTERCHANGE IN MARITIME INDUSTRY

Thorsten Kuhlmann, Rainer Lampig, Christian Massow and Jens Schumacher

BIBA - Bremen Institute of Industrial Technology
and Applied Work Science at the University of Bremen
P.O. Box 33 05 60, 28335 Bremen, Germany
jsr@biba.uni-bremen.de

Abstract

One of the main objectives of the European ESPRIT-project EDIMAR[1] is to create, implement, test and evaluate an EDI based communication infrastructure between the various partners involved in the shipbuilding process. EDIMAR is dedicated to exploit the potentials of both the STEP and EDIFACT approaches to product and process data communication through a concept, which combines their complementary nature (business versus engineering data). This, together with an inter-organisational workflow system based on EDI, will facilitate the realisation of a virtual enterprise for shipbuilding processes.

This paper, focused on the inter-organisational workflow aspect, gives an overview of the problem-domain and motivation behind the EDIMAR project. Concepts are outlined and a brief overview of the future inter-organisational workflow system is given.

Keywords: Electronic Data Interchange, Virtual Enterprise, Workflow, Decentralised Production

1 Introduction

The trend towards global markets and the increasing customer orientation give rise to new manufacturing paradigms like Agile Manufacturing and the Extended or Virtual Enterprise. Due to the growing of production in temporary networks these paradigms require advanced communication/co-operation facilities and infrastructures. Large company-wide information and

---

[1] ESPRIT-Project 20.624 **EDIMAR** – Electronic Data Interchange for the European Maritime Industry

control structures are unable to cope with this changing in an evolving environment. Due to the increasing complexity of distributed production management there is a strong need for integratable systems to support the automatic co-ordination of business activities, thus unburdening the human actors.

Future systems have to act according to predefined business processes. On the other hand they have to be flexible enough to survive in an unpredictable environment. Thus the problem is two fold. The first issue is the modelling of processes in order to define the systems behaviour in general. The other one is the execution of processes based on a process-model which might be invalid at runtime caused by a changing project behaviour.

Process execution becomes more complicated in a distributed manufacturing environment where sub-processes are executed at geographically different sites and in different organisational units. Workflow Management Systems (WfMC, 1994) are considered to provide the needed procedural automation of business processes. These systems are well suited for the application in well structured domains. In case of less structured tasks available tools are not sufficient. This is the domain of GroupWare. For several reasons a Virtual Enterprise isn't an ideal application domain for existing Workflow Management Systems. The most important one is the fact that a Virtual Enterprise consists of a *temporary* network of independent companies. Regarding communication, the links between the involved partners are more volatile compared to a classical manufacturer-supplier relationship, e.g. in the automotive industry. Thus it is necessary to rely on existing standards. The EDIMAR approach is to integrate workflow systems on an inter-organisational level via EDI.

2 EDI in Maritime Industry

Electronic data exchange will be one of the key elements for the European maritime industry in order to become more competitive in a market which is expanding and thus known for being a (promising) battlefield. One of the European strengths is in the short development and production lead time. To protect as well as to increase this advantage, the shipbuilders, suppliers, class societies and ship owners require to exploit state-of-the-art information and communication technologies supporting integration throughout the entire ship life cycle. To achieve this goal, the ongoing ESPRIT-project EDIMAR is to create, implement, test and evaluate EDI based communication infrastructure between the various partners involved in the ship production process. This infrastructure is to automate ordering, delivery, invoicing and payment process of ship mechanical systems and equipment as well as for supporting the design refinement process which is an intermediary activity between ordering and delivery for such make to order products. In future the entire production process has to be understood as a Virtual Enterprise project facilitated by all the different companies involved. An inter-organisational workflow system linking the various autonomous companies and thus trace the information flow across company borders is a necessary pre-requisite to support enhanced co-ordination and to make the Virtual Enterprise alive.

Prerequisites for such advanced digital communication are i) standardised message formats (e.g. EDIFACT) capturing the semantics of the procurement process and ii) a standardised message content based on a STEP product model enabling system interoperability on the level of engineering tasks.

The goal of EDIMAR is to exploit the potentials of both the STEP and the EDIFACT approaches to product and process data communication. A concept will be developed which combines their complementary nature, i.e., business versus engineering data. This, together with an inter-organisational workflow system, will facilitate the realisation of a virtual enterprise for shipbuilding processes.

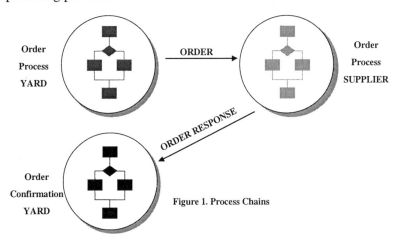

Figure 1: Process Chains

Major results of EDIMAR are envisaged to be:

- a procurement process model exploiting the potential of pure digital data exchange and system interoperability
- EDIFACT message types for the procurement of ship mechanical systems and equipment
- a STEP product model (Application Protocol) enabling the representation of ship mechanical systems product data

- an EDI communication infrastructure featuring secure and compatible information exchange for the entire production process
- a prototype implementation of the business chain scenarios for purchasing and design refinement in a real world environment with realistic test data amongst shipyards suppliers and the classification society.
- a distributed workflow component supporting process definition and process execution across the boundaries of autonomous organisations

The focus of this paper is on the latter topic, i.e., the inter-organisational workflow.

3 Integration of EDI, Workflow and GroupWare

For requirement definition purposes the consortium analysed some core business processes at the beginning of the project. The order process chain, depicted in figure 1 is an example.

As described in various publications, processes vary from the structured to non-structured. A structured process is usually subject to automation. Regarding inter-organisational data exchange companies apply EDI for that purpose with EDIFACT as the emerging standard for message-type definition. Both orders and order-responses are predefined EDIFACT messages. Non-structured processes are difficult to support with IT-Technologies. Telephone and fax are tools which are currently applied. The trend towards the application of GroupWare systems is increasing. Within these two extremes one kind find semi-structured processes. Together with the structured processes this is the application domain of workflow systems. Currently none of the involved partners applies such a workflow system. The reason may be a lack of awareness due to the novelty of this kind of tools. On the other hand the application domain of workflow systems is limited to (semi-)structured processes. A process consists of a set of activities, each of them may be a leaf level entity or a sub-process. Several analysed processes showed that sub-processes, regarding their degree of structure, vary from being structured to a completely unstructured behaviour. Thus workflow systems may be only applied to a structured sub-process of the entire process. The application of a technology focusing on a specific part of a process leaving the rest of the entire process more or less unsupported seems to be not useful.

Thus the goal is to find a solution which supports all types of processes, i.e., structured, semi- or unstructured. The EDIMAR approach is first applied to workflow systems which operate on top of an existing infrastructure, i.e., groupware systems like Microsoft Exchange or Lotus Notes. *ProZessware* provided by the German company Onestone and *Keyflow* provided by Keyfile Inc. are examples for those kind of workflow systems. These workflow systems will be used to support the in-house-processes like ordering etc. (Depicted in figure 1).

Another step (see figure 2) which is done in parallel is to integrate EDI and workflow.

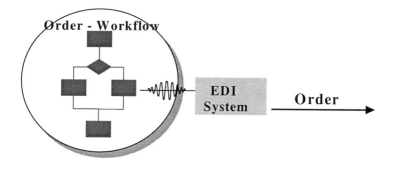

Figure 2. Integration of EDI and Workflow

The goal is to trigger the transfer of an EDI-message by an event which occurs in the workflow system. On the receiver side the arriving message will be processed by an EDI system. This in turn will cause an event in the workflow system thus triggering a process.

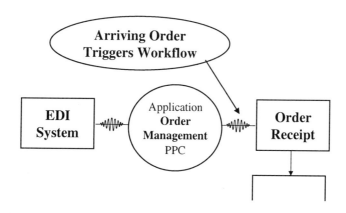

Figure 3. EDI-Message triggers Workflow

4 Assistance for Unstructured Processes

The analysis of processes has shown that several negotiations take place between the involved actors on an intra- or interorganisational level. Ordering- or invoice-processes can be automated, but a change in the order has to be negotiated, at least the supplier will insist. To support decision making on a case based level it is necessary to provide some assistance. The goal is to co-ordinate activities and to solve conflicts. In practice these negotiations are relatively unstructured and very difficult to track. Austin and later on Searle, developed an approach to model interaction between humans, the so-called *Speech Act Theory*. Basic element of human communication is a speech act. Speech acts aim to yield actions. Such an action can effect the real (physical) world or can change the mental states of talkers and listeners. The speech act approach serves already as a base for agent communication languages (Finin et al, 1994).

The assistant will be based on electronic mail and implements different kinds of speech act-expressions as messages such as request, order accept, or reject. Currently available mail-tools (part of groupware systems) provide a so-called inbox where incoming messages are stored. Frequently using e-mail causes an inbox which is overloaded with messages that has to be searched for relevant e-mails. The problem is that the communication-context is lost when applying an e-mail tool. Thus a prerequisite for the success of our approach is to preserve the context in which a communication was started until it comes to an end. Therefore the assistant will open a folder when a communication is set up and all messages within a communication context are added to the folder. Another issue is the traceability of the message exchange. Messages can contain due dates for an answer or a flag indicating an expected type of answer. The assistant detects automatically if answers don't come on time and informs the user or sends a reminder. If all expected answers arrive users are informed by the communicator and can undertake further actions.

Steiner (1993) claims that a similar approach implemented by Winograd called *The Communicator* failed because the set of co-operation primitives, i.e., message types, was fixed. Our approach to overcome this problem is to allow free-form messages but to keep the communication context.

5 Conclusion

Currently the EDIMAR consortium is analysing the core processes of shipbuilders and their suppliers. The next step will be the detailed specification of EDIFACT messages which will be applied in future. The proposed inter-organisational workflow system will be prototypically installed and evaluated within an industrial testbed. The EDIMAR prototype aims to show how the execution of structured, semi- and unstructured processes can be supported thus allowing a higher level computer based communication compared to existing EDI connections

References

FININ, T., MCKAY, D., FRITZON, R., and MCENTIRE, R., "KQML: An Information and Knowledge Exchange Protokol", *Knowledge Building and Knowledge Sharing*, K. and Yokoi, T. (eds.), Ohmsa and IOS Press, 1994.

STEINER, D.D., "Kooperative Mensch-Maschine Arbeit", *Verteilte Künstliche Intelligenz*, Müller, J. (Ed.), Wissenschaftsverlag, Mannheim, Leipzig, Wien, Zürich, 1993

WfMC – Workflow Management Coalition, The Workflow Reference Model, Document Number TC00-1003, Issue 1.1, 29-Nov-94, http://www.aiai.ed.ac.uk:80/WfMC

ADVANCED SUPPLY CHAIN MANAGEMENT STRATEGIES FOR THE MARITIME INDUSTRY

R. Ahlers and J. Brodda

BALance Technology Consulting; Contrescarpe 45; D-28195 Bremen; Germany
balance@balance-bremen.de

Abstract

Marine supply chains are increasingly coming into the focus of restructuring and productivity improvements of shipyards and their suppliers. Material cost, counting for more than 60% of the total ship cost, offer a high potential for cost savings and logistical improvements. Beyond the cost for the material itself, bought-in-services and subcontracts, the cost for the administrative processes involved, i.e. marketing, co-operative engineering, purchasing etc., are substantial. New methods of work in combination with advanced information and communication technology available on the market offer great opportunities for process improvements. The shipbuilding industry in Europe is at the very beginning to apply classical Electronic Data Interchange (EDI) and new Electronic Commerce (EC) technologies. This paper discusses the different marine supply chains processes and describes basic technical solutions. Further some basic activities of the industry with this respect including R&D measures performed under the auspices of European R&D programmes are described. This includes the discussion of cost for the application of the technology and the potential for overall cost-savings.

1 Introduction

The shipbuilding industry is characterised by a high competition on the world market. To avoid the further loss of market shares it is necessary to improve the inter- and intra-organisational production and business processes. Investments in the last 10 years within shipyards world-wide led to increasing levels of automation and process integration with substantial improvements of productivity in "blue collar" areas. Most advanced shipyards developed from craft-skill-based workshop technologies towards highly robotised shipbuilding factories. Beside the consequent development of all CAD/CAM processes the shipyards also improved their organisational and logistical functions. This was necessary to serve the needs of those highly integrated production areas, but also to improve the productivity of "white collar" functions.

Most developments were oriented to improve functions and processes inside the individual companies. Whereas, new and advanced Information Society Technologies (IST), namely, Electronic Data Interchange (EDI) and Electronic Commerce by means of Internet and Multimedia technologies, open up new fields for business improvements through inter-company process integration. These technologies will sustainable change and enhance shipbuilding supply chains and co-operative engineering processes. Many other branches have started to improve their supply chains and to reduce costs by outsourcing. Due to the variety and high complexity of it's supply chains the shipbuilding industry is still at the beginning of this optimisation process. The different problems and parameters for a supply chain management strategy in the maritime industry and a method which solves some of the problems can be taken care by the application of a dedicated methodology and a toolset which is described in this paper. By using the method the risk and the expenses for inter-organisational information technology projects will be reduced.

The practical part of this paper will discuss the state-of-the-art in EDI and Electronic Commerce technologies and its application in shipbuilding supply chains. On the basis of actual trends in the shipbuilding industry towards more co-operative working, outsourcing and system supplies, the potential application areas of EDI/EC technologies will be discussed including its commercial implications on the process, i.e. cost savings and lead time reductions. First maritime EDI applications have shown a high cost reduction potential. Therefor European yards have started the EDIMAR project to develop an EDI based network for technical and commercial information. The project has developed common implementation guidelines and first promising realisation results for steel procurement processes are presented. At least a general cost calculation and a benefit analysis for maritime procurement processes are shown. It is clear that not only the use of the EDI technology but the restructuring of the business processes promises a high optimisation potential. For companies with low EDI traffic some possibilities for a cheap use of this technology are outlined. Comprehensive a perspective for future maritime logistic processes is given. EDIMAR and other projects have proven the functionality in different test scenarios by adapting technology ready for application, i.e. available products and services. This draws also the scenario for ongoing projects activities and on future development needs.

2   Motivation to Look Into Supply Chain Management

Competition in shipbuilding is constantly increasing in the shipbuilding industry for many years. After long phases of recession in the 70's and 80's the markets are improving. However, through new capacities coming into the market the competitive position of many shipyards has not improved. Searching for alternative solutions to improve the competitive position the shipbuilding industry is following world wide a trend towards further outsourcing of processes and services to benefit from a better specialisation and cost performance of smaller and self-responsible companies, i.e. marine equipment manufacturers and sub-contractors. Compared to the total cost of a ship this trend leaves the shipyards today with a share of 50 – 70% material cost, 20 – 35% manufacturing cost (labour and overhead), 5–10% engineering/design cost and 5-10% sales and administration cost.

Some of the potential advantages of outsourcing have been bought in for the price of dramatically increasing overhead and management cost. This is because many companies have not properly prepared themselves to keep control of services and processes which they so far performed by themselves. On the other hand shipyard personnel often are not used to adequate management techniques and tools to manage external resources and the purchasing process effectively. Therefore, material and services overhead cost are summing up to 5 – 8 % of the total ship cost not saying anything about the time losses through incomplete and inadequate information in the process.

This substantial share of cost, which is very often not clearly visible, but hidden in other cost positions, provide a very good motivation and a large potential for cost savings.

3   Elements of the Maritime Supply Chain

Elements of the maritime supply chain can be found in almost all processes of ship newbuilding. The respective work and effects cannot be limited to the purchasing functions, but has to be considered as an integrated element in almost all functions throughout the shipbuilding process. It already starts with the suppliers seeking for markets and acceptance of their products and it continuous after the ship delivery through life cycle supporting functions in the area of maintenance and repair. Besides the shipyards and the suppliers maritime supply chains involve many external partners directly and indirectly (Figure 1) and requires an extensive communication process including specially applied management procedures.

More specific the different elements of the supply chain may be distinguished in the following six business processes:

Marine Equipment Type Approval

Before entering into the market marine equipment suppliers have to obtain type approvals from classification societies for their products. This is a major entrance barrier into the market and as well a time critical, lengthy and expensive process for the suppliers. It mainly involves the suppliers and the classification societies. The procedures involve laboratory tests and complex administrative procedures. For some products testing of the individual products are requested beyond type approval.

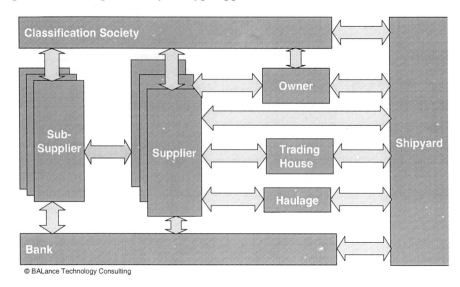

Figure 1: Partners in the Supply Chain

Pre-Selection of Equipment and Materials (Engineering and Design Process)

A process of vital importance for the supplier is the engineering and design process of the shipyard. The optimal situation for a supplier is to be no. 1 choice on the ship-owner's maker list, which requires after good quality and reliable products continuous marketing and sales efforts to maintain the position in the market. But even then it is necessary to be "at hand" for the designer either in form of good catalogues and fast accessible technical information, technical advisory and support services and maybe through good personal relations.

Procurement Process

Often in parallel, sometimes in a sequential order or even before the detailed design process has started, purchasing activities begin with inquiries in the market by requesting quotations from suppliers. This is not necessary for those products where the shipyards have negotiated framework contracts with the suppliers including fixed price structures. The bidding process is followed by the order process including sending the formal orders and receiving respective order responses including confirmations respectively changes to the order. Since shipbuilding is a very dynamic process with highly concurrent engineering processes order changes are frequently necessary. In some special cases the purchasing process will be handled through trading houses, which may receive better prices than single shipyards through some special framework contracts and access to different markets.

Material Delivery Process

The purchasing process itself is followed by close tracking of the order, especially with respect to the delivery date. For some supplies the timely delivery is of vital importance for the shipbuilding schedule. Therefore a continuous contact to the suppliers will be maintained and even shipping and transport are subject of close tracking. However, all the paperwork including transport data, delivery notes, despatch advices, invoices and storage intake control are subject of this process. It may also comprise the handling of certificates which may accompany the supplies. These have to be handled and administered carefully and become later an element of the overall documentation for the ship.

On Site Assembly, Functional Testing, Approval

Whoever is responsible for the assembly of materials and components (shipyard or supplier) will rely on good documentation for the assembly procedure. Access to remote information through direct contacts or advanced media can be important for fast and reliable mounting on site. This is followed by functional testing of systems which may involve again the classification societies. Beside the technical testing this is also a very formal procedure with excessive amounts of documentation and administrative procedure. Again the availability of all required information, certificates etc. is important for fast and reliable procedures.

Guarantee Process, After Sales Services, Maintenance and Repair

After the delivery of the ship normally all involved parties, i.e. the owner, the ship, the classification society and the shipyard file comprehensive sets of all documentation for the ship. For all events like potential guarantee processes, renewing the class, regular maintenance or emergency repair it is essential to have fast and reliable access to all documentation of the ship. Documentation needs to be small in size, but comprehensive and supportive in its content.

Understanding the different supply chain processes and working on the supplier base to derive most valuable information on the meaning of the different suppliers for the shipyard is essential to develop and evaluate new and advanced strategies. Some shipyards have developed complimentary strategies to treat different supplier groups differently. This can just be done on the basis of detailed knowledge. It must be stated that many shipyards do not have this knowledge and therefore cannot launch appropriate measures respectively cannot control the impact of their respective investments.

4 Requirements of Shipbuilding Supply Chains

The needed cost reduction in the shipbuilding industry is, like in other branches, not only a task of the manufacturers but also for their suppliers. Other branches like e.g. the consumer goods and the automotive industry have started cost reduction programs together with their suppliers a couple of years ago. The shipbuilding industry is still at the beginning of such initiatives. But, to copy only the concepts of other branches will not be enough because of the special structure of this industry.

The automotive industry (serial mass production) as well as the aircraft industry (serial production) e.g. have much more power to succeed with new supplier chain management concepts because of their structure and their amount of products. The annual average production per automotive manufacturer (per pieces) is 170,000 times higher than in the shipbuilding industry (project industry). But there are seven times more shipyards active on the world market than automotive companies. Compared to the shipyards the annual average production of aircraft companies are 24 times higher but there are 70 times more shipyards operating on the world market than aircraft companies. Aircraft and automotive industry are much more concentrated by a higher product throughput per company, which gives the manufacturer the possibility to accomplish new supplier management concepts and offers the suppliers benefit by long term co-operations.

Beside the structure of the shipbuilding branch the amount of yard suppliers is still another problem. The share of supplier parts for a container ship is approximately 60% which means nearly 1.000.000 supplier parts. Compared to that figure, a VW Golf has approximately 11.000 supplier parts. European yards (capacity: 100cgt/year) have approx. 2500 suppliers and select approx. 1000 of them per ship (e.g. cargo vessel). This shows the complexity of the needed supply chain management processes of yards. In many cases, there is a project-dependent supplier structure, which leads sometimes to a short duration of co-operations. Some suppliers are only needed for a special type of ships (container, cruise liner etc.) and sometimes, the interval between two similar ship type orders is a couple of years. That means, the expanse for both (yards and suppliers) for organising the co-operation is really high in relation to the duration of the co-operation.

The heterogeneous structure of co-operation partners (technology suppliers, suppliers for small batches and supplier for standard parts, classification societies, ship model basins, etc) leads to different requirements for the inter-organisational information exchange.

In opposite to other branches the shipbuilding industry handles not only with standard parts. A high amount of supplier parts are raw materials (e.g. steel plates, pipes, profiles) or make-to-order" items (e.g. cabins, engines, deck machinery). These complex product structures influences the supply chain organisation.

Figure 2: Important parameters of a supply chain management strategy

All the mentioned points (Figure 2):

- Kind of production (serial mass production, serial production, project industry, etc.)
- Supply chain structure (amount of suppliers, project dependent supplier, etc.)
- Kind of co-operation partners (technology suppliers, standard part suppliers, engineering offices, classification societies, etc.)
- Kind of supplier products (standard parts, raw material, make-to-order-items)

influence the supply chain management strategy of companies and require special attention of the shipbuilding industry.

5 New Strategies and Technology Trends

Beyond outsourcing strong tendencies towards more global sourcing of materials, more system related purchasing (reducing the supplier base!) and more collaborative engineering can be identified within the major shipbuilding groups world-wide. In spite of high potentials for cost reduction in these strategies, there are risks, which may jeopardise the anticipated success. Major concerns are with the delivered quality of supplies, the timely delivery of ordered materials and components and, to come in control of the entire process, the need for new and advanced management skills in combination with a better information and communication system environment.

Benchmarking studies in the shipbuilding industry for comparable ship types show margins of 15 % and more between prices for external material cost. The shipyards have started to realise those margins by putting more price-pressure on the suppliers, but also by the standardisation of technical solutions, teaming-up with other shipyards to achieve stronger buyer-power and by reducing their supplier base through more system related enquiry's.

On the other hand these trends in general require also good strategic concepts from the marine equipment manufacturers for the future. Since the trend towards outsourcing in the first place effects the configuration of strategic alliances with marine equipment suppliers in geographically close regions, the building of global co-operation alliances with some material/component key-suppliers and service-providers may be more adequate. The general step-by-step process of outsourcing through shipyards is shown in Figure 3.

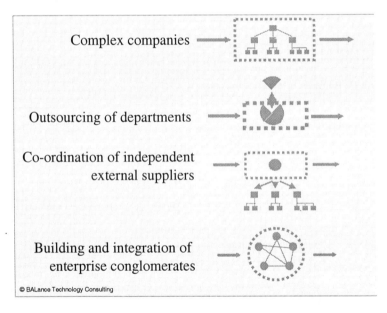

Figure 3: Migration towards a virtual enterprise

Beneath the effect to achieve commercial benefits through the outsourcing process itself, e.g. through higher workloads and relatively lower overhead costs, the availability of new and advanced information and communication technology allows the cost-effective realisation of those concepts. As an ultimate consequence shipyards, theirs suppliers and others integrated into the process may migrate towards a Virtual Enterprise (VE). A Virtual Enterprise by definition is a set of temporary linked individual companies clustered to fulfil a timely restricted business process and behaving for that business process as an integrated enterprise enabled by advanced technologies.

On the basis of the individual supplier analysis of a shipyard it is essential to apply the right strategy with the right partners (marine equipment suppliers) and to assign the right technology for the implementation of co-operative working solutions. An analysis of the supplier base can be used to make appropriate decisions. From this analysis indicators and strategic decisions can be derived with which partners technical solutions towards paperless purchasing and/or collaborative engineering should be developed on high priority. Those suppliers of shipyards which provide high value components with a low amount of purchasing documents, but a high amount of technical data to be exchanged must be considered for collaborative engineering solutions. Those who supply "bulk materials" or standard products which require frequent and periodic exchange of purchasing documents, may be better considered for paperless purchasing procedures.

New technologies, basically information and communication technologies, tremendously effect the way of working within and between companies. Since this is true for almost 40 years now, the shipbuilding industry seems still to be at the starting point for an organisational revolution caused by this. The given background of newly available technology, e.g. internet, EDI, geographically distributed client server environments etc., allow far reaching concepts for integrated supply chain management for shipbuilding applications. Principle examples for this can be found in other industries, e.g. just in time delivery solutions in automotive and aircraft industries.

The technology to be applied is very often described by the name "Virtual Enterprise Technology" (VET). VET is anticipated to play an increasing role in the support of emerging collaborative networks. Virtual enterprises are defined as a set of temporary linked individual companies clustered to fulfil a timely restricted business process and behaving for that business process as a integrated enterprise enabled by advanced information and communication technology. For example a shipyard and a set of key suppliers team-up to fulfil a ship newbuilding contract. Virtual enterprises can be build-up for different applications, e.g. supply chains, design chains, distributed manufacturing and assembly processes. Because of their temporarily nature and a heterogeneous portfolio of participating companies the mechanisms applied need to be flexible, standardised and easy to reconfigure. An open communication infrastructure, openness of software systems, agreed data exchange standards, harmonised workflow and a dynamic intra- and interorganisational reorganisation process are vital success parameters for VEs.

To achieve the expected benefits, it is further essential that the shipyards and their suppliers build up new and powerful managerial skills combined with continuous qualification programmes for their employees.

In the last ten years the European shipbuilding industry including also suppliers to some extend started to prepare the baseline for this kind of future working. Within individual projects international standards for the exchange of data have been always in focus. For example, major contributions have been made to the international discussion and development of maritime application protocols of the ISO standard STEP and to the definition of industrial specific message types according to the UN standard EDIFACT. Through the establishment of EMSA (European Maritime STEP Association) in 1994, Special Interest Groups for Networks, Electronic Data Interchange (EDI) and Product Data Management (PDM) and many bilateral international co-operations the industry achieved a better understanding for the needs and benefits of co-operative working. The industry is now at the point to show an increasing interest for putting VE-technology into operation.

Mainstreams for the future collaborative electronic based supply chain management are computer supported co-operative work, electronic exchange of commercial data (e.g. orders, invoices, etc.), electronic exchange of technical information (e.g. drawings) and the use of electronic supplier catalogues (Figure 4).

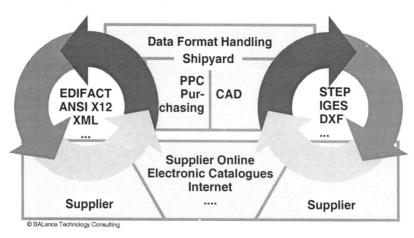

Figure 4: Mainstreams in EDI

Most likely a hybrid solution combining the advantages of different technologies should be implemented for individual business process needs. The major challenge is to find the right configuration by using all enabling technologies and to keep the application flexible for fast adaptation according to a fast changing technological platform. BAL.SILK (BALance - Strategy for Information Logistic Concept realisations) supports the selection, configuration and realisation process for all business process chains (see next chapter). Electronic Data Interchange (EDI) and Electronic

Commerce are the most promising technologies to improve supply chain management even in the shipbuilding industry.

One of the application challenges is that the structure and the level of technological development may be extremely different between the co-operating partners. The portfolio ranges from fully developed and computerised companies which also apply appropriate management abilities to the change of the processes to those companies who have hardly applied any computerised solutions for their own process handling. The shipyards have to think about the right way to build up solutions which allow most of these companies to be integrated into advanced co-operative working concepts. The way as chosen by many other industries to just put enough pressure on suppliers and force them into solutions which are favourable for the customer but complicated, inadequate and expensive for supplier cannot be applied by the shipyards. This is because the shipyards are a very heterogeneous group of companies itself which does not create enough market-power. Even co-operational agreements between bigger shipbuilding groups in Europe are not consequently used to create and us this market-power. Further, the supplier base is comparable big and consist of many small and medium sized enterprises which are by far not prepared for advanced working concepts.

New very promising technologies which have been developed for Internet applications may help to overcome the old problem of too high cost for the application of classical EDI solutions to small and medium sized enterprises. As a result it can be stated that the availability of technology for all level applications is as such that they almost offer solutions also for the incorporation of these companies. Different projects performed under the framework of European support programmes etc. have substantially contributed to some of these developments. MARVEL OUS (Maritime Virtual Enterprise Linkage – Open User Syndicate) draw a baseline to the situation of standards for Maritime Virtual Enterprises and edited a basic book on standards. EDIMAR (Electronic Data Interchange for the European Maritime Industry) developed some adapted EDIFACT messages to the need of maritime purchasing applications, contributed to the definition of STEP AP 226 and developed and adapted workflow tools and concepts to shipbuilding purchasing applications. The new project MARIFLOW (A Workflow Management System for the Maritime Industry) is now working on workflow applications to quality data chains including applications of EDI functionality for the exchange of quality certificates for steel plates. In these projects and more others functionality and potential of different technologies and standards have been proved by setting up demonstration networks and scenarios covering Computer Supported Co-operative Work (CSCW), Workflow Management Systems, Classical EDI and Extensible EDI (XDI) concepts by means of internet technology. It is now about time to continue working on these platforms and to create numerous and manifold reference applications to verify and develop commercial benefits and to create new starting points for further developments.

6 BAL.SILK – The Method for Effective Inter-Organisational IT-Implementations

To reduce the risk and the expanse for inter organisational information technology (IT) projects, a systematic realisation method is needed. This method which is called BAL.SILK method (BALance Strategy for the Information Logistic Concept realisations) was developed and successful approved in practise also for EDI projects. It is developed for the installation of inter-organisational information systems and considers the technology and network aspects, different organisational structures of the co-operating partners and the cost/benefit aspects of such realisations.

SILK includes the whole range from the of business process chain analysis, support of the evaluation process of important process chains up to the tool supported realisation of selected chains. This focused method guarantees a cost effective solution of information logistic concepts and improves the organisational and information logistic processes. BAL.SILK was developed and improved over at least five years by the partners of BALance Technology Consulting and was proved in the automotive supplier industry as well as in the shipbuilding industry. The method marks out for the flexible interconnection of inter- and intra-organisational processes, the support of group- and workflow technologies and the consideration of organisational aspects.

It uses methodology specific developed tools as well as tools which are available at the clients. This makes the implementation easier. In general, the method is divided into five general steps (Figure 5):

- Analysis of business process chains
- Determination of robustness and weak points
- Definition of nominal concepts
- Evaluation
- Realisation

The analysis of **business process chains** focuses on the determination of the companies' organisation and the process chains. To reduce the analysis expanse (analysis only as much as absolutely needed), it is necessary to select the relevant chains for information logistic as soon as possible. Parameters for the selection of process chains are among other things the strategic goals of the company, the communication intensity respectively the media interrupt within dedicated process chains and the determined company lacks. The orientation of the SILK-method is not on different company areas

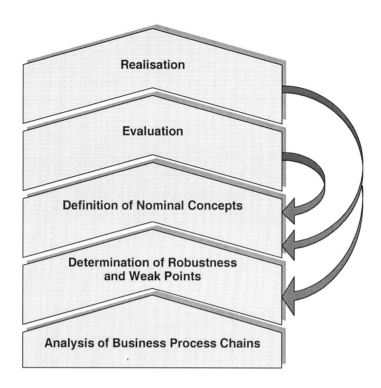

Figure 5: BAL.SILK method for the realisation of information logistic concepts

(e.g. departments) but on the process chains which also includes inter-organisational processes. For the description, evaluation and the support of the selection BAL.SILK uses well known tools as well as especially for this method developed tools. The analysis results are models of selected process chains and a data dictionary.

The list of **robustness and weak points** of the chosen chains are presented. Indicators for weak points are e.g. high information run times, low use of available information systems, high data redundancy and high manual finishing expanse.

Within the **definition of nominal concepts** the most important chains for the improvement are selected. The nominal concepts includes the organisational description; and the selection of information systems, interchange formats and message-types. The technical concept includes the selection criteria for the needed networks and network services. The future process chains and their alternatives are described.

For the **evaluation**, the possible technology solutions described in the nominal concepts will be compared. The criteria are among others the realisation and the running costs, the quality of the realisation, the time needed for the realisation and the needed organisational changes. The expanse has to be compared with the expected benefit. All changes, which will be made in this phase of SILK, have to be reflected to the nominal concept. At the end of this process, decisions will be made for the following realisation procedure and the technology will be selected.

During the **realisation** phase, the progress and the quality is controlled, training and qualification will be supported and decisions about changes have to be made. A balanced management of goals, milestones, resources, costs and quality is managed by BAL.SILK.

BAL.SILK was used for analysing order process chains for steel in some yards. The results are described within this chapter and some general conclusions are made. Within the project a high communication intensity and a lot of media breaks over the inter-organisational process chains were observed. The weak points in this process chains of a couple of yards were evident. Beside the high manual expanse for the generation and administration of the order data, time breaks within the process chains have been some days. This time is needed to exchange information between the yard and the steel supplier because of incomplete information. Additionally a lot of discussions are needed via telephone because of unclear defined orders.

For one of the yards a nominal concept has been defined for the EDI support of steel order chains. Networks, network provider, communication protocols were selected as well as EDIFACT as the message standard. Different EDI systems were tested and proposals were made by considering the different requirements of the company. During the evaluation phase of the different proposals, a rough cost calculation was made and compared with the expected benefit. Therefor mainly the cost reductions and process time improvements were taken into consideration. The feasibility of organisational changes were evaluated. During the realisation phase, a lot of attention has to spent to the organisational changes. It was really difficult to change the old rules inside the companies like the signature rights. A test installation was made and after a half of a year the realisation phase was finished successfully. The last point of the realisation phase was the preparation of an EDI contract. It includes the description of the technical realisation and the rules in case of need. Compared to the nominal concepts, there are only some marginal changes especially on the message content. In relation to the weak point description eminent optimisation potentials were shown. Especially the EDI realisation for steel ordering processes reached human expense reductions for the shipyard of approx. 70%.

This realisation shows the potential of EDI applications in the shipbuilding industry. As a general assumptions of the described project a cost reduction potential of 3 – 6% compared to the total cost of a ship today seems be possible. Compared to other industries and compared to some promising field tests these figures can be considered to be conservative. In comparison to investments in the manufacturing area the risk ratio (ratio of investment to potential earnings) is lower, but needs more managerial involvement and consequent reorganisation. Further international co-operation in this field will increase the potential and will strengthen the basis for commercial solutions.

As mentioned before, to know the yard individual supplier basis is essential to choose the right partners for implementing EDI solutions. The return on investment of such projects depends on this selection. Some general tendencies were discovered by using BAL.SILK in the analysing phase of the above described project (Figure 6).

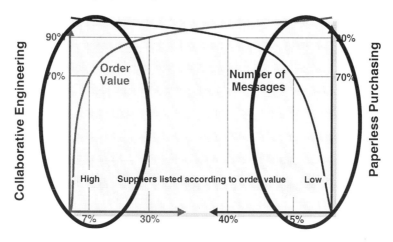

Figure 6: Typical supplier analysis and recommended co-operation fields

With approx. 15% of the yard suppliers for low order values nearly 70 % of the purchasing messages have to be handled. This supplier group is a good candidate for implementing paperless EDI purchasing procedures. The supplier products with high engineering expanse are products with higher order values. 70% of the higher order values were handled by 7% of the yard suppliers. For this group the IT support of collaborative engineering, e.g. by using EDI for technical data will optimise the inter-organisational procedures. The figures are not the same for every yard, but the tendency is the same in many yards.

From this analysis indicators and strategic decisions can be derived with which partners technical solutions towards paperless procurement and/or collaborative engineering should be developed on high priority.

7   Maritime EDI Network Implementation in Europe

The knowledge that Electronic Data Interchange will have a high benefit for the shipbuilding industry if implementation costs could be reduced by common definitions and realisations has led to an European project. A large European consortia of shipyards, suppliers and classification societies has initiated the ESPRIT project EDIMAR (Electronic Data Interchange for the European Maritime Industry) to install an EDI based network (Figure 7).

Figure 7: Partner of the EDIMAR project

EDIMAR created, implemented, tested and evaluated an EDI based communication infrastructure between the various partners involved in the ship production process. This infrastructure was to automate ordering, delivery, invoicing and payment process of ship mechanical systems and equipment as well as for supporting the design refinement process which was an intermediary activity between ordering and delivery for such "make-to-order" products. The project aimed to act as a vehicle for migration from currently paper-based system to future EDI system. An inter-organisational workflow system linking the various autonomous companies and thus traced the information flow across company borders as a necessary prerequisite to support enhanced co-ordination. EDIMAR was an end-user driven project, aiming at the optimum usage of available communication technology and developing the missing links and tailor the existing software modules to their needs. The participation of all relevant industry types ensured the consideration of all important requirements and a profitable realisation.

In general, the commercial information (orders, order changes, etc) was generated by using in-house systems like PPC systems (Production Planning and Control) with application specific formats. These data is transformed into a neutral format by using an EDI system and delivered to the co-operation partner (suppliers, banks, etc.) via networks. The partners integrate the information into their in-house system after transforming the information into their specific format. That means in practise the reduction of manual input failures, communication time and process time, which leads to lower stock level (the order processes are quicker), higher order safety (the order and production point can be closer together), higher process transparency (inquiry of the order process status is possible over company boundaries) and fast data check (automatically check of e.g. orders against order responses are possible).

As mentioned before, the supplier product structure influences the EDI infrastructure. Available solutions of other branches were used or adopted to the requirements of the maritime industry. But in many cases, this is too difficult because of the complex product structure. In shipbuilding even major supply-products are not standard of-the-shelf products. Within the EDIMAR project, three product classes have been defined (Figure 8).

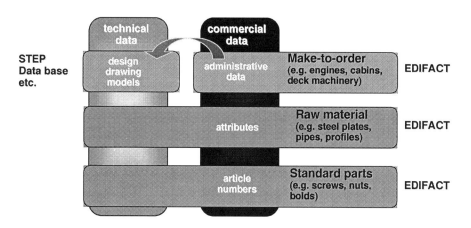

Figure 8: Classification of supplier products

The first group is the group of standard products which can be described by product or article numbers. Today, Electronic Data Interchange (EDI) is an often used technology in many branches like consumer goods and automotive industry. These branches mainly handle with standard products and therefor, they have clear logistic structures with long-term co-operations. Therefore, EDIMAR uses their experiences and realisations.

But beside that, the project defined solutions for raw material and "make-to-order products". Orders for raw material like steel plates, pipes, profiles etc. need a detailed description by attributes (measures, classification, etc.). These attributes has been structured to enable EDI applications for this kind of products.

Ordering of "make-to-order" products such as engines, cargo securing systems, cranes, boilers, etc. are accompanied by a significant number of engineering information. The follow-up process of joint design-refinement between shipyard and supplier is normally highly data-exchange intensive. The need of procurement and engineering information respectively product data for "make-to-order" products requires the combined use of two different standards - EDIFACT (Electronic Data Interchange for Administration, Commerce and Transport) standard for the commercial messages and the STEP (Standard for Exchange of Product Model Data) standard for the product model description.

One example to integrate both standards is shown in Figure 9. For the exchange of technical information, an envelope message has to be created. This message includes a description of the transmitted technical data like project name, project number, file format etc., which makes it easier for the receiver to appoint the data to the right department, right application and responsible person in the company. The technical data and the describing message have to be transmitted together to the receiver. Additional commercial information (EDIFACT messages) can be added to the technical messages. The transformation of the technical data into a neutral format (e.g. STEP) will be done by the technical application system (e.g. CAD) itself and will not be influenced by the EDI system.

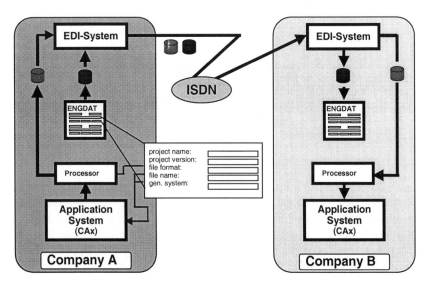

Figure 9: EDI for technical data

EDIMAR has to adapt the messages to the requirements of the maritime industry. Therefor common implementation guidelines have been developed. That means, the project has defined and realised different messages using EDIFACT standards. Also, the project has developed and used an industry specific extension to the STEP standard for exchange of engineering data (the AP226 for ship mechanical systems). Particularly for one-of-the kind supplier parts administrative and technical information are needed. Therefore the EDIMAR project has established a link between the EDIFACT and the STEP standard.

The EDIMAR project has achieved the following tasks:

- **Specific maritime EDIFACT messages (EDIFACT Subsets)** for selected commercial business and engineering processes have been defined. These business processes included orders, order responses, order changes, despatch advice's and invoices for standard material, raw material as well as for make-to-order items. Messages for the order process chains have been implemented on the basis of the EDIMAR Subset descriptions.

- For the electronic exchange of technical information the STEP standard has been used within the project. Therefor an Application Activity Model and a STEP Application Reference Model for **Ship Mechanical Systems (AP226)** have been developed. The models have been presented on ISO-STEP meetings.

- For the exchange of procurement information EDI interfaces have been developed and tested as a first prototype. An **EDI System** has been installed and is now available as a commercial service of BALance (BAL.DIS). **STEP Processors** for AP226 (crane models) have been developed. The EDI environment to support the management of technical data and commercial data for has been integrated.

- To support the co-ordination of distributed business processes in temporary engineering and production networks **an inter-organisational workflow system** has to be installed. These distributed workflow components based on the EDI communication infrastructure will support process definition and process execution across the boundaries of autonomous organisations. Prototype implementations and tests have been made with two different systems in one location.

- A **scenario** has been implemented and shown all project results by using real business data.

The EDIMAR results focusing on commercial and technical EDI and on inter-organisational work flow systems will lead to a complete electronic working environment. This will reduce the ship construction costs, the time to market and the lead time for European shipbuilders, enhanced inter-organisational co-operation in ship production and improve the quality of data exchange between industries.

8   Benefit of EDI Realisations in the Shipbuilding Industry

As said above the cost involved in the complex functions of supply chain management are substantial and very much worth to seriously think about an improvement. Nevertheless these cost are very often hidden in other costs and therefore, often not easily to identify or to separate. Overhead cost by nature the potential for cost reduction is difficult to prove and just be approached through consequent managerial efforts and cross-departmental thinking and re-organisation. However, a considerable overall cost-reduction for ship newbuildings can be anticipated by the application of new technologies and new ways of collaborative working if the technology is seriously taken and consequently applied.

The commercial benefits maybe generated at both ends of the collaboration, the shipyards and the suppliers. In comparison to investments in the manufacturing area the risk ratio (ratio of investment to potential earnings) is lower, but, to say this again, needs more managerial involvement and consequent reorganisation. The benefits through the application of advanced Electronic Commerce and EDI technology in the different processes of the supply chain may sum up to about 5% of the total cost of the ship, which is a considerable share. The biggest share can be realised through decreasing material overhead cost at the shipyard and at the suppliers. However major achievements can be expected in the design area as well as in the area of Sales and Administration (Figure 10).

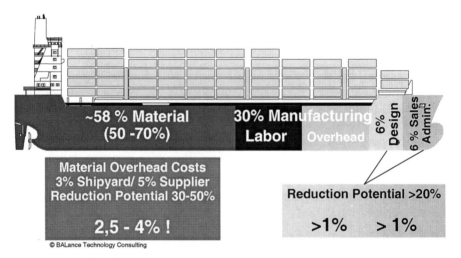

Figure 10: Potential for cost reduction

At the supplier side some more effects can be generated through the use of advanced multimedia marketing instruments, i.e. electronic catalogues with technical information elements either on CD-ROM and/or through suitable Internet representations. This may include product descriptions in standard formats which are ready to build in for the designer in his product model. Further the consequent building of organisational interfaces towards the shipyards including building the ability for the structured exchange of data by means of EDI can also create very positive effects for the opening of new markets and the maintenance of existing one's.

Potential effects at the suppliers are the building of a special differential advantage in the market, possibilities for direct marketing (without regional sales agents), a faster penetration of the market with new products, a faster/cheaper change of the marketing strategy and a closer link to the customer once the new links have been positively established.

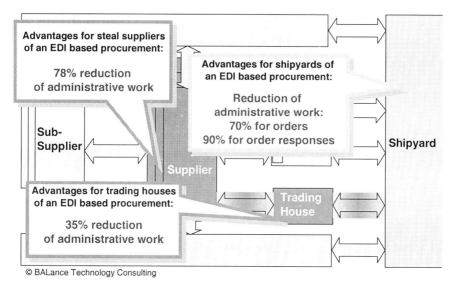

Figure 11: Benefits through EDI based Steel purchasing.

Pilot installation and demonstration cases have shown that the anticipated targets for cost reductions could be achieved easily (Figure 11). This is also confirmed by some comparable applications in other industries However, the full benefit of the investment can just be achieved if new and EC/EDI based shipyard/supplier relations can be build up fast and consequently so that as many suppliers as possible can be linked in a short time frame. Risks can be minimised if shipyards and suppliers in the starting phase do not invest in own systems, but use commercial data clearing services (e.g. BAL.DIS the BALance Data Integration Service). As long as the number of interlinked suppliers or other co-operational partners is low or the amount of data to be transformed is limited those commercial services offer the economical solution. By developing more co-operational links one or all partners can successively migrate into an own system which can be slowly build up in parallel to an already working solution.

Other benefits have been proved through tremendous lead time savings during the entire purchasing process, but also in other follow-up processes. Better data accuracy, less mistakes through data coding and a better basis for decision making processes have been reported to be other major achievements which can be forecasted, but just proved through the consequent application and use of new and advanced technology and management methodologies. There is no lack in technology, even if for many special applications suitable solutions still need to be developed. But for initial earnings the technology is ready for application.

9 Costs of EDI Realisations, Technical Prospects and Organisational Challange

The costs of an EDI implementation project can be distinguished between investment costs and running costs. The investments include costs for:

- EDI-software and implementation,
- qualification of EDI-software administrators,
- configuration and test of communication software,
- adaptation of in-house systems (programs for data selection, test, error handling etc.),
- interface development for in-house systems,
- re-engineering of organisational structures,
- definition of EDI-contracts,
- implementation of security modules etc.

The communication costs and the costs for the integration of new partner relationships are running costs.

Beside the realisation expanse the investment costs specially for small and medium enterprises with a low amount of EDI partners and low message exchange frequency are an important factor. To reduce the investment costs as well as the expanse for training and qualification on EDI-systems, an EDI broker service (Figure 12) should be used for new established EDI projects. The EDI broker service of BALance is BAL.DIS (BALance Data Integration Service) which can be used instead of company owned EDI-systems. By using this service every company can send their in-house file to the service. The service will convert the data into a neutral message and deliver it to the co-operation partner. The company has to pay a charge per message which is much more cheaper for low message exchange traffic than the investment into own installations. After increasing the amount of EDI partners and the message exchange traffic an own system can be installed and a high return on investment can be guaranteed in a short time.

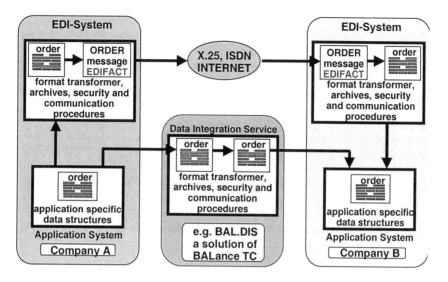

Figure 12: Principles of EDI

It should be noted that the crucial points of EDI realisations are not the technology but the organisational aspects. In our experience, the technical problems include only 10% of the realisation expanse. The other 90% of the expanse is needed for the solution of organisational problems. That means e.g. the restructuring of the process chains and the change in the company culture (suppliers are not longer slaves but they are partners). To attain the possible optimisation potentials, the partners have to find common solutions. It is estimated that approximately 30% of the total benefit of EDI can be realised by the substitution of traditional communication means and the other 70% by the adaptation of the processes to the new environment. That shows the importance of organisational viewpoint of these technology. Therefor BAL.DIS provides more than Value Added Network Services, which are concentrating on exchange and tracking of transactions. BAL.DIS analysis the business processes and opens possibilities to optimise the inter-organisational co-operations.

The paper based exchange of structured information should be replaced by electronic based message exchange as complete as possible to avoid parallel processes (electronic and paper based) and additional costs (Figure 13). Therefor the customer (company A) has only one EDI interface to the world. The company sends all messages to BAL.DIS, where the messages can be transformed into any other format. After that procedure BAL.DIS is able to send the message to an EDI-system of the co-operation partner (standardised or any other format) or a fax system (if no EDI system is available) or to the dummy EDI-application BAL.PUR (BALance PURchasing Module). This module is able to receive messages, store the information in an own data base and transmit messages. It is mainly used for companies without any in-house systems.

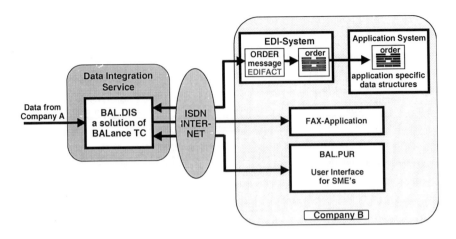

Figure 13: BAL.DIS avoids parallel interfaces to different suppliers

BAL.DIS offers a complete and cheap EDI service specially for companies with low exchange traffic and keeps the way to an own EDI system open for the future.

10 Conclusion

The shipbuilding industry is characterised by the complexity of its product, concurrent processes and a large number of external companies taking part in shipbuilding processes. Enabling these companies to a more efficient co-operation is one of the major challenges for European shipbuilders towards major cost-reductions. One possibility to overcome the cost barrier is to outsource certain parts of the product development as well as of the production. This in turn increases the expanse and the costs for organising the supply chain.

The complexity of maritime supply processes requires high effort for their management, but information and communication technology is available to optimise the inter-organisational processes. It has been shown that EDI for technical and commercial data could be used successfully in the maritime industry. The needed effort to realise Electronic Data Interchange is higher than in other branches, but the potentials are also higher. The significance of organisational aspects should not be underestimated for EDI realisations.

Especially the reorganisation of the purchasing process and the logistical process between shipyards and their suppliers through the application of Electronic Data Interchange and Electronic Commerce Technology show promising potentials. Very actual new developments in the area of Internet programming languages (XML) which are allowing also the exchange of structured data on this basis are very promising to also overcome cost problems of classical EDI for small companies, which do not even run own purchasing systems. Nevertheless, all applications in this field have to consider the heterogeneous structure of the shipyard's supplier base. Therefore all solutions needs to be flexible to the outside, but streamlined to the inside.

The problem to start respective applications in shipyards is not a problem of the availability of technology. A management decision has to be taken, pilot applications have to be implemented and necessary re-organisation and qualification programmes have to be started in parallel to the configuration of the technical solution. Once the technology is in place and the organisation has learned to handle it the potential to quickly earn commercial benefits is very high.

References

AHLERS, R.,: Installation Method for Electronic Data Interchange in the Maritime Industry. In: Johansson, K.; Koyama, T. (Ed.): Proceedings of the 9th International Conference on Computer Applications in Shipbuilding, Yokohama, Japan, 13-17 October 1997. The Society of Naval Architects of Japan, Tokyo; S. 511-526.

AHLERS, R.; WARSCH, C.: Electronic Data Interchange in the Shipbuilding Industry. In: Brodda, J.; Johansson, K. (Ed.): Proceedings of the 8th International Conference on Computer Applications in Shipbuilding (ICCAS 94); September 5-9, Bremen, Germany.

AHLERS, R. et al (1999), "EDIMAR - Electronic Data Interchange for the European Maritime Industry", Internal Project Report No. 2 Esprit Project EDIMAR, January 1999

BLOOS, L; PESTER, W.: Technologie-Vorsprung wird von den Reedern kaum honoriert. VDI-Nachrichten; 22.12.1995.

BRODDA, J., AHLERS, R. (1995), "Effective use of EDI, including MARIS programme relationships and interactive partnerships between shipyards and their suppliers", Proceedings of the CESA (Committee of European Shipbuilders' Association) Conference "European Shipbuilders World Class Performance through new Partnerships with Suppliers", November 1995, Brussels, Belgium.

BRODDA, J.: Electronic Commerce – Chance and Challenge in Shipyard/Supplier Relations; Machinery Marketing Conference of the MMA (Machine Maritime Association) on Development and Marketing of Shipboard Machinery and Equipment for the Commercial and Naval Markets, New Orleans, United States, 19-20 November 1997. http://www.marmach.org/.

BUXMANN, P. (1999), "The Future of EDI – XML as a basis for building bilateral business processes", Brochure of Competence Center XML, University Frankfurt, Germany 1999.

EDIMAR D-2-1: Definition of the commercial messages content (standard parts, raw material make-to-order products) and EDI engineering meta data. EDIMAR project deliverable D-2-1.

EDIMAR D-3-1: Application Activity Model for Ship Mechanical System and Information needed to be represented in AP 226 for shipbuilding processes. EDIMAR project deliverable.

EDIMAR D-3-2: AP226 Application Reference Model in EXPRESS and EXPRESS-G and AP226 STEP clause 4 documentation including AP 226 CDC document. EDIMAR project deliverable D-3-2.

EUROPEAN COMMISSION – DG III/D (Ed.): Task Force "Maritime Systems of the Future", A Competitive Maritime Industry in Europe. European Commission, DG III/D; Rue de Loi 200 Wetstraat, B-1049 Brussels.

KENDALL, J. (1998), "Standards and Protocols for the Realisation of Virtual Enterprises in the Maritime Industry", Public Document Esprit Project MARVEL OUS, January 1998.

KUHLMANN, T.; MAßOW, C.; LAMPING, R.: Inter-Organisational Workflow based on Electronic data Interchange in Maritime Industry. In: Johansson, K.; Koyama, T. (Ed.): Proceedings of the 9th International Conference on Computer Applications in Shipbuilding, Yokohama, Japan, 13-17 October 1997. The Society of Naval Architects of Japan, Tokyo; S. 505-510.

MANZANARES, E.: Lead time Reduction as a Result of EDI Supplier Connections. Machinery Marketing Conference of the MMA (Machine Maritime Association) on Development and Marketing of Shipboard Machinery and Equipment for the Commercial and Naval Markets, New Orleans, United States, 19-20 November 1997. http://www.marmach.org/.

ÖZEL F. (1996), "Analysis of Cost-Benefit through the Application of Electronic Data Interchange in Shipbuilding", Master Thesis at the University of Bremen, Germany 1996.

TIENPONT, A.: Networking – Philosophy behind co-operation between yards and suppliers in the Netherlands. Proceedings of the European Shipbuilders World Class Performance Through New Partnerships with Suppliers; Brussels, Belgium, 28-29 November 1995.

IT Application for Ship Management and Ship Operation

Egil Rensvik

Norwegian Marine Technology Research Institute (MARINTEK)
Egil.Rensvik@marintek.sintef.no

Abstract

This chapter covers IT applications found useful for ship operation and ship management. It reflects a change in the acceptance of IT systems on board ships and at the shipowners office. The software itself has become more reliable and common use of PC computers in society illustrates the use and importance of this technology. Through several projects in Norway we have made progress in improving ship operation as it relates to safety, efficiency, routine work load reduction and competence development for the crew and personnel ashore. Transport logistics efficiency is crucial for sea transport as competition with rail and road transport increases. Integration of applications and efficient exchange of information between different parties in the transport chain shows promising results. Based on the availability of information, we see a need for developing "decision support functions" for different levels in the organization. Efficient use of IT systems requires organizational adoption and competence development. These areas are likely to cost more then the IT systems itself. We still see a need for improving the IT systems to be more user friendly, as well as eliminating the need for an IT expert on board every ship.

1 Introduction

Shipping today must balance ISM[1] implementation, which requires a great deal of the internal resources, while at the same time dealing with the problem of availability of qualified officers in the fleet. The Bimco studies showed that there was a lack of 18,000 officers in the worldwide fleet in 1995. The study indicates that this is likely to increase to 40,000 in year 2005. The experience from Norwegian shipping companies indicates that this negative trend is developing even faster, which will present an even bigger challenge for the future.

---

[1] ISM-International Safety Management Code

New computer technology seams to develop faster then expected some years ago. There is a danger that a lot of personnel in the shipping area can not cope with this rapidly changes. This is a challenge for the industry to be able to make products that is easy to use and maintain.

New international requirements like implementation of the ISM code, has taken a lot of resources in all shipping organizations. Even if there are many positive effects of this work, a focus of attention has been changed from the technical aspects to the management aspects.

The question is can we get the benefit of all the technology, get the added value from the IT systems, and will the shipping industry be an interesting and high status business area in the future? The best approach to these challenges is to develop the solutions in close co-operation between the users, manufacturer of equipment, software companies and researchers. The role for the maritime educational institute is also of great importance.

1.1 Norwegian shipping research

Maritime R&D in Norway been coordinated through the "MARITIM" programme in The Research Council of Norway. This programme is covering the areas of:

- Transport Logistics
- Ship Operation
- Environmental aspects
- Ship Yard developments and
- Ship Equipment technology

The focus and the reason for covering all these areas has been to be able to set up cluster –oriented projects, which involves parties from different part of the supply chain. This means the shipyard, suppliers, shipowner and their customers can sit together in the same R&D project.

The recent years, Maritime R&D in Norway has been focused on utilizing the benefits of Information Technology in the shipping industry, and especially for ship operation and ship management. This includes involvement from the shipowner companies, the supplying industry, software producers and classification societies. The research activities have focused on developing products with practical installations on board several newbuildings and existing ships. The following are some of these applications.

2 Integrated maritime IT - The Höegh[2] project

Development of IT for ships started many years ago with "stand alone" systems for automation and instrumentation functions. In the last few years, availability of standard PC, PC-network and satellite communication technology has provided the opportunity to integrate the systems on board the ship itself as well as between the ship and the land organization.

The installation of the integrated network on board the Höegh Monal (figure 1) and Höegh Morus shows the use of main automation systems integrated with MiTS[3] protocol and linked to the management network through a "gateway", (figure 2). Use of standard protocol like MiTS (figure 3) is essential for guaranteeing flexibility when choosing different manufacturers of part systems. The management network consists of a Windows NT server and three workstations for the officers.

Figure 1 Høegh Monal, open hatch, bulk container ship

The following list represents the primary applications that are available on the integrated management solution:

- Reporting System - includes automatically recorded data, like ships position, engine performance, cargo condition and manual input from the officers, i.e. deck log, port log, machinery log. The important factor in this case is the effectiveness in reducing work load for entering of

---

[2] Höegh – Norwegian Shipping Company

[3] MiTS – Maritime Technology Standard, "open integration network mechanism", IEC TC80/WG6.

input data. Today's paperbased reporting systems force users to write the same information several times in different forms. It is projected that a lot of this paper work will be reduced through users of computer application. Another advantage is that the data exchange between ship and shore does not require high speed datalinks and can be updated regularly, one or two times a day. The database structure from this project is basis for the proposed AP 234[4] standard.

- Weather Routing - provides the officers on board with access to weather charts. These weather prognoses received from Meteorological Institutes, are used as a decision tool for selecting the best route to the next port. This requires a high speed data communication shore to ship and the datafiles can be in the order of 0.75-1.0MB. The cost of these transmissions is likely to be reduced in the years to come.

- High Speed Data Communication with Inmarsat B, 64 kbit/s, - gives better performance for transferring datafiles than the standard A system with 9.6 kbit/s. For ships sailing in coastal waters, a possibility for switching between GSM and Inmarsat will be a cost-efficient solution.

- Load calculator - in this installation it is linked to the management network and will read data from the "Gateway process". Stability, share forces, etc for the ship can be continuously calculated.

- Maintenance Management System - connected to the management network and uses "condition monitoring data" to trigger Maintenance tasks. This has usually been "counting of running-hours from rotating machinery", but in this case both the technical conditions from the main engine and faults from the fire alarm systems are used to trigger the maintenance and inspection tasks.

- Interactive Electronic Manuals (from several companies integrated in a structured database) - provides quick access to relevant information related to the actual task. This can be a maintenance task, trouble shooting or requirement for spare parts for overhaul.

- Computer Based Training Modules - cover familiarization training, training on technical systems, basic training, etc.

- Condition Monitoring of Main Engine - includes the system on board, but also transfer of information to the shipowners office, for simplification of trouble shooting by providing the chief engineer and the inspector with the same information at the same time.

---

[4] AP234 – ISO TC 184/SC4-T23

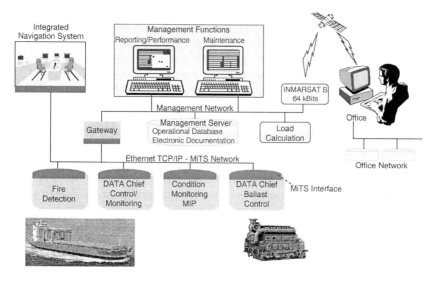

Figure 2 Information system

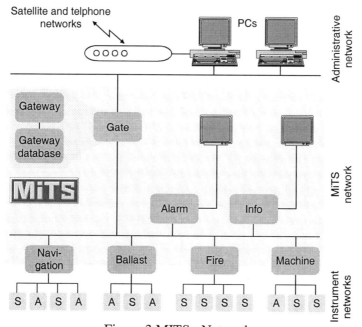

Figure 3 MITS - Network

Our experience so far has provided valuable information which will lead to improved applications in the future. These improvements are applicable to both newbuilding, with totally automatic data recording, and for existing ships with reduced functionality and more manual input of data. (Figure 4). Höegh Fleet Services[5] uses the same "infrastructure architecture" for their all of their newbuildings. In parallel, they are working further to implement the working procedures for the land organization for improving ship performance and maintenance management. One example of this includes new structures in Maintenance Management systems, which have been developed in close cooperation with software companies. We also see that several automation systems manufacturers have started developing similar infrastructures, providing a link between ship instrumentation, throughout management level and communication to the management systems at shipowners office. This development indicates that there will be several industrial products in the near future.

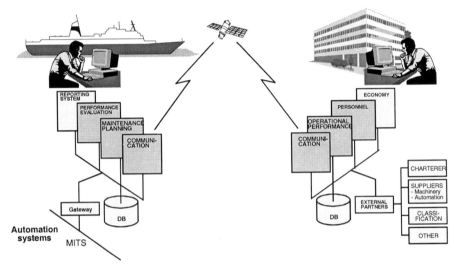

Figure 4 Information exchange, decision support

3 New classification society regulation

Use of IT includes automatic recorded condition and performance status of critical systems and components. These functions in combination with standard reporting and Maintenance Management reporting, have become more useful for trend analyses and for documentation to external parties like the port authorities and classification societies. The benefits include a more systematically recorded status of the machinery for use both to class and the shipowner, decreased number of physical inspections and reduced number of "opening up" inspections on equipment. Tests made by the classification

---

[5] Höegh Fleet Services- Höegh Ship Management Company.

societies show promising results and will improve business relationships and reduce costs for the shipping company in the future. Important aspects are that most of the shipowners have ships in different classification societies, which leads to an increased need for standardization of information exchange from ships to the different classes. This standardization work has been coordinated through EMSA[6], fig. 5.

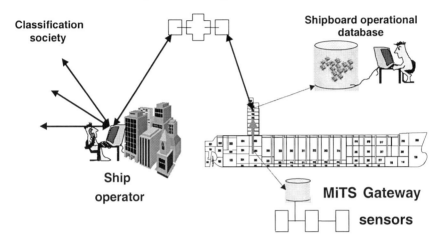

Information exchange between ship and shore

Figure 5 Classification society, integration and standardization

4 Interactive electronic documentation

The traditional paper based technical manuals and documentation of ship systems have varied widely and are often of poor quality. One step in the direction of improving this situation is to start producing this documentation in a more standard electronic format. This in itself will not improve the manual unless work is done to design a structure that is easy to implement in an integrated solution for practical use on board the ship. These practical applications shows the structure of the documentation. These are made by manufacturer of equipment in an electronic form, using the SGML[7] and XML[8] standard with the Document Type Definition (DTD[9]) from the

---

[6] EMSA - European Maritime Step Association

[7] SGML – ISO 8879- Standard General Markup Language

[8] XML - See www.w3c.org

[9] DTD – ISO - Document Type Definition

Norwegian project "IT in Ship Operation[10]" (figure 6). This is now integrated between this database, as shown in figure 7 and the Maintenance Management System. The chief engineer or the mechanical engineer can from the Maintenance Task Procedure, link up to the actual description of the system which includes spare parts requirements, troubleshooting, instructions for assembling the equipment and guidelines for operation and repair. It is also possible to search directly in the database and use the information found in preparation for work to be done or for training of junior mechanical personnel. In order to have an efficient integration of documentation from several suppliers to take place, standards for exchange of these data are essential.

Figure 6 Interactive Electronic Documentation

Several shipping companies are requiring these kinds of solutions as part of the newbuilding process, resulting in better and more easily accessible documentation. Other benefits include improved quality of documentation and reduced work for the supplier through automated updating of their product databases as well as cost savings through improved exchange of the data.

---

[10] IT in Ship Operation Programme – Norwegian R&D programme 1994-98.

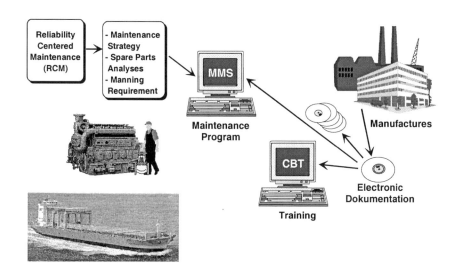

Figure 7 Maintenance optimization

5 RCM -analysis

As a part of the ISM code, continuous improvement of the maintenance process is required. The methods used to ensure continuous improvement are "RCM- Reliability Centered Maintenance" and "CIM – Continuos Improvement of Maintenance". The principal concepts is shown in figure 8.

RCM are an analysis method first developed and applied by the aviation industry in the late 60's. The results from the analysis forms a basis for the maintenance engagement (strategy, tasks, etc.) for the function and equipment subject to analysis. A normal analysis comprises:

- selection of systems subject to analysis
- collecting input for analysis (maintenance routines, operation manuals, equipment data sheets, P&IDs, inspection routines, failure data etc.)
- function analyses, FMECA and maintenance assignment
- expert assessments
- reporting of results

In the research programme "IT in Ship Operation", MARINTEK established procedures for RCM-analysis for ships, including functional breakdown of vessel, cause and consequence analysis and assignment of effective maintenance tasks and spare parts. Further, a ranking list of all systems on the pilot ship with respect to criticality were established. RCM-analysis for the most critical system on a merchant ship (main engine, cargo system, el-power generation, steam system, steering system) were completed. Finally,

MARINTEK completed and evaluated work packing for maintenance of Ulstein Bergen Auxiliary Engine based on RCM-results.

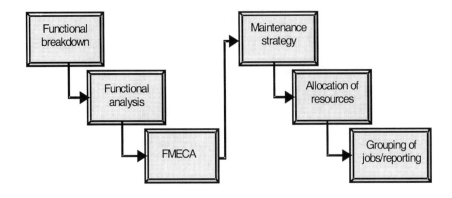

Figure 8 Main parts in RCM

5.1 Continuous Improvement

The RCM project described in section 5, developed a model for continuous improvement of maintenance and spare part stock which can be included in maintenance management systems, (MMS's). This model facilitates the continuous improvement process by introducing decision support features. The MMS will continuously monitor the actual maintenance history and spare part consumption, flagging deviations from the original plan. The results of the RCM-analysis are then used in the planning process. The ultimate objective is that the MMS itself will direct the user's focus towards the non conformities and guide him/her through the decision process. Figure 9. shows developed module for continuous improvement (Continuous Improvement Module-CIM) of maintenance and spare part stock.

6 Competence Development

Over the past ten years, the use of computer based training or CBT, has become more common. In the maritime field, the most recent development in the area of competence development have been made by manufacturers of equipment. Increasingly, these companies are taking on the responsibility to make documentation and training packages available as part of system delivering. Software companies are constantly improving special training modules for more basic training. It is important that all of these CBT modules are used in combination with the shipping companies overall competence management system and not as "stand alone" training packages. Companies with which MARINTEK has been working closely show clear indications that a complete "learning system" approach yields the greatest success in competence development and management. Figure 10 shows the introduction to "Familiarization training" for a Norwegian shipowner. This module consists of graphic and video presentation of the subject matter. It guides the "student" through the technical information, and ends up with a question sheet for a final test of the competence of the student.

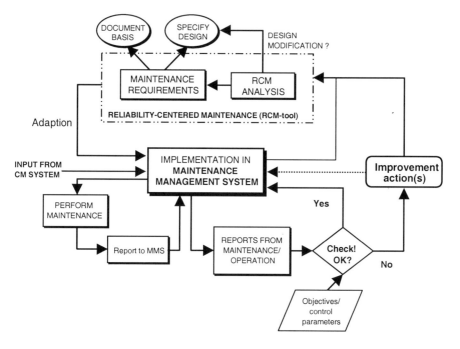

Figure 9 CIM – Principal concepts

In the future, it is clear that "internet/WEB" technology will become an important tool in closing the gap between the ship, shipping company and the "competence source", such as the manufacturer. We see great potential in combining "CBT" modules with "Distance" advice from Subject Matter experts, testing of training results, and the interactivity between the trainer and the "student".

MARINTEK is been involved in projects such as "Flexible learning and Safety-Net[11] where MARINTEK is managing a European Commission funded project with partners from 7 countries. Figure 11. This project includes 12 demonstrations modules for competence development for personnel doing safety-critical work within maritime, offshore port and

---

[11] Safety Net/EC project:

railway industries. A total number of 3,000 candidates took part in the demonstration phase of "Safety-Net". Presently MARINTEK is managing another EC-project "DISCOVER" investigating the potential of PC based "Virtual environment for team training". These technologies will supplement training programs that currently rely on large, expensive, full-scale simulators.

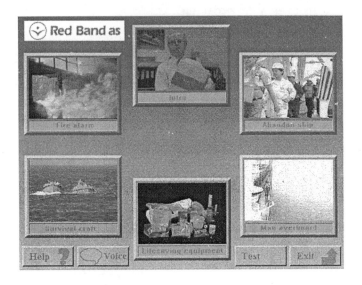

Figure 10 Familiarization training

Important factors for the future will be "experience transfer and experience feedback". Having the luxury to gain knowledge through practical sailing period and learn from older, more experienced personnel is decreasing. It is very important that we investigate methods by which the knowledge of experienced personnel can be effectively transferred to the new generation of ship's crew and to the inspectors and land organization. IT will play an important role in accumulating experience, structuring information from operations and making support tools for improving the training process.

7   Transport Logistics

Being a country outside the mainland of Europe, Norway must to improve transport logistics when transporting cargo from the long Norwegian coast to the consumers in central Europe. Project areas that focus both on Norway and the EC cover the physical transport, supply chain management and transport means. Important for the future is the information availability for those in the lead in this field. The example in figure 12 shows the intermodal transport chain including the different parties involved in the chain.

Figure 11 Flexible training system

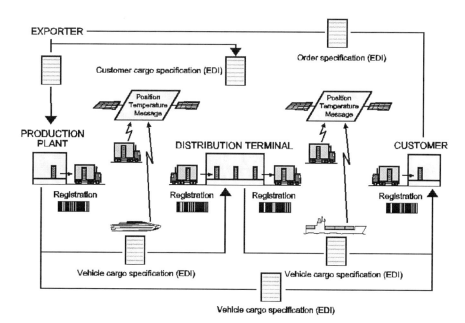

Figure 12 Unit cargo Logistics (Door-to-door)

In this field, we see structural changes where companies merge to gain a stronger position in the market. One example of this type of project is "Supply chain management", which covers both the IT part and physical cargo logistics from the manufacture of the cargo, through supplying the cargo to the main terminal, over the sea leg and on to local distribution to the customer. The efficient information exchange between the different parties involved in the intermodal transport chain is essential for cost-efficiency in the international market. The applications under development in this field are related to the cargo itself, dangerous goods classes, tracking of cargo and payment. The described model show a complex exchange of information between the parties and needs for "reference models", like the TRIM model (see figure 14). This model is useful when designing the different IT applications. The TRIM model has been developed through an EC funded project called "Interport". One example of an application for fleet optimization from MARINTEK has been "Turbo-router" program. Figure 13. This program has tracking functions and can be used for optimization of the ship capacity and the sea transport logistics.

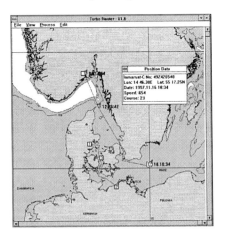

Figure 13 Fleet scheduling, optimization and tracking

8   Emergency Management – Improved Safety with IT systems on the bridge

The ship bridge today contains a wide range array of electronic equipment for navigation purposes. Emergency systems, like the fire alarm system, closing of fire doors, monitoring of stability of the ship, etc are stand alone systems. In an emergency situation, the officers on the bridge have to be well trained and have extensive experience to efficiently operate the different systems. The integrated "Emergency Management System"(EMS) has been developed to give a better overview, provide decision support and meet the requirements in SOLAS.

This main functions in the system cover:

- Fire alarm and handling of the situation, spreading of the fire, extinguishing, evacuation of passengers.
- Damage stability, cargo and ballast tank levels, and damage assessment, prediction of the development of the situation over time, and possible measures to be taken to increase the stability.

Ship machinery and systems technical condition, availability of power in critical maneuvering situations, etc.

After the first test of the system on board the Norwegian passenger ship "The Coastal Express - Polarlys", Cruiseline companies have specified that these types of systems be included on all of their newbuildings.

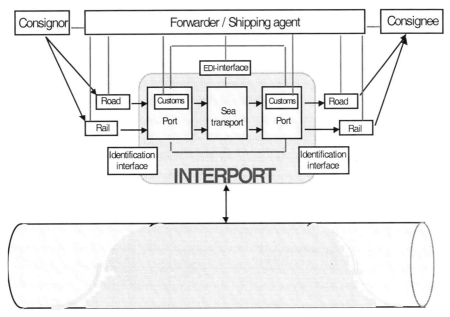

Figure 14 Intermodal transport chain

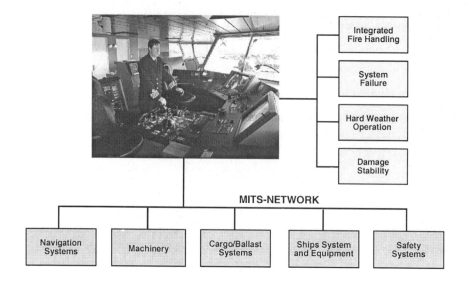

Figure 15 Emergency Management System

9 Future development of maritime IT

From Norwegian R&D perspective, IT gives wide ranging possibilities for making both simple and sophisticated products for use in the shipping industry. Important factors to keep in mind when developing these systems are challenges posed by implementation and the acceptance from the crew and personnel in the land organization. How do we encourage practical people to use the systems and how do we change the work process to make the most out of the system? MARINTEK has been working closely in the R&D projects with shipping companies and software producers developing the systems, making them match the needs as closely as possible. The problem is often that the need changes when customers see the possibilities, while those who have not been involved in the development are skeptical of the new systems. Important in new system development is to:

- make the system easy to use and maintain.
- reduce the complexity and number of new functions in the starting phase
- make the systems reliable and robust.
- develop systems in such a way so that crew members do not have to be data experts.
- make it possible to do remote diagnosis from the manufacturers trouble shooting and make software updates at the system management level.
- use standards and reference models if available.

Through common projects which involve several shipping companies and, with a practical approach, Norwegian R&D has been able to increase the validity and reliability of the new systems by involving the people that will actually use the systems in the development process. In the end this gives a better system result. It also enables the designers and developers to sort out what are useful modules and what is just nice to have.

Norwegian R&D programme is now based upon projects in several shipping organizations, which use the knowledge gained from the "IT in Ship Operation" program 1994-98. The plan is to take the best practices and implement these in each of the companies involved. This will also involve a close cooperation with the manufacturing and software industries.

References:

IT in Ship Operation

http://www.marintek.sintef.no/mt23doc/mitd/

http://www.marintek.sintef.no/sikt/

MARINTEK:

http://www.marintek.sintef.no

MiTS

http://www.itk.ntnu.no/SINTEF/MITS/

TRIM:

http://www.noemie.informatics.sintef.no/trim/

SAFETY NET

http://www.marintek.sintef.no/marintek_eks/organisation/departments/avd-23/4-main.html

STEP: Its Rationale, its Development and its Structure

Jon Owen

University of Bradford, UK
j.owen2@bradford.ac.uk or jon@leva.leeds.ac.uk

Abstract

This chapter gives a brief history of the development of standards and specifications for product data exchange, and some of the problems inherent in the early developments. Methods to reduce or eliminate these are then discussed, followed by a description of the methods used to develop the Standard for the Exchange of Product model data (STEP) and its resulting structure.

1 The historical context

Until the end of the 1970s, industrial enterprises that wished to exchange computer-aided engineering (CAE) data in electronic form had three possibilities:

1. the data from one system was re-keyed (manually) into the second;
2. two special programs were written, called direct translators, that converted the data from one system into the form required by the other, and vice versa;
3. each enterprise purchased the same CAE system, allowing the native form of the data to be exchanged.

None of these alternatives was particularly attractive. The first was very time-consuming and error-prone; the second required specialised knowledge - that was often commercially sensitive - of both of the CAE systems involved. The third alternative meant that one CAE system had to be used for an entire project, which caused difficulties for companies that were suppliers to many main contractors. It also meant that one general-purpose CAE system had to be used, where a number of more specialised systems might have been more appropriate.

Data often needed to be exchanged not only between different enterprises that were co-operating on a project, but also between different departments of the same enterprise. The solutions outlined above apply to both scenarios.

A so-called neutral format for computer-aided engineering data would allow such data to be captured in a form that was independent of all CAE systems. With this approach, the vendor of each system provides two pieces of software, called a pre-processor and a post-processor, that translate from and to the data in the form used by that CAE system. Thus, data is created in the sending CAE system, translated to the neutral format by the pre-processor, sent to the receiving system as a neutral format file, translated from the neutral format by the post-processor into its own native form, and then worked on in the receiving CAE system.

The physical - neutral format - file could be written to a magnetic tape or disk and mailed to the receiving site, or it could be transmitted using a network. The method of sending it is irrelevant to the neutral format approach.

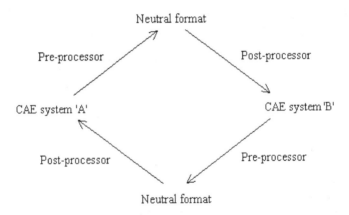

Figure 1: Transferring data using a neutral format

The first main advantage of this approach is that each vendor needs to provide only two pieces of software, for translating between the CAE system native form and the neutral format, rather than two for every system with which data needs to be exchanged. In addition, commercially sensitive information remains confidential to each vendor: there does not need to be any co-operation in writing direct translators, where knowledge of two sets of proprietary data structures is required.

The first neutral format for CAE data was published in 1980, and was called IGES (Initial Graphics Exchange Specification). It enabled the specification of data that traditionally appeared on engineering drawings - geometry and annotation - in addition to properties and associations, and provided facilities for structuring this data into views and onto layers. An example file is shown below. It comprises five sections: a human-readable prologue; a global section giving information about the file itself; a directory entry section giving details of levels, fonts, colours and so on; a section that gives the parameter values of each entity, and a terminate section that gives the number of records in each section, which acts as a checksum to ensure that no information has been lost in transmission. Note that there is a considerable amount of white space in the file.

```
Example IGES file
S        1
1H,,1H;, 12HExample test,    6HZ.IGES,    5HLuigi,    11Hversion 4.0,
G        1
  32,   38,   6, 308,   15,  12HExample test, 1.00000E+00,    2,    2HMM,
G        2
    1,  0.00000E+00,  13H940126.090223,  1.00000E-06,  0.00000E+00,
G        3
  8HJon Owen,  37HCADDETC, University of Leeds, England,   6,    0;
G        4
        100        1        0        1        0        0        0
000000000D        1
        100        0        0        3        0               circ arc
1D       2
        100,  0.00000E+00,   5.00000E+00,   5.00000E+00,
1P       1
                             3.50000E+01,   5.00000E+00,
1P       2
                             1.08527E+01,   3.44236E+01;
1P       3
S        1G       4D       2P       3
T        1
```

Figure 2: An example IGES file

2 The development of neutral formats

IGES continued to be developed after its initial version. Rational B-spline curves and surfaces were added in 1983, to complement existing facilities for parametric curves and surfaces, together with further pre-defined properties. Provision for electrical, piping and finite element applications were added in 1986, constructive solid geometry representations in 1988 and boundary representations in 1991. Several versions became US national standards.

The USA also developed the Product Definition Data Interface (PDDI) for the transfer of manufacturing information, and started work on PDES, the Product Data Exchange Specification. In Europe, collaborative research and development projects funded by the European Commission, notably the CAD*I project, contributed considerable expertise and knowledge to the fields of CAE and product data exchange.

The French aerospace industry produced a national standard called SET (Standard d'Echange et de Transfert). It was initiated in 1983, and was developed originally because of the lack of functionality in IGES for some curves and surface representations - some of which were added to a later version of IGES - and to reduce the size of the physical file. Software was developed and made available to vendors to help with the writing of the pre-processor and the post-processor, thus ensuring that certain tasks in all software were written once rather than many times by separate vendors.

The German automotive industry produced both VDA-FS and VDA-IS. The former was a short specification (which later became a German national standard) for the transfer of curves and surfaces. The latter defined subsets of IGES, an idea that was taken up later by the US Department of Defense in its MIL-D-28000 standard. It also included translation algorithms, so that a processor could convert from a high-level geometric subset to lower-level information in a standard way, although with some loss of information or precision.

3   Problems with the early neutral formats

Although the neutral formats worked in practice, and enabled CAE data to be exchanged successfully between enterprises, there were problems associated with them.

Firstly, there was often no distinction between material in the specification for the different audiences that would read it. For example, an application expert might want to know what particular geometric representations were available in the specification. However, this information was often included in the same section as information needed by someone developing the software to read and write the physical files containing this information. In practice, the software developer needs to know only about the format of the data and the file - not the content - whereas the application expert is interested in the content and not the details of how this is represented in a file.

Some of the neutral formats were written in a natural language, such as English, French or German. Such languages are open to different interpretations by different readers, causing ambiguity. There was little use of formal specifications in the early neutral formats.

Although the entities were classified as 'geometry', 'annotation' and so on, there was no documented requirement that indicated why one particular entity had been included or, more importantly, for what purpose it was supposed to be used. For example, a circular fillet could be modeled by the sending system using either a circular arc, a general conic or a parametric or rational spline curve; whichever was chosen would have implications for the translation into the receiving system, during which the key idea of the entity being a fillet might be lost.

In addition, there were no subsets of the specifications defined, until this was recognised as a problem. This meant that CAE vendors were free to choose which entities they supported. In turn, files generated by one system would contain legal entities that were not recognised by the receiving system, and so information would be lost. In practice, data is invariably sent from one system to another, and then back again. This process is repeated, possibly many times, during which successive losses of information could be very costly.

This last problem was compounded by lack of independent conformance testing services. Ideally, an independent laboratory would test the pre-processor and the post-postprocessor of a particular vendor to check that it performed according to the specification. Without such a service, users were reliant on the claims of vendors that their software worked correctly on the complete standard.

Finally, a distinction needs to be drawn between specifications and standards. Although the former undergo considerable review, they can be the product of a single company or group of companies. This means that the specifications will necessarily reflect the expertise and strategy of those companies. On the other hand, a standard is developed democratically, with world-wide - or at least national - review, to ensure that the interests of a single company do not dominate.

4   The design principles of STEP

With several competing national standards available, and problems inherent in them that could not easily be corrected, in the mid 1980s an international effort to develop a single, world-wide standard was started. It was known informally as STEP: Standard for the Exchange of Product model data, and was developed under the auspices of ISO (the International Organization for Standardization). It initially had expert contributions from the USA, Japan and several western European countries including France, Germany and the UK. Since then, expertise has been contributed from many other parts of the world, including Australia, China, South Korea, Eastern Europe and the former Soviet Union.

Several key methods and technologies were used in the development of STEP, with the objective of avoiding the ambiguities of the existing neutral formats.

The application, logical and physical specifications were to be separate. This would not only allow experts to concentrate on their particular discipline (finite elements, geometry, physical file, product structure) but would also enable different implementation methods to be applied to the same information structures. It was recognised that some models would be generally applicable, or context-independent: these include provision for geometry, topology, units, shape and product structure. Other models, such as those for two-dimensional engineering drawings, three-dimensional facetted boundary-representation geometric models, and three-dimensional configuration-controlled design, would be context-dependent. The latter would use the former as resources for constructing the more specific models, so that all models used for exchange would be based on the same source, defined by experts in that discipline.

None of the information modelling languages available at the time that STEP started to be developed satisfied all of the requirements of the STEP community. Consequently, a formally-defined modelling language - EXPRESS - was defined as part of STEP itself to allow, in turn, the definition of conceptual and application models. Further, information modelling methods were to be used to help to define requirements.

The physical file implementation method was also to be specified using a formal language. This approach facilitates the use of automatic software to help produce pre-processors and post-processors. It also reduces the possibility of ambiguous definitions.

Finally, conformance requirements were to be documented as part of the standard, so that it would be clear what a vendor would have to implement in order to be able to claim that his or her software supported the standard. Test data was to be produced and standardised, which could be used both by vendors during the development of their software and by users to check that the software did work correctly.

As a result of these requirements, the standard was divided into classes of parts which reflect these axioms of STEP development:

name of class	part range
introductory	1-9
description methods	11-19
implementation methods	21-29
conformance testing methodology and framework	31-39
integrated resources	41-99 and 101-199
application protocols	201-299
abstract test suites	301-399
application interpreted constructs	501-599

The STEP standard is officially ISO 10303. The EXPRESS language is defined in ISO 10303-11 (Part 11), the physical file in 10303-21 (Part 21) and the geometry resources in 10303-42 (Part 42).

These classes are shown diagrammatically. Those classes of parts that have a relationship with one another have an edge in common. The class of application protocols encloses the entire diagram, and acts as the interface with the outside world.

The major relationships between the document classes are as follows:

formal description methods are used to define the integrated resources;

application protocols are developed in a particular application context, based on the integrated resources using the description methods (and may include application interpreted constructs);

an application protocol is combined with an implementation method to form the basis of an ISO 10303 implementation;

an ISO 10303 implementation is tested for conformance to the standard using the conformance testing methodology and framework, and the abstract test suite associated with the application protocol.

The different classes of parts are now described in turn, with the exception of the description methods (primarily EXPRESS), details of which can be found elsewhere. These strands are then brought together with a more detailed view of the architecture of STEP, and a more detailed examination of the inter-relationships between the various models and languages.

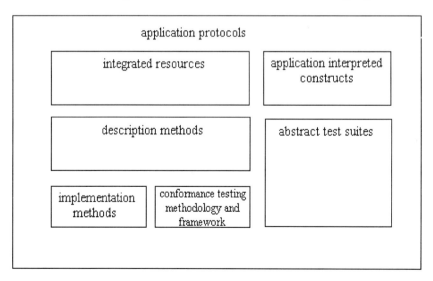

Figure 3: The document classes of STEP

5   The integrated resources

The integrated resources are documented in separate parts in the 40-series and 100-series class of parts. However, the models comprise a single integrated model which provides a general-purpose set of resources from which more specialized application protocols can be built.

The fundamentals of product description and support are documented in Part 41, and comprise:

1. generic product description resources;
2. generic management resources;
3. support resources.

The first of these provide a common framework for representing product data. The support resources provide models for commonly used engineering information, such as measures and units, dates and times, and a grouping mechanism.

The generic product description resources comprise:

- application context schema;
- product definition schema;
- product property definition schema;
- product property representation schema.

The application context schema allows a frame of reference to be defined for product data, by modelling the stage of life cycle in which the data is used, and details of the application that uses it. A product may have many different configurations (versions or variants) which may be modelled using the product definition schema. This also allows the relationships between the different configurations to be modelled. Each product definition may have a number of properties, which are then defined and represented using the last two schemas. Two common properties are shape and material, the first of which is modelled explicitly in the product property representation schema (although it could equally well be documented in Part 42). Part 41 provides a general-purpose framework for information about products. Consequently, it has placeholders for properties about a product, but does not define how the properties might be represented: instead, it provides a framework for the definition and representation of properties in general.

It should be noted that the style of modelling in the integrated resources is often perceived initially by readers to be the opposite way to that expected. A product "has" properties; a property "has" representations: one would expect that the first entity would have explicit attributes of the second, and hence "include" that information. However, although the STEP approach initially appears complex, it gives great flexibility: a property can be represented and added easily to an existing product definition without compromising the original definition.

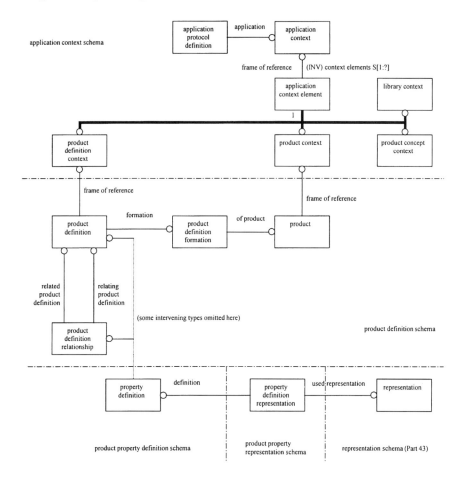

Figure 4: The generic product description resource (simplified)

The support resources comprise the following schemas:

- action
- approval
- certification
- contract
- date and time
- document
- affectivity

- external reference
- group
- person and organization
- security classification
- support
- units and measures

The last of these can be used to illustrate the nature of these support resources. A comprehensive set of units is provided that enable any physical quantity to be modelled. The basic physical quantities - length, mass, time, electric current, thermodynamic temperature, amount of substance, luminous intensity - can be used to create others, such as area (length times length) or force (length times mass divided by time squared).

A radius might be expressed as a measure with unit, with the value component being a length measure ("5.0") and the unit component being a named unit, which is an SI unit with a name ("meters") and a prefix ("milli"). Alternatively, a model may specify that all length measures are expressed using millimeters. However, if an application protocol only requires length measures, it does not need to import the whole of the measures schema: it can select just those constructs of interest.

The generic management resources provide a means of associating information with other information. For example, the security classification schema provides a resource for defining levels of security. However, it does not specify what those levels are, nor to what they may be applied: it merely provides a general-purpose mechanism for their definition. When an application protocol is being constructed in which specific security classifications are needed for a particular object, the security classification schema is used in conjunction with the generic management resources to provide this facility. For example, Part 203, the application protocol for configuration-controlled three-dimensional design, defines the levels of security to be unclassified, classified, proprietary, confidential, secret and top secret: no other levels are allowed. It then specializes this part of the model further by requiring that every security classification is associated with:

- a classification officer (from the person and organization schema);
- a classification date (from the date and time schema);
- an approval, because the classification is applied to designs.

Each security classification may also have an (optional) declassification date, by associating it with a second date and time. This general-purpose mechanism in Part 41 means that security classifications may be applied not only to designs, but to documents, products, processes and so on. Whenever such a facility is needed in an application protocol, the general-purpose mechanism from the integrated resources can be specialized according to the industrial requirements.

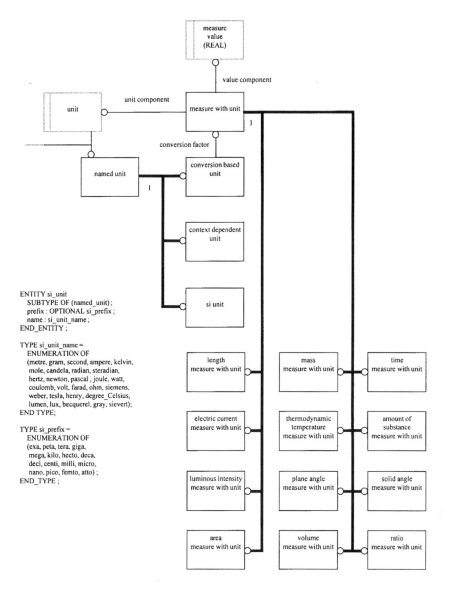

Figure 5: The measures schema (simplified)

The other parts in the 40-series and the 100-series provide additional integrated resources from which application protocols can be constructed. For example, Part 42 contains general-purpose geometric resources. As well as providing facilities for geometry and topology, there is a geometric model schema which can be used to represent the shape of objects.

The link - or integration point - between the geometric model schema and the generic product description resources is by the geometric representation item, sets of which comprise a shape representation. Put another way, the shape of the product may be represented by several geometric representation items. However, as far as Part 41 is concerned, the shape is simply one property of the product: details of the possible representations are irrelevant at its level of abstraction.

If the geometric model schema is now examined in more detail, a geometric representation item is one of the following:

- shell based surface model;
- face based surface model;
- shell based wireframe model;
- edge based wireframe model;
- geometric set, comprising points, curves and/or surfaces;
- sphere;
- block;
- right angular wedge;
- torus;
- right circular cylinder;
- right circular cone;
- half space solid;
- boolean result;
- solid model.

In turn, the last of these is one of:

- solid replica;
- csg solid;
- manifold solid brep;
- swept area solid;
- swept face solid.

In turn, some of these entities also have subtypes.

The structures in the model allow complex solid models to be defined using constructive solid geometry. A solid model is a csg solid, , which can be the result of applying a boolean operator (union, difference or intersection) to a pair of boolean operands. These may be csg primitives (a sphere, block, torus, and so on) or may be the result of a previous boolean operation, or other types of solid model such as a swept area solid. A complex 'tree' of operators and operands can be constructed to define the required shape of the object. However, as far as Part 41 is concerned, all this is the details of how one property - the shape - of an object is represented.

These geometric resources may be used selectively by an application. Even in this small part of the geometry resources that has been shown, there are many ways to describe the shape of an object. However, an application protocol may select just those representations that are relevant for the industrial context, and not use the others. In this way, any application protocol that uses (for example) facetted boundary representations will have two benefits. The first is that other application protocols that use the same representation will use precisely the same structures and formulation. The second is that the representation has been modelled by experts in the geometry field, and so will not have to be re-invented each time an application protocol needs to use it.

6 Building an application protocol

If there were no application protocols in STEP, a software vendor would be free to choose which entities to implement from the integrated resources. This would replicate problems from the previous generation of neutral formats: that entities would be used for purposes for which they had not been intended, and that entities would be used out of context. Vendor-defined subsets would proliferate.

Consequently, the idea of the application protocol was developed. It satisfies an industrial need directly, and has four major components:

1. a scope, supported by an activity model;
2. requirements, supported by an application reference model;
3. an application interpreted model;
4. conformance requirements.

The application activity model is usually written in IDEF0, and depicts the activities that use the information that is of interest. In practice, additional activities and information will be included, in order to show the scope of the application protocol in a wider context. The application reference model is written in an information modelling language, such as EXPRESS or EXPRESS-G.

Where as the application reference model is written using the terminology of the application itself, the application interpreted model uses the nomenclature of the integrated resources. A mapping table is provided to show how the two are related. The application-interpreted model is built from the integrated resources to satisfy the requirements. This process of building the application-interpreted model is called interpretation.

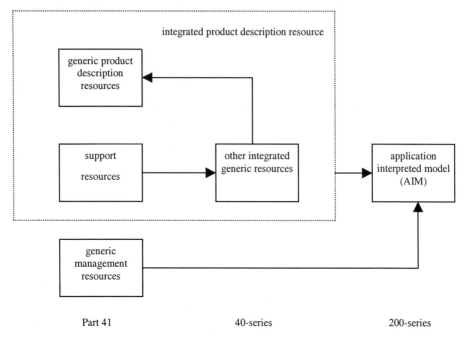

Figure 6: Building an application protocol

In practice, some constructs in the integrated resources are used in many application protocols, such as particular types of geometry model. Rather than have to interpret groups of such constructs from the beginning each time they are needed, application interpreted constructs were introduced. These are building blocks which may be used during the interpretation process, and provide a basis for sharing information structures between different application protocols.

As noted in the previous section, constructs from the integrated resources may be used directly, but they may also be modified in certain restricted ways. For example, the integrated resources support boundary representations of solid models, but in certain application protocols, the surface types may be restricted to use only planar surfaces (facetted boundary representations) or elementary surfaces (which preclude the use of higher-order sculptured surfaces). Similarly, the integrated resources include a comprehensive model of units, but a particular application protocol may require only length, and further constrain this to be measured only in millimetres or inches. This highlights the fact that the integrated resources are a resource to be used when constructing an application protocol.

The STEP application protocols cover a wide range of engineering disciplines (aerospace, automotive, building and construction, maritime, chemical and process, electrical and electronic) and different stages of the product life cycle (conceptual and detailed design, analysis, manufacture, testing and so on).

7 The implementation methods: the physical file and the SDAI

Where as the structure and content of the data is determined by an application protocol, its format, or means of accessing it, is specified by the implementation method. By separating these, it is possible to have different implementation methods of the same information.

The first implementation method to be developed in STEP was the physical file. This allowed information to be translated from a CAE system by a pre-processor, written to a physical file which was sent to another site, and then translated from the STEP file into the receiving system by a post-processor.

A STEP physical file comprises two sections: a header section followed by a data section. The former contains administrative information about the file itself. The second contains the engineering data. However, rather than use a potentially ambiguous language - such as English - to describe the file, STEP uses a formal description, based on Backus-Naur Form. This is used to specify the syntax of the file unambiguously.

In the extract that follows, square brackets mean that the construction enclosed within them is optional, braces (curly brackets) mean that the enclosed construction may be repeated zero, one or many times, the vertical bar denotes alternatives, literal symbols are enclosed in string quotes, and other productions in lower case.

```
real ::= [ sign ] digit { digit} "." { digit } [ exponent ] .
sign ::= "+" | "-" .
digit ::= "0" | "1" | "2" | "3" | "4" | "5" | "6" | "7" | "8" | "9" .
exponent ::= "E" [sign ] digit {digit } .
```

Thus a real number may be represented as an optional sign, followed by one or more digits, a decimal point, followed by zero, one or many digits and an optional exponent. The exponent is the letter E, followed by an optional sign and one or more digits. With this syntax, "1.0" and "+1." are syntactically correct real numbers, whereas ".1" and "+1" are not.

In the same way, the whole syntax of the physical file can be specified:

```
STEP_physical_file ::=
    "ISO_10303_21;" header_section data_section
"END_ISO_10303_21;"

data_section ::=
    "DATA;" entity_instance_list "ENDSEC;"
```

and so on.

This approach means that much of the writing of the pre-processor or post-processor can be automated, by using parser-generation techniques. It also saves having to describe rules of the syntax informally in English, such as "the data section begins with the word 'DATA' in upper case, followed by a semicolon with no intervening spaces, followed by a list of entity instances, and the word 'ENDSEC', again followed by a semicolon with no intervening characters".

In the figure, the example STEP physical file has been laid out to help human readability. In practice, it would be stored as a stream of characters, with no carriage returns. White space has therefore been reduced considerably, with no fixed-format information. The header section is analogous to the start and global sections of the IGES physical file, and there is no need for the terminate section because each section is enclosed by keyword delimiters.

The second implementation method is the SDAI: the standard data access interface. This provides a standardised software interface to data structures that contain the information required. The important point is that the software that uses the interface does not need to know the structure of the underlying data.

The SDAI is a functional interface that is described independently of any computer programming language. Further parts in the 20-series class define language bindings of the SDAI, which document how the interface is realised in individual languages such as C++ and Java.

8   Conformance testing

Conformance testing is supported in STEP in several classes of parts.

The 30-series class of parts describes the conformance testing methodology and framework. An overview provides definitions of terminology, distinguishes between different types of testing, and sets out the framework for conformance testing. Such testing assumes that there is a laboratory that undertakes the testing and a client that supplies the software to be tested.

```
ISO-10303-21;
HEADER;
FILE_DESCRIPTION ( ('example ATC for Part 304 conformance project'),
'1') ;
FILE_NAME ('ATC.S21', '1994-04-01T00:00:01',
          ('JO', 'RJG'),
          ('CAE Group', 'Dept of Mech Eng', 'University_of_Leeds',
'UK'),
          'Lupine++', 'Ray Goult', 'authorisation for sending file:
unknown') ;
FILE_SCHEMA (('facetted_brep_aic')) ;
ENDSEC;
DATA;
#1 = FACETED_BREP_SHAPE_REPRESENTATION ( ( #2 ), #3,
   ( 'aic_fac_brep',
     'the definition of a b-rep model with planar faces bounded by
poly_loops' ) ) ;
#2 = FACETED_BREP ( #4 ) ;
#3 = GEOMETRIC_REPRESENTATION_CONTEXT ( 'context_1',
'context_for_tetrahedron', 3 ) ;
#4 = CLOSED_SHELL ( #5, ( #6, #7, #8, #9 ) ) ;
#5 = CONNECTED_FACE_SET ( #10 ) ;
#6 = FACE_SURFACE ( ( #11 ), #12, .TRUE. ) ;
#7 = FACE_SURFACE ( ( #13 ), #14, .TRUE. ) ;
#8 = FACE_SURFACE ( ( #15 ), #16, .TRUE. ) ;
#9 = FACE_SURFACE ( ( #17 ), #18, .TRUE. ) ;
#10 = TOPOLOGICAL_REPRESENTATION_ITEM ( #19 ) ;
#11 = FACE_OUTER_BOUND ( #20, .TRUE. ) ;
#12 = PLANE ( #21 ) ;
#13 = FACE_OUTER_BOUND ( #22, .TRUE. ) ;
#14 = PLANE ( #23 ) ;
#15 = FACE_OUTER_BOUND ( #24, .TRUE. ) ;
#16 = PLANE ( #25 ) ;
#17 = FACE_OUTER_BOUND ( #26, .TRUE. ) ;
#18 = PLANE ( #27 ) ;
#19 = REPRESENTATION_ITEM ( ) ;
#20 = POLY_LOOP ( #28, #29, #30 ) ;
#21 = AXIS2_PLACEMENT_3D ( #28, #31, #32 ) ;
#22 = POLY_LOOP ( #28, #33, #29 ) ;
#23 = AXIS2_PLACEMENT_3D ( #28, #32, #31 ) ;
#24 = POLY_LOOP ( #28, #30, #33 ) ;
#25 = AXIS2_PLACEMENT_3D ( #28, #34, #32 ) ;
#26 = POLY_LOOP ( #29, #33, #30 ) ;
#27 = AXIS2_PLACEMENT_3D ( #33, #35, #36 ) ;
#28 = CARTESIAN_POINT ( 0, 0, 0 ) ;
#29 = CARTESIAN_POINT ( 0, 0, 100 ) ;
#30 = CARTESIAN_POINT ( 0, 100, 0 ) ;
#31 = DIRECTION ( -1, 0, 0 ) ;
#32 = DIRECTION ( 0, -1, 0 ) ;
#33 = CARTESIAN_POINT ( 100, 0, 0 ) ;
#34 = DIRECTION ( 0, 0, -1 ) ;
#35 = DIRECTION ( 1, 1, 1 ) ;
#36 = DIRECTION ( 1, -1, 0 ) ;
ENDSEC;
END-ISO-10303-21;
```

Figure 7: An example STEP physical file

This class of parts describes what the both laboratory and the client undertake during conformance testing; in other words, who is responsible for doing what. It should be noted that the client need not be the vendor of the software: it may be a company that uses the software, or perhaps an industrial alliance of such companies. However, provided that the client is able to undertake the designated responsibilities, this does not matter. Other parts in the 30-series describe how to conformance test a physical file implementation or an SDAI implementation, both within the same framework but with different detailed steps.

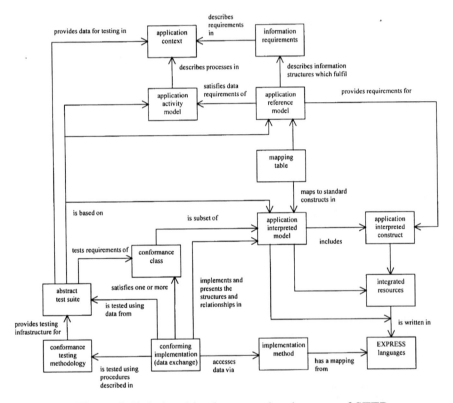

Figure 8: Relationships between the elements of STEP

Fundamental support for conformance testing is also provided by the abstract test suites. For each application protocol, there is a standardised set of test data that is used during conformance testing of that application protocol. The data is specified in an abstract form that can be translated so that it can be used for conformance testing either a physical file implementation or an SDAI implementation. This independence from the implementation method means that data does not have to be specified for every STEP implementation method: the form in which it is specified merely has to map onto each of the implementation methods (in the same way that there is a mapping from EXPRESS to each of the implementation methods).

There is also support for conformance testing in each of the application protocols and each of the implementation methods. A questionnaire is provided in each of these parts that the client must complete as part of the conformance testing process. This allows the options (or possibly the subsets) of the application protocol that are supported by the software to be specified, so that appropriate tests may be selected from the standard set of tests.

It should be noted that software that has been successful in conformance testing might still not inter-operate correctly with other such software. One obvious reason for this is that the two items of software might support different legal options within an application protocol, so that there is a mismatch of functionality. For example, software that is "STEP-203 compliant" might produce legal advanced boundary representations that cannot be read by other "STEP-203 compliant" software that (legally) processes facetted boundary representations. Such terminology needs to be treated with considerable caution: the particular conformance class should also be quoted in such claims.

9 The architecture of STEP

Having described - briefly - the different document classes of STEP, and the relationships between them, it is now possible to address the overall architecture of STEP, and the relationships between its elements.

In the figure, the arrow at the end of each of lines joining a pair of boxes denotes the direction of the relationship. For example, the "application reference model" "satisfies data requirements of" the "application activity model" (and not the other way around).

In the upper and central part of the figure, the components of an application protocol are depicted: the application context, the information requirements, the application activity model, application reference model, application interpreted model, the mapping table, and the conformance class. The relationships between them are also shown. In particular, the importance of the application context and of the mapping table should be noted.

The application interpreted model includes application interpreted constructs and interprets the integrated resources: this is the interpretation process that constructs a model to satisfy the requirements of the application protocol. (In addition, the application reference model of an application protocol might drive further development of the integrated resources, if provision has not already been included in the latter for every requirement.)

Both the application interpreted model and the integrated resources are written in the EXPRESS language, and each implementation method has a mapping from EXPRESS.

The conformance testing parts of the standard are depicted in the lower left corner of the figure: the abstract test suite provides data and the 30-series class provides the procedures for testing.

A conforming implementation is the combination of an implementation method and the application interpreted model, that has been tested successfully using the standardised data and procedures.

Each application protocol is built from a standardised set of integrated resources, developed by experts in each of the disciplines. The application interpreted model is combined with an implementation method to provide the basis for a software implementation, which can then be tested using standardised procedures and data. Implementations of several STEP application protocols have already been used to exchange industrial data successfully on many projects.

Further information

Details of the status of the STEP parts can be found on the Web site:

http://www.nist.gov/sc4/www/stepdocs.htm

For more detailed introductions to product data exchange, to STEP itself, and to the EXPRESS languages, the reader is referred to the following textbooks:

BLOOR, M. S. and OWEN, J., "Product data exchange", 1995, ISBN 1-85728-279-5, UCL Press, London, UK.

OWEN, J., "STEP: an introduction". Second edition, 1997, ISBN 1-874728-11-9, Information Geometers, UK.

SCHENCK, D. A. and WILSON P. R., "Information modeling the EXPRESS way". 1994, ISBN 0-195-08714-3, Oxford University Press.

THE EXPRESS DATA SPECIFICATION LANGUAGE

Jorulv Rangnes[1]

[1]EPM Technology, Grenseveien 107, P.O.Box 6629, 0607 Oslo, Norway
Jorulv.Rangnes@epmtech.jotne.no

Abstract

EXPRESS has become the preferred modelling language for electronic commerce and product data technology standards. Its main purpose is to enable the definition of complete product information in both a human readable and computer sensible-way. The language provides data structure and classification means, as well as comprehensive constraint mechanism and executable statements. Knowledge to express is required for people developing and reviewing data models and for those concerned with implementation. EXPRESS is designed to be independent of any particular implementation technology. However, implementation views can be produced in a straightforward and even automatic way.

This chapter provides an explanation of the EXPRESS language through a Meta-modell using express itself. By reading this document the reader should get to understand express and get familiarised with the combination of the textual notation of express, as well as it's graphical notation EXPRESS-G, which is the way that PDT data models are documented, such as those published by STEP.

This information is primarily captured from information in the standard and books published about EXPRESS. This should be consulted for consistency and a complete reference. In this chapter the documentation about the Meta-model is limited to the objects and their constraints. A complete Meta-model in HTML is maintained at WWW.EPMTECH.JOTNE.COM/EXPRESS.

1 Introduction

Product data modelling or object technology has got its home under the umbrella of Product Data Technology (PDT) which includes all information pertinent to a product's design and operational life. Although we have been practising PDT solutions through single-vendor systems in the last decades, it is first when product models are made available as internationally accepted standards that the real exploitation of PDT can start. ISO TC184/SC4:

Industrial data develops a suite of such PDT standards whereas STEP, being published as ISO 10303: Product data representation and exchange is probably the most well known.

As part of the descriptive methods of STEP, the EXPRESS language is used to specify all the normative parts of this compound standard, and that also are used by a series of other PDT standards including of course all SC4 sister standards. EXPRESS has therefore a significant importance within PDT to capture information requirements, but also to be unambiguous and computer-sensible so that implementation views can be carried out in an easy and straightforward manner.

2 EXPRESS – language description

2.1 Overview

EXPRESS is classified as textual conceptual schema language. It provides also a graphical notation – EXPRESS-G and complimentary languages for instantiation – EXPRESS-I and mapping – EXPRESS-X.

EXPRESS is an entity relationship model with generalisation and constraint specification. It divides the information modelling into parts. It provides a *wrapper* for collections of related definitions, a way to express a definition of an information unit and to represent value domains. The wrapper is called a SCHEMA, an information unit is called an ENTITY and the value domain is called a (data) TYPE. The properties of an ENTITY are specified by attributes, which is the relationship between the ENTITY and the domain value. Since an attribute can specify another ENTITY as its domain, the ENTITY can also be a domain value.

EXPRESS is case insensitive and built from reserved words that include keywords, some operators and the names of standard constants, functions and procedures. The textual language is the full specification that both is human readable and most important computer sensible. EXPRESS is not a programming language. However, this comprehensive language provides an easy and straightforward way of defining implementation forms.

For the further explanation of EXPRESS, a graphical subset of EXPRESS named EXPRESS-G is introduced.

2.2 EXPRESS-G

EXPRESS-G is a formal graphical notation for the display of data specifications defined in the EXPRESS (textual) language. The notation supports a subset of EXPRESS. It is designed to only use non-graphic symbols and thus require a minimum of computer graphics capabilities.

EXPRESS-G is represented by graphics symbols forming a diagram. There are three types of symbols:

- *Definition symbols* – denoting data type and schema declarations.
- *Relationship symbols* – describing relationships that exist among *Definitions*.
- *Composition symbols* – enabling a diagram to be displayed on more than one page.

EXPRESS-G supports simple data types, named data types, relationships and cardinality. It also supports the notation for more than one schema.

It does not support for the comprehensive constraint mechanisms provided by the EXPRESS language. However, providing an asterix for the appropriate construct indicates constraints.

The symbols for EXPRESS-G is shown in the flowing table.

aSchema	The Schema symbol is only used within a schema-level diagram and for showing the possible schema interfacing. The schema symbol has two possible relationship, the USE FROM represented by single, solid line, and the REFERENCE FROM represented by a single, dashed line. Explicit schema interface, will provide the interfaced objects with an arrow pointing to the relationship line, Implicit schema interface need not this since every object is interfaced.
anEntity	The ENTITY symbol is used within a entity-level diagram denotes an object within a schema. An entity symbol can have three types of relationship lines. The line terminator – the circle is used as an arrow indicating the "direction" of the relationship. - attribute lines, thin, solid line for mandatory attributes and thin, dashed line for optional attributes. The attribute name is provided adjacent to the relationship line, possible together with the aggregate type. - supertype lines are thick solid lines that can be branched. Supertype constraints may be indicated at the branch. Constraint that applies to the entity or any attribute are indicated by an asterix.

aDefined Type	The defined TYPE symbol is used within an entity-level diagram and denotes the type within a schema. The type has relationship lines to its (underlying) base type without any naming, but potentially indicating the aggregate. Constraint that applies to the entity or any attribute are indicated by an asterix.
aSelect	The SELECT type symbol is used within an entity-level diagram. This type has relationship lines to its underlying types.
anEnum Type	The ENUMERATION type symbol is used within an entity-level diagram. Listing of the enumeration items are not provided.
aPrimary	Primary type symbols is used within an entity-level diagram. The primary type such as STRING, LOGICAL, BOOLEAN, NUMBER, REAL, INTEGER are denoted as the name inside the symbol.
Page,Ref#	Page reference symbol denoting a reference to another page. The relationship line from the referencing symbol is used, but without the terminating symbol.
Page,Ref#	Page reference symbol denoting a reference from another page(s). The relationship line has no other information.
Schema.def Alias	The REFERENCE FROM schema-interface symbol used in entity level diagrams. The interfaced object is denoted by dot notation. An alias name might be provided.
Schema.def Alias	The USE FROM schema-interface symbol used in entity level diagrams. The interfaced object is denoted by dot notation. An alias name might be provided.

2.3 EXPRESS – presented through a Meta-model.

EXPRESS is a highly semantical language, and the formal specification is published as ISO 10303: *EXPRESS language reference manual*. This document provides the overview of EXPRESS through using the EXPRESS notation to dually explain the semantics and for the reader to get used to reading such specifications.

For further references this model of EXPRESS is referred to as an EXPRESS Meta-model [1], and it is a conceptual view of the language as opposed an implementation view that are provided by STEP implementation forms and software.

The Meta-model is specified as two schemas, the MetaExpress schema and the Support schema. The focal point is the MetaExpress schema that makes use of constructs defined by the Support schema.

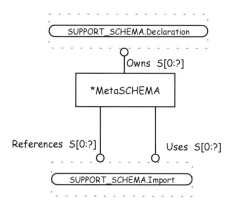

Figure 1 Entity level-diagram for metaExpress

2.3.1 The METAEXPRESS Schema

```
SCHEMA METAEXPRESS;
REFERENCE FROM SUPPORT_SCHEMA
  (Declaration,
   Import,
   NamesUnique,
   NameList);
```

2.3.1.1   MetaSCHEMA

The metaSCHEMA entity assembles a collection of declarations, including any imported via a USE FROM and REFERENCE FROM interface.

(The constructs defined within the schema, e.g. the 'owns' attribute in addition to the things imported by the USE FROM interface are owned by the schema. Constructs imported through the REFERENCE FROM interface may be mentioned, but they are not owned, e.g. they cannot exist independently and cannot exist unless they are used to support one of the owned constructs.)

```
ENTITY MetaSCHEMA;
Owns:       SET OF Declaration;
References :     SET OF Import;
Uses:       SET OF Import;
WHERE
InScope   :      NamesUnique(Namelist(owns) +
   NameList(Uses) + NameList (References));
END_ENTITY;
```

Formal Propositions:

    InScope   The name of the declarations made in this schema, plus any imported declarations shall be unique.

```
*)
END_SCHEMA;
```

2.3.2 SUPPORT_SCHEMA

```
SCHEMA SUPPORT_SCHEMA;
REFERENCE FROM METAEXPRESS
   (MetaSCHEMA);
```

2.3.2.1 *CharSet*

Provides the set of characters that can be used by an EXPRESS string value
```
TYPE CharSet = STRING (1) FIXED;
END_TYPE;
```

2.3.2.2 *EXPRESSname*

Represents a list of names
```
TYPE EXPRESSname = STRING;
WHERE
Conforms   :     ParseOK(SELF);
NotUsingReservedWords  :    NOT SELF USEDIN ROLEOF
   ImportedItem.AliasName OR
   NOT SELF USEDIN ROLEOF Declaration.Name;;
END_TYPE;
```

2.3.2.3 *ListOfNames*

```
TYPE ListOfNames = LIST OF EXPRESSname;
END_TYPE;
```

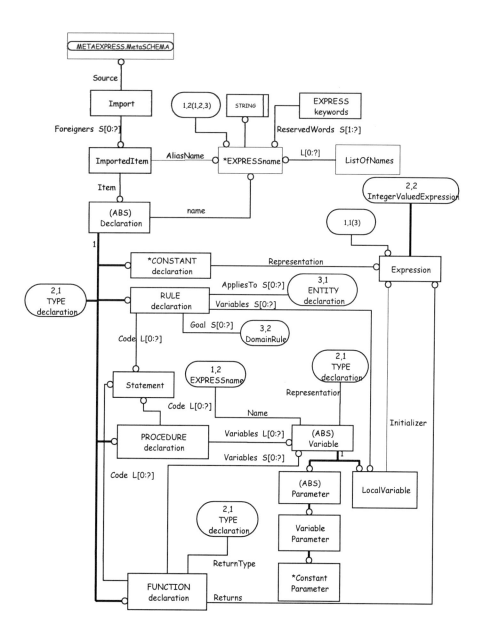

Figure 2 SUPPORT_SCHEMA EXPRESS-G diagram1 of 3

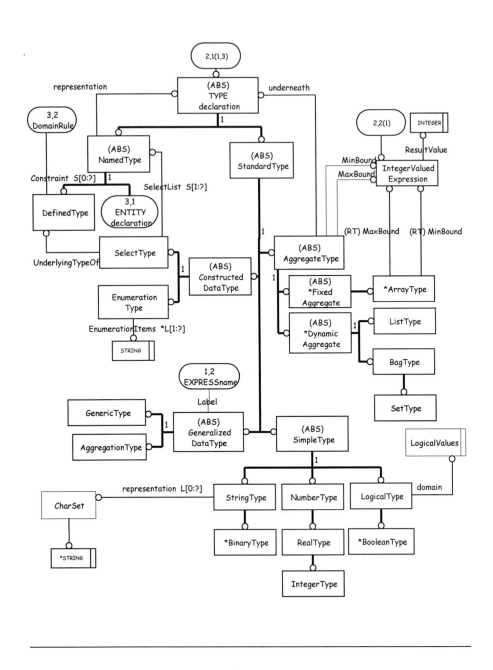

Figure 3 SUPPORT_SCHEMA EXPRESS-G diagram 2 of 3

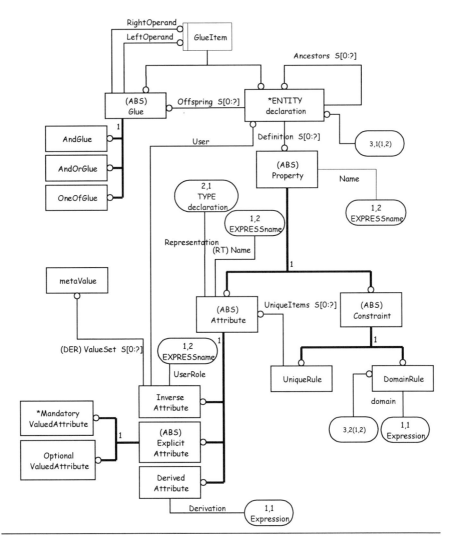

Figure 4 SUPPORT_SCEMA EXPRESS-G diagram 3 of 3

2.3.2.4 *LogicalValues*

```
TYPE LogicalValues = ENUMERATION OF
   (TRUEVALUE,FALSEVALUE,UNKNOWNVALUE);
END_TYPE;
```

2.3.2.5 *GlueItem*

The GlueItem selects between the Glue entity and an entity data type.
```
TYPE GlueItem = SELECT
    (ENTITYdeclaration,Glue);
END_TYPE;
```

2.3.2.6 *AggregateType*

Aggregation data types have as their domains collections of values of a given base type. These base types are called elements. Express provides for the definition of one fixed aggregation data type (ARRAY) and three dynamic aggregation data type (BAG, LIST, SET)

The bounds (and therefore the size) is established by the upper an lower bounds.

Its subtypes have different semantics.
```
ENTITY AggregateType
ABSTRACT SUPERTYPE OF (ONEOF(FixedAggregate,
    DynamicAggregate))
SUBTYPE OF(StandardType);
underneath :      TYPEdeclaration;
MaxBound    :     OPTIONAL IntegerValuedExpression;
MinBound    :     OPTIONAL IntegerValuedExpression;
END_ENTITY;
```

2.3.2.7 *AggregationType*

An AGGREGATE type is used to indicate that any aggregate type is acceptable as an actual paramet of a function or procedure.
```
ENTITY AggregationType
SUBTYPE OF(GeneralizedDataType);
END_ENTITY;
```

2.3.2.8 *AndGlue*

```
ENTITY AndGlue
SUBTYPE OF(Glue);
END_ENTITY;
```

2.3.2.9 *AndOrGlue*

```
ENTITY AndOrGlue
SUBTYPE OF(Glue);
END_ENTITY;
```

2.3.2.10 ArrayType

An ARRAY type has as its domain indexed, fixed-size collection of like elements.

The lower and upper bounds which can be numeric expressions must evaluate to an integer.

An ARRAY type can optionally specify that array elements shall by unique by using the UNIQUE keyword

It may also specify that an array value need not contain an element at every index point.

```
ENTITY ArrayType
SUBTYPE OF(FixedAggregate);
SELF\AggregateType.MaxBound   :
    IntegerValuedExpression;
SELF\AggregateType.MinBound   :
    IntegerValuedExpression;
WHERE
UniqueOccurences  :    InformalFunction;
Sparseness :     InformalFunction;
END_ENTITY;
```

Formal Propositions:

UniqueOccurences   If the UNIQUE keyword is used, duplicates shall not occur

Sparseness   If the OPTIONAL keyword is used, an array item need not contain an element at every index position

2.3.2.11 Attribute

An attribute describes material characteristics.
```
ENTITY Attribute
ABSTRACT SUPERTYPE OF (ONEOF(InverseAttribute,
   ExplicitAttribute, DerivedAttribute))
SUBTYPE OF(Property);
SELF\Property.Name       :      EXPRESSname;
Representation   :    TYPEdeclaration;
END_ENTITY;
```

2.3.2.12 BagType

A BAG type has as its domain unordered collections of like elements
```
ENTITY BagType
SUBTYPE OF(DynamicAggregate);
```

```
END_ENTITY;
```

2.3.2.13 *BinaryType*

A BINARY type is a specialization of the STRING type. Legal values are '0' and '1'.
```
ENTITY BinaryType
SUBTYPE OF(StringType);
WHERE
OnlyTwo  :
    BinaryChars(SELF\StringType.Representation);
END_ENTITY;
```

2.3.2.14 *BooleanType*

A BOOLEAN type is a specialization of the LOGICAL type, that exclude the UNKNOWN value.
```
ENTITY BooleanType
SUBTYPE OF(LogicalType);
WHERE
ExludeUnknown    :      SELF.domain<>UNKNOWNVALUE;
END_ENTITY;
```

2.3.2.15 *CONSTANTdeclaration*

A named value that never changes.
```
ENTITY CONSTANTdeclaration
SUBTYPE OF(Declaration);
Representation   :      Expression;
WHERE
NeverToChange    :      InformalFunction;
END_ENTITY;
```
Formal Propositions:

NeverToChange   Once a constant has been given a value, it is illegal to use it in any situation that will, or has the potential to, alter that initial value.

2.3.2.16 *ConstructedDataType*

There are two types of constructed data types in EXPRESS: ENUMERATION and SELECT. These data types have similar syntactic structures.
```
ENTITY ConstructedDataType
ABSTRACT SUPERTYPE OF (ONEOF(SelectType, EnumerationType))
SUBTYPE OF(StandardType);
END_ENTITY;
```

2.3.2.17 *Declaration*

An EXPRESS construction created directly within the schema: constant, type, entity, rule, function or procedure. Each declaration has a name that conforms to the EXPRESS grammar.

(The names of the declaration subtypes are changed to reflect that it is not allowed to use a reserved word as a name).

```
ENTITY Declaration
ABSTRACT SUPERTYPE OF (ONEOF(CONSTANTdeclaration,
   TYPEdeclaration, RULEdeclaration, FUNCTIONdeclaration,
   PROCEDUREdeclaration));
name:      EXPRESSname;
END_ENTITY;
```

2.3.2.18 *DefinedType*

Defined type is declared by the TYPE declaration. A defined type is assigned a type identifier by the user and is referenced by this identifier.

Defined types are used to encapsulate information and to add semantics to its underlying types.

```
ENTITY DefinedType
SUBTYPE OF(NamedType);
Constraint :    SET OF DomainRule;
END_ENTITY;
```

2.3.2.19 *DerivedAttribute*

A derived attribute get its value from the evaluation of an expression.

```
ENTITY DerivedAttribute
SUBTYPE OF(Attribute);
Derivation :    Expression;
END_ENTITY;
```

2.3.2.20 *DynamicAggregate*

Dynamic aggregates have a fixed lowerbound and a optional upper bound. The lower bound establishes the minimum - and the upper bound establish the maximum number, of values to populate the aggregate. When the upper bound is not given, there is no limit on the size of the population.

```
ENTITY DynamicAggregate
ABSTRACT SUPERTYPE OF (ONEOF(BagType, ListType))
SUBTYPE OF(AggregateType);
WHERE
```

```
LoBoundNeeded,     :        EXISTS(MinBound);
LoBoundLimit       :        MinBound>=0;
BoundOrdered       :        (EXISTS(MaxBound) AND (MinBound <=
   MaxBound)) OR NOT EXISTS (MaxBound);
END_ENTITY;
```

2.3.2.21 ENTITYdeclaration

An ENTITY type is a declaration which describe an object in terms of properties: attributes and constraints.
```
ENTITY ENTITYdeclaration
SUBTYPE OF(NamedType);
Definition  :      SET OF Property;
Ancestors   :      SET OF ENTITYdeclaration;
Offspring   :      SET OF Glue;
WHERE
InScope     :      NamesUnique(Namelist(Definition));
END_ENTITY;
```

2.3.2.22 EXPRESSkeywords

```
ENTITY EXPRESSkeywords;
ReservedWords      :       SET [1:?] OF EXPRESSname;
END_ENTITY;
```

2.3.2.23 EnumerationType

An ENUMERATION type has as its domain an ordered set of names. The names represent values of the enumeration data type
```
ENTITY EnumerationType
SUBTYPE OF(ConstructedDataType);
EnumerationItems  :     LIST [1:?] OF UNIQUE STRING;
END_ENTITY;
```

2.3.2.24 ExplicitAttribute

An explicit attribute is an attribute which value is maintained by the application.
```
ENTITY ExplicitAttribute
ABSTRACT SUPERTYPE OF (ONEOF(MandatoryValuedAttribute,
   OptionalValuedAttribute))
SUBTYPE OF(Attribute);
END_ENTITY;
```

2.3.2.25 FUNCTIONdeclaration

A FUNCTION is an algorithm that returns a result value of a given type.
```
ENTITY FUNCTIONdeclaration
SUBTYPE OF(Declaration);
```

```
ReturnType :       TYPEdeclaration;
Code:       LIST OF Statement;
Variables  :       SET OF Variable;
Returns    :       Expression;
END_ENTITY;
```

2.3.2.26 *FixedAggregate*

FixedAggregates have fixed, mandatory lower and upper bounds. Each element in the aggregate has a value (null or otherwise).

```
ENTITY FixedAggregate
ABSTRACT SUPERTYPE
SUBTYPE OF(AggregateType);
WHERE
BoundsNeeded      :       Exists(MinBound) AND
   EXISTS(MaxBound);
BoundsOrdered     :       MinBound <= MaxBound;
END_ENTITY;
```

Formal Propositions:

BoundsNeeded	Both expressions in the bound specification, MinBound and MaxBound shall evaluate to integer values. Neither shall evaluate to the indeterminate (?) value.
BoundsOrdered	The lower bound shall not be greater than the upper bound.

2.3.2.27 *GeneralizedDataType*

The generalized data types are used to specify a generalization of certain other data types, and can only be used in certain very specific contexts (as formal parameters of a FUNCTION or a PROCEDURE)

```
ENTITY GeneralizedDataType
ABSTRACT SUPERTYPE OF (ONEOF(GenericType, AggregationType))
SUBTYPE OF(StandardType);
Label       :      OPTIONAL EXPRESSname;
END_ENTITY;
```

2.3.2.28 *GenericType*

A GENERIC type is used to indicate that any type will be acceptable as an actual parameter of a function or procedure.

```
ENTITY GenericType
SUBTYPE OF(GeneralizedDataType);
END_ENTITY;
```

2.3.2.29 Glue

The Glue entity is used to hold subtypes together: when an entity has several subtypes, the specialization of this "glue" specifies how those subtypes behave.

```
ENTITY Glue
ABSTRACT SUPERTYPE OF (ONEOF(AndGlue, AndOrGlue,
    OneOfGlue));
RightOperand      :       GlueItem;
LeftOperand       :       GlueItem;
END_ENTITY;
```

2.3.2.30 Import

The Import entity identifies declarations made within a specific schema which are to be imported into another schema. (an easy handle for the metaSCHEMA entity in the metaEXPRESS schema)

```
ENTITY Import;
Foreigners :      SET OF ImportedItem;
Source     :      MetaSCHEMA;
END_ENTITY;
```

2.3.2.31 ImportedItem

The ImportedItem entity is a declaration to be imported into a schema. It optionally has an alias. when the alias is present, it replaces the natural name in the scope of the importing schema.

```
ENTITY ImportedItem;
Item:      Declaration;
AliasName  :      OPTIONAL EXPRESSname;
END_ENTITY;
```

2.3.2.32 IntegerType

A INTEGER type represent the subset of natural numbers which are whole numbers.

```
ENTITY IntegerType
SUBTYPE OF(RealType);
END_ENTITY;
```

2.3.2.33 InverseAttribute

An inverse attribute is an attribute whose value is the set of all entity values which use an entity value of the type as an attribute value. The inverse attribute is used to constrain the cardinality and further relationship.

```
ENTITY InverseAttribute
SUBTYPE OF(Attribute);
```

```
User:         ENTITYdeclaration;
UserRole   :     EXPRESSname;
DERIVE
ValueSet   :     SET OF metaValue := UsedIn(SELF,User.Name
    + Userrole);
END_ENTITY;
```

2.3.2.34 *ListType*

A LIST type has as its domain sequences of like elements
```
ENTITY ListType
SUBTYPE OF(DynamicAggregate);
END_ENTITY;
```

2.3.2.35 *LogicalType*

A LOGICAL type represent the three logic states TRUE, UNKNOWN, FALSE
```
ENTITY LogicalType
SUBTYPE OF(SimpleType);
domain     :     LogicalValues;
END_ENTITY;
```

2.3.2.36 *MandatoryValuedAttribute*

A mandatory attribute is an explicit attribute that requires a non-null value.
```
ENTITY MandatoryValuedAttribute
SUBTYPE OF(ExplicitAttribute);
WHERE
Mandatory  :     EXISTS(Representation);
END_ENTITY;
```

2.3.2.37 *NamedType*

Named type is a type defined by the user. It can only be populated as one of its two subtypes: TYPE and ENTITY.
```
ENTITY NamedType
ABSTRACT SUPERTYPE OF (ONEOF(DefinedType,
    ENTITYdeclaration))
SUBTYPE OF(TYPEdeclaration);
representation  :     TYPEdeclaration;
END_ENTITY;
```

2.3.2.38 *NumberType*

A NUMBER type represents the set of all natural decimal numbers:negative, zero, positive, rational and irrational.
```
ENTITY NumberType
SUBTYPE OF(SimpleType);
```

```
END_ENTITY;
```

2.3.2.39 *OneOfGlue*

```
ENTITY OneOfGlue
SUBTYPE OF(Glue);
END_ENTITY;
```

2.3.2.40 *OptionalValuedAttribute*

An optional attribute is an explicit attribute which accept a non-null (?) value.
```
ENTITY OptionalValuedAttribute
SUBTYPE OF(ExplicitAttribute);
END_ENTITY;
```

2.3.2.41 *PROCEDUREdeclaration*

An algorithm that acts on its input parameters
```
ENTITY PROCEDUREdeclaration
SUBTYPE OF(Declaration);
Variables :     LIST OF Variable;
Code:       LIST OF Statement;
END_ENTITY;
```

2.3.2.42 *Property*

A property is (part) of the definition of an entity.
```
ENTITY Property
ABSTRACT SUPERTYPE OF (ONEOF(Attribute, Constraint));
Name:       OPTIONAL EXPRESSname;
END_ENTITY;
```

2.3.2.43 *RULEdeclaration*

A RULE defines a constraint on one or more populations of entities.
```
ENTITY RULEdeclaration
SUBTYPE OF(Declaration);
AppliesTo :     SET OF ENTITYdeclaration;
Variables :     SET OF LocalVariable;
Code:       LIST OF Statement;
Goal:       SET OF DomainRule;
END_ENTITY;
```

2.3.2.44 *RealType*

A REAL type represents the subset of all natural decimal numbers which are rational or irrational numbers.
```
ENTITY RealType
```

```
SUBTYPE OF(NumberType);
END_ENTITY;
```

2.3.2.45 *SelectType*

A SELECT type is an implicit abstract supertype in the sense that it can only be populated as one of the data types in the select graph. A select can only be used as the underlying type of a DefinedType.

Each item in the select list shall be a named data type

```
ENTITY SelectType
SUBTYPE OF(ConstructedDataType);
SelectList :        SET [1:?] OF NamedType;
UnderlyingTypeOf :      DefinedType;
END_ENTITY;
```

2.3.2.46 *SetType*

A SET type is a specialization of the BAG data type and shall not contain two or more elements that are instance equal.

```
ENTITY SetType
SUBTYPE OF(BagType);
END_ENTITY;
```

2.3.2.47 *SimpleType*

A simple data type covers the most fundamental data representations: numbers, strings and logicals. These data types are considered to be axiomatic.

```
ENTITY SimpleType
ABSTRACT SUPERTYPE OF (ONEOF(NumberType, StringType,
    LogicalType))
SUBTYPE OF(StandardType);
END_ENTITY;
```

2.3.2.48 *StandardType*

A standard type is one of the types predeclared by EXPRESS. It can only be populated as one of its subtypes: EnumerationType, selectType, AggregateType, Pseudotype and SimpleType

```
ENTITY StandardType
ABSTRACT SUPERTYPE OF (ONEOF(SimpleType, AggregateType,
    GeneralizedDataType, ConstructedDataType))
SUBTYPE OF(TYPEdeclaration);
END_ENTITY;
```

2.3.2.49 StringType

A STRING type is a list of characters
```
ENTITY StringType
SUBTYPE OF(SimpleType);
representation    :     LIST OF CharSet;
END_ENTITY;
```

2.3.2.50 TYPEdeclaration

A TYPE defines the characteristics and domain values. There are two main subtypes (specializations): standard types and named types. The standard types are predefined in EXPRESS. Named types are built using named types and standard types.
```
ENTITY TYPEdeclaration
ABSTRACT SUPERTYPE OF (ONEOF(NamedType, StandardType))
SUBTYPE OF(Declaration);
END_ENTITY;
```

2.3.2.51 metaValue

Holds a value of an entity, attribute, local variable, parameter or data type. (This entity is out of scope and therefore is presented as a stub only)
```
ENTITY metaValue;
END_ENTITY;
```

2.3.2.52 BinaryChars

```
FUNCTION BinaryChars
  (Str:LIST OF CharSet):BOOLEAN;
    REPEAT i := 1 TO SIZEOF (Str);
      IF ((Str[i] <> '0') AND (Str[i] <> '1')) THEN RETURN
(FALSE);
      END_IF;
    END_REPEAT;
    RETURN(True);
END_FUNCTION;
```

2.3.2.53 InformalFunction

```
FUNCTION InformalFunction
  (str: INTEGER):Boolean;
    Return(False);
    (*Informal*)
END_FUNCTION;
```

2.3.2.54 Informal_Function

```
FUNCTION Informal_Function
```

```
   (i:INTEGER):INTEGER;
     ;
   END_FUNCTION;
```

2.3.2.55 *NameList*

```
FUNCTION NameList
  (Container : declaration):ListOfNames;
  ;
END_FUNCTION;
```

2.3.2.56 *NamesUnique*

```
FUNCTION NamesUnique
  (Names : ListOfNames):LOGICAL;
    LOCAL
      SetOfNames : SET OF ExpressName := [];
    END_LOCAL;

    REPEAT i := 1 TO SIZEOF(Names);
      SetOfNames := SetOfNames + Names[i];
    END_REPEAT;
    RETURN (SIZEOF(Names) = SIZEOF(SetOfNames));
END_FUNCTION;
```

2.3.2.57 *NotUsingExpressKeywords*

```
FUNCTION NotUsingExpressKeywords
  (str:Declaration):BOOLEAN;
    (*Change parameters and add code*)
    RETURN(i);
END_FUNCTION;
```

2.3.2.58 *ParseOK*

```
FUNCTION ParseOK
  (Name : ExpressName):LOGICAL;
    RETURN (False);
  END_FUNCTION;
END_SCHEMA;
```

References

DOUGLAS A. SCHENCK and PETER R. WILSON, (1994), *Information Modelling: The Express Way*. Oxford University Press, ISBN 0-19-508714-3

EPM TECHNOLOGY, (1998), EPMxpx - Structural Data Mapping Language for data sets defined in ISO 10303-11: The EXPRESS language.

ISO 10303 Industrial automation systems: ISO TC184/SC4/*WG5 N65 (P2) Industrial Data part 11: The Express Language Reference, (1994).

SHIP HULL PRODUCT MODEL

M. Ventura[1], J. Vitória[2] and C. Guedes Soares[3]

Unit of Marine Technology and Engineering, Technical University of Lisbon
Instituto Superior Técnico, Av. Rovisco Pais, 1049-001 Lisboa, Portugal
[1]mventura@beta.ist.utl.pt [2]jvitoria@mar.ist.utl.pt [3]guedess@alfa.ist.utl.pt

Abstract

The need for data exchange in shipbuilding motivated the concept of a neutral data model that may support the information requirements during the complete life cycle of a ship - the Ship Product Model. A brief survey of the related research work done in the last years is presented, together with its impact on the evolution of the international standards. Focus is set on the emerging STEP standard, its structure and the methodology used for its development. Finally, the role of the Application Protocols, is discussed as well as their internal structure and how industrial specific business cases are being used to support their development.

1 Introduction

1.1 Data flow in shipbuilding and maintenance

The design, production, assembly and maintenance of a ship require the management of an extraordinary volume of data. The complexity of the ship implies that different design, engineering analysis and manufacturing software (CAD/CAE/CAM) systems are used throughout the design and production process. Due to the conditions of the market, parts of both design and production are often sub-contracted to different companies, which may even be located in remote sites. So, either within a single company or between different companies, a large amount of data exchange is required.

In the traditional paper based environment a time consuming and error prone re-input of information was necessary, but in the current status of technology a great deal of data is already in digital format and can be processed by translators. The development of proprietary translators between the native formats of specified systems has been the approach but it is not an effective solution since the number of translators needed raises quite quickly with the number of systems available. The definition of a neutral format, independent from system vendors, is a much better solution, since each system must provide only one import and one export translators. Such format must cover the extent of data needed by the applications used by the industry and must have the agreement of all the parts involved, which led to the development of standards.

When the work on neutral formats started the CAD systems were changing from 2D drafting systems to 3D surface and solid geometry modelling systems. Therefore, the first standards were mainly concerned with the exchange of graphical data either in the form of technical drawings or as 3D geometric models.

Currently CAD systems are changing to 4D systems (they include the time dimension) that create and support a complete database which stores both the geometric and the non-geometric data required to manufacture, assemble and maintain the product. To cope with this evolution, the data exchange standards have been extended in their scope to make possible the transfer of the complete data defining the product instead of only the geometry.

1.2 Product Data Model

Ship data includes not only geometry but also topology, material specifications, structural scantlings, assembly, production planning and costs. The concurrency of design disciplines and manufacturing creates an additional requirement of configuration management to maintain the consistency of the data available to the different departments of a company or to all the companies involved in the process.

The implementation of basic product model technology at the shipyards requires a standard description of a ship's product model data, modification to CAD information system architectures, and the development of translation mechanisms.

Ship data must be generated in a comprehensive and consistent format independently of the individual application systems and the data generated at each stage should be re-used and completed throughout the following stages. In other words, there is the need to have a formal specification of a data structure that:

- describes as completely as possible all information related to a ship
- has a neutral format, independent from system vendors, commonly agreed on and available
- allows for the complexity and concurrency that is usual within this industry.

Such a data structure is the Product Data Model. A product model is a set of objects and relationships between the objects. While the objects describe the assemblies and components of the products, the relationships describe the architecture of the product. The Ship Product Model have been developed in the last years through the work done in research projects

2 Development of Standards for Product Data Exchange

2.1 Research background

Several projects have contributed to the development of the neutral format standards and the ship product model such as:

- CADEX   EU (1982-92)
- CAD*I   EU/ESPRIT (1984-89)
- SEAWOLF   US Navy (1987-1995)
- NIDDESC   US (1986-93)
- NEUTRABRAS   EU/ESPRIT (1989-92)
- MARITIME   EU/ESPRIT (1992-95)
- ShipSTEP   EU (1994-96)
- MariSTEP   US (1996-99)
- SEASPRITE   EU/ESPRIT (1996-99)

The results of such projects have contributed to the development of national and international standards such as IGES and STEP.

The Initial Graphical Exchange Specification (IGES) was developed to support the storage and transfer of basic 2D geometry between different CAD systems. IGES 1.0 was approved as ANSI standard September 1981 and the current version 5.3 was issued in 1996.

Although widely used for geometry exchange, the initial IGES data transfers had problems because the specification did not cover all the constructs used in CAD systems. After a series of enhancements, another problem was raised due to the fact that the specification allowed multiple correct representations of the same information and each CAD vendor was implementing only a unique subset. The lack of validation procedures for the translators was another cause for complains.

The US Navy defence program of the SEAWOLF class attack submarines was one of the first shipbuilding projects to generate a 3D solids model to support design and manufacturing. Under the split design/construction strategy used in the program, Tenneco's Newport News Shipbuilding and Drydock Company was responsible for the overall design and detail design of the submarine's forward end, while General Dynamics' Electric Boat Division was responsible for designing the submarine's aft end and for constructing the two first ships. The volume of data flowing between the two shipyards and the suppliers was the motivation for the SEAWOLFF Digital Data Exchange Project, in which scope IGES translators were implemented. Exchanges of 3D structures and 2D drawings between two shipyards were successfully accomplished (DeVale and Guilbert, 1994).

The experience with IGES demonstrated that drawings and basic geometric data could be exchanged between drafting and modelling systems. However, geometry exchange is only part of the problem. The large volume of data included in the technical drawings specifying structure and piping could be more easily re-used if available in a computer readable format. With this motivation, it was decided in 1985 to enhance IGES including product data, approving Product Data Exchange Specification (PDES) as a new work item. In the beginning of the 90's, the name PDES was changed to *Product Data Exchange using STEP*. However, it soon became evident that a mechanism, independent of any system, was needed to describe product data throughout the lifecycle of a product. To fulfil this need, it was decided to initiate at international level a standard for product data exchange and sharing, the STandard for the Exchange of Product model data (STEP – ISO 10303). STEP was designed to overcome the problems identified with early neutral formats such as the lack of distinction between the application, logical and physical levels, the inexistance of a formal specification, requirements not clearly documented and no conformance requirements defined.

The project CADEX (CAD Geometry Data Exchange) running from 1982 to 1992, was aimed at ensuring the European influence on the new STEP standard, involving a number of European CAD systems in the development of processors. CADEX has produced five AP's: AP204 "Manifold Solid Boundary Representation", AP205 "Surface Models" and AP206 "Wireframe Models". The project CAD*I (CAD Interface) started in 1984 was a five years research work targeting the exchange of geometry and shape information (curves, surfaces and solid models), the interface to Finite Element Analysis applications and drafting information in the area of mechanical engineering. The results of this project in the specification of a neutral file format and the information model for the description of technical drawings have provided a valuable input to the development of STEP.

In 1986, by initiative of the U.S. Naval Sea Systems Command (NAVSEA) and the Shipbuilding Research Program, the Navy/Industry/Digital Data Exchange Standards Committee (NIDDESC) was formed to develop standards for product model exchange for the maritime industry (Murphy,

1994). The information models previously developed in SEAWOLF were used as a starting point to the ship product model, which was divided into six main areas: *Ship Structures, Ship Piping, Ship HVAC, Ship Electrical and Cableways,* and *Ship Outfitting and Furniture*. The final goal was to develop the corresponding AP's which should be submitted to ISO. Two other models, Configuration Management and Ship Library Parts should also be developed to be included in each of the AP's. These models were issued in 1993. Meanwhile, and in accordance with the ISO recommendations of the Paris meeting (1985) to continue the development of existing national standards in parallel to the STEP effort, NIDDESC has also developed two AP's to enhance the transfer of CAD drawings and 3D piping (1990) that have been included in the version 5.1 of the IGES specification issued in 1991.

The MariSTEP project was developed in response to an invitation from the Defence Advanced Research Projects Agency (DARPA) to submit a full technical and cost proposal based on the project abstract titled "Development of STEP Ship Model Database and Translators for Data Exchange Between U.S. Shipyards". The objectives of this project were the implementation of a neutral file transfer capability between the product models at the U.S. shipyards, and the development of a U.S. marine industry prototype product model database to facilitate the future implementation of translators and product model data architectures by U.S. shipyards and CAD system developers.

A major component of this effort was the implementation of product model technology at each shipyard, including not only the geometric representations, but also attribute and relationship data for the total product life cycle of the ship or class. The effort required the development of a translation mechanism to exchange product model data among the various shipyards, owners, and vendors, and support of a product model database for data storage and retrieval. Regarding the product model, this program built on the AP's developed by NIDDESC. During this project, the shipyards have analysed the processes used, devised a plan for implementing a Product Model Database and then implemented that plan to develop a database. During the development, a prototype of a neutral Product Model Database (PMDB) should be implemented and populated with a typical ship data set, and the shipyards' internal data sets should be enhanced in accordance. Finally, translators should be implemented to permit data exchange of these STEP Product Models in a format consistent with the NIDDESC/STEP AP's.

The European project NEUTRABRAS, "Neutral Product Definition Database for Large Multifunctional Systems", carried out between 1989 and 1992, building on the work of CAD*I, has targeted the formal definition of a ship product model the specification of a format for a neutral database with a pilot implementation, and the development of prototype translators between existing shipbuilding systems and the neutral database (Welsh and Brun, 1992). The neutral database was required to be defined using the EXPRESS modelling language, should be complete in the scope, covering the relevant attributes throughout the life cycle, to have a flexible structure and to have an open architecture, suitable for use in distributed systems. This project was carried in a close relationship with the US project NIDDESC.

The European successor of NEUTRABRAS was the project MARITIME, "Modelling and Reuse of Information over Time", that started with the AP's as provided by NIDDESC. The technical goals of the project were to develop a life-cycle product model for maritime products, ships in particular, taking into account the perspectives of the shipyard, the classification society and the owner, to define information exchanges scenarios for the design and maintenance of ships, develop a technology for extracting the relevant subsets from neutral product databases, demonstrate the product model in pilot tests and contribute to the ISO standardisation process in the development of the APs.

From the joint effort of NIDDESC and MARITIME within ISO, it was decided to develop the ship structures model, which should be split into 3 AP's - AP216 (Ship Moulded Forms), AP218 (Ship Structures) and AP215 (Ship Arrangements) - and the AP217 (Ship Piping).

2.2 Current STEP Research

The development of STEP within the industry has taken almost ten years to reach the current position in which the core AP's are reaching the first ISO ballot stage.

Currently, STEP implementation is being made mainly in the scope of the EU funded project SEASPRITE and the US funded project MariSTEP.

SEASPRITE (Software Architectures for Ship Product Data Integration and Exchange) is an ESPRIT project started in 1996 and ending in June 1999. The fundamental objective of the project is to facilitate the transition of the European maritime industry from an inefficient paper based environment to a fully interoperable electronic based environment. The project is specifically aimed at the creation of a capability that fully supports the comprehensive inter-organisational electronic interworking in the areas of ship hull design, construction, in-service survey, maintenance and repair. The targets of SEASPRITE are to:

- Develop a Ship Hull Product Data model to support the business requirements of the overall maritime industry.

- Develop state-of-the-art software to support an electronic business environment.
- Carry out data exchanges that support specific business scenarios to meet the business requirements.

Both SEASPRITE and MariSTEP are focussing on the core AP's for ship arrangements, moulded forms and structures, with MariSTEP additionally implementing AP217 – Ship Piping Systems. The implementations however are being based on the information requirement models. In order that these can become stable and internationally accepted, the business cases supporting the implementation efforts were handed over to the European Marine STEP Association (EMSA) and will be published as EMSA protocols.

EMSA protocols are the information requirements for data exchange within specific busines case domains. These protocols are based on exact subsets of the official STEP AP's and will be withdrawn when STEP publishes AP's covering their scope.

3 Development of STEP

The International Standard ISO 10303 is organised as a series of parts, each published separately. The parts fall into one of the following series, described in ISO 10303-1: description methods, integrated resources, application interpreted constructs, application protocols, abstract test suites, implementation methods and conformance testing.

Twelve parts were approved as International Standards in 1994 and are referred to as STEP Version1.0. These parts have also been approved as an ANSI standard under the name PDES.

3.1 Application Protocols

For development purposes, the product model can be divided into separate parts, Application Protocols (AP's), each covering a key element of the product for its whole life cycle. The AP's are developed based on industry requirements defined and collected from the analysis of realistic data exchange situations designated by business cases. Basically, an AP is composed of the following main parts:

- A Scope, to describe the industrial requirements that the AP addresses and that can be documented by an application activity model (IDEF0), by a planning model (IDEF1X, NIAM or Express-G) or simply in plain English

- An Application Activity Model (AAM), to describe and decompose the activities, input and output objects, controls and modifiers
- An Application Reference Model (ARM), to describe the information objects required, their structure and attributes
- An Application Interpreted Model (AIM), to map the requirements to the types of objects understandable to other CAD systems. The AIM includes an Express schema (short form), an Express schema (long form) and a mapping table.

The *Ship Product Model* can also be divided into separate parts defined by the following key elements:

- Ship arrangements
- Ship structures
- Ship mechanical systems
- Ship moulded forms
- Ship mission systems
- Ship distribution systems
- Ship outfit and furnishings

The reasons for this division are the distribution of modelling work and the need to exchange subsets of the product model between agents in the marine industry, not to mention the practical aspects of exchanging the data associated with an entire ship. Each separate part is described by one or more different application protocols. The full series of planned shipping Application Protocols (AP) is shown in the figure 1 indicating those which are under development at the present time.

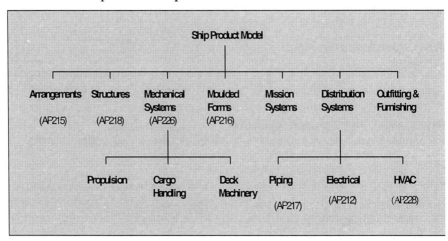

Figure 1 Planed and currently developed Ship Product Model AP's

4 Use of business cases to develop STEP Application Protocols

The approach that has been adopted by the SEASPRITE project for the further development of the STEP protocols is to concentrate in some important business cases so as to identify the subset of the Ship Product Model that is required to carry out those cases, and to establish these subsets. The business cases considered involve (Kendal, 1999):

- Hull form optimisation
- Hull cross-section design approval
- Subcontracting during design and manufacturing
- Handover of as-built condition

4.1 Hull Form Optimisation Business Case

When a shipyard develops a new ship design, one of the first stages is to establish the shape of the hull and its associated hydrodynamics characteristics. The initial requirements are drawn up by the shipyard and are then transferred to the test model basin for hydrodynamic testing. Information flows back and forth between the two companies, testing and alterations are made to the design until a satisfactory solution is reached. Due to the large variety of software applications that are used within the industry and the large financial cost associated with developing and maintaining interfaces, this information is currently transferred between different systems mostly by paper drawings and manual inputs.

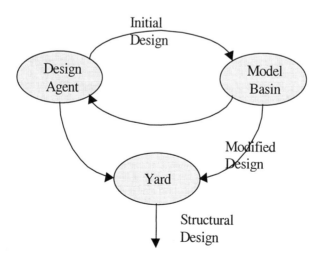

Figure 2 Hull Form Optimisation Business Case

The aim of this business case is to identify a subset of the Shipbuilding STEP AP Application Reference Models (ARM), that can be used to perform data exchange between a shipbuilder and a test model basin, for the testing and development of a ships hull moulded form. Results of the implementation will be provided as input to the STEP Shipbuilding AP development. This will validate the Shipbuilding ARMs and improve their quality and the companies involved in the implementation will benefit from early prototypes of electronic data exchange. This process will ensure that the implemented technology meets the needs of the end user.

The data exchange in this business case is related only to the moulded hull form (AP216). The business situation considered here is the dialogue between the shipbuilder and the test model basin, during the design stage, in order to define the final hull shape (figure 2). Typically this information consists of text, graphs, tables and 3-D CAD representation of the ships hull form. One example case that has been used as a test case is the hull of a VLCC. Figure 3 show its bow shape as imported by the CADShip system (Ventura and Guedes Soares, 1998).

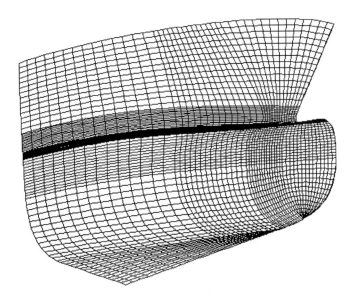

Figure 3 Bow of VLCC transferred using STEP

4.2 Hull Cross-Section Approval Business Case

This environment is one process during building of new ships, here designated by hull cross section approval. The process is also often referred to as section scantling. Hull cross-section information is commonly exchanged between shipyards - or engineering offices - and classification societies during the design phase of the ship life cycle (figure 4). The exchanges have the purpose of plan approval of the shipyard design. A hull cross-section is the collection of all those parts of the ship structure at a specified longitudinal position that are relevant for longitudinal strength.

Currently the required data for approval is mostly transferred using technical drawings. The drawings are output from ship design and construction systems. At the classification society's office, the drawings are either checked manually against the rule books, or they are entered into an approval software system. Based on this input, the classification society produces an approval report highlighting deficiencies of the ship design if any. The deficiencies may be noted down by red-marking the drawing. In case of computer-aided approvals an automatically produced report returns detailed results to the shipyard.

Already for the near future it is envisaged to use digital data exchange among the ship design and production systems and the analysis packages of the classification societies. The implementations based on this business case specification will contribute to the new way of working. They will imply that electronic copies of three dimensional ship designs are sent to classification societies via e-mail or similar means. Nowadays, hull cross section approval is still based on two dimensional data, with all the limitations this means for secure analysis. Without major human interaction the ship design data will be read into a ship structural analysis and approval package. Deficiencies of the design will be recognised and corresponding notes be added to the received model. The validated and marked digital model will be returned. It will be imported into the construction system of the design office and changed to satisfy the classification society comments.

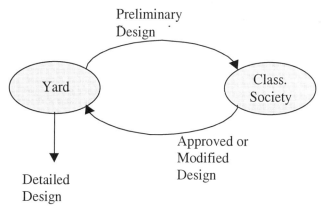

Figure 4 Midship Section Approval Business Case

This future scenario leaves the roles of the players in this business case untouched; design and analysis are strictly separated. However, with the new data exchange technology, the process can be made more efficient. The analysis tools can be given to the designers so that they can check their draft designs immediately, so that no cross-company communication would be required. The classification societies would finally be handed a ship design that has already been verified and which only needs approval. In summary, the verification by analysis may in the future be done by the shipyard or design office themselves. This, however, requires a seamless communication between ship construction and structure approval systems, as aimed for by this business case specification.

The majority of the business case is based on the AP218 but also includes parts of AP215 to cover the exchange of the information specifying the compartments arrangement.

4.3 Engineering and Production Sub-Contracting Business Case

The scenario (figure 5) starts with the available basic design of a yard. This yard will play the role the Main Contractor (MC) subcontracting a part of the detailed design. The Engineering Sub-Contractor (ESC) will then in parallel to the MC carry out their design. It is possible to update modifications made by the MC into the system of the ESC. Backwards the MC has to add the data received from the ESC into his system. Collecting all design data the MC will send a complete detailed design to a Production Sub-Contractor (PSC).

The reality shows that there is no straight flow of data and several iterations have to be used to complete the detailed design and to send the necessary modifications to the production yards. So it will be necessary to use also tools for data controlling.

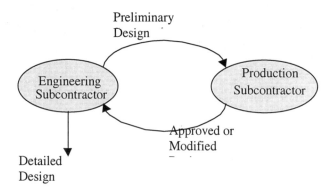

Figure 5 Engineering and Production Subcontracting Business Case

The situation in the shipbuilding industry today shows that different design systems are used. Not all of them are specific shipbuilding system but they have at least integrated shipbuilding tools. The systems involved in the scenario have also very different roots. There are only two possibilities to exchange design data today, both on drawing level. The exchange of paper drawings will create an additional effort at the MC side to integrate the received information into his system. The second way is to use for drawing exchange the existing neutral formats. But this means a loss of a lot of background information available in a product model but not in a drawing. The same situation we can find in the opposite way for updating the system of an ESC. The PSC as the end user of all produced data needs a lot of the detailed design data to be able to control his robots. A lot of manpower has to be used and the risk of making errors is always present following that old fashioned way. In general a drawing can't substitute product data how they are use in many yards today.

One example used as a test case is a transverse bulkhead. Figure 6 shows the bulkhead as imported by the CADShip system (Ventura and Guedes Soares, 1998).

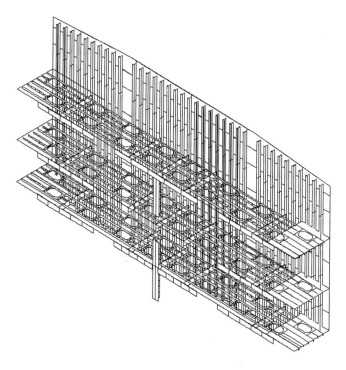

Figure 6 Transverse bulkhead transferred using STEP

4.4 As-Built Data Business Case

The scenario (figure 7) represents the situation at the end of the construction of the ship, when the complete information and specifications of the ship are held by the shipbuilding yard to the ship owner and to the classification society.

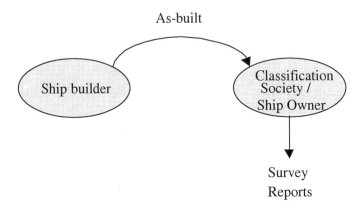

Figure 7 As-Built Data Business Case

Nowadays, this means that a large number of paper based drawings and specifications is supplied. Then the classification society converts the paper drawings into digital drawings to store in the database that is going to provide support to survey results and maintenance during the operational life of the ship.

4.5 Method for development of business case requirements

The aim of a business case is to identify a subset of the STEP Shipbuilding AP Application Reference Models (ARM) in order to perform data exchange and achieve the stated business benefits. Results of the implementation will be provided as input to the STEP Shipbuilding AP development. This will validate the Shipbuilding ARM's and improve their quality and the companies involved in the implementation will benefit from early prototyping of electronic data exchange.

The methods employed to define the requirements are thus similar to those used for developing the shipbuilding AP ARMs. The logical steps used in SEASPRITE in the process of developing a business case are as follows:

- Identify the information requirements
- Map these parameters to the entities in the Ship Product Model (entire ARM)

- Identify the Building Blocks required
- Create additional building blocks if required
- Compile the Building Block schemas as a single schema and resolve all cross-references
- Refine the schema by removing any redundant entities
- Document the schema as an EXPRESS model
- Carry out a pilot implementation to test the ARM
- Feed the results back into the ISO process

The data modelling is done using the EXPRESS language and the EXPRESS schemas are documented as building blocks. This is shown in figure 8.

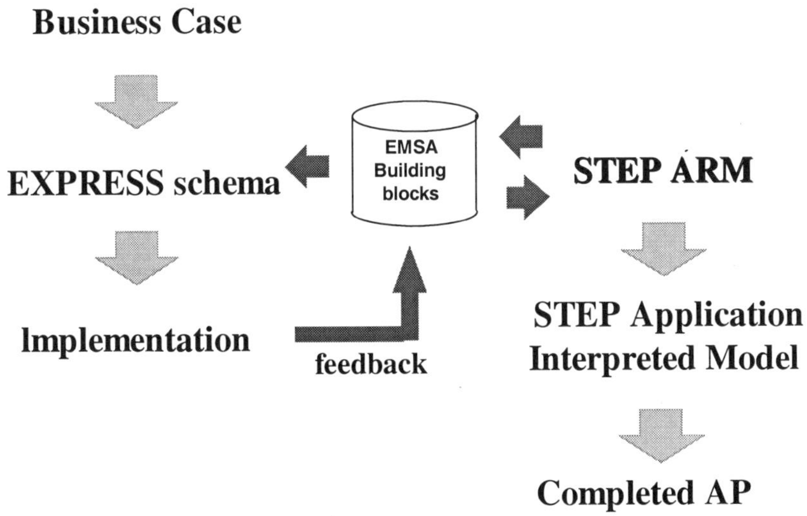

Figure 8 Business case requirements development methodology

5 Conclusions

Five years after the publication of version 1.0, the development of the STEP standard is an ongoing task. The international standardisation is a slow process and the APs that will constitute the Ship Product Model continuously being improved. The AP216, AP218 and AP215, which the core APs of the ship hull model, are in an advanced stage and have been already used in the implementation of translators to be included in existing commercial applications.

The translators implemented in the SEASPRITE project have successfully demonstrated data transfer of ship moulded forms and ship structures between some of the main software systems used by the shipbuilding industry. STEP processors are planned to be included in the next generation of software offered by several classification societies.

The business cases based on which the translators were developed will be published as industry standard EMSA Protocols in order that the data models remain stable. This will allow the translators to be exploited in the near future to allow data sharing and exchange in relevant business situations of ship design and production.

References

DEVALE, E. and GUILBERT, J. "Production Integration Via Solids Modeling", *Journal of Ship Production*, Vol.10, No.3, 1994, pp.202-214.

KENDALL, J. "Ship Product Data Interchange to Support Ship Design Processes", *Proceedings of ICCAS'99*, 1999.

MURPHY, J. "NIDDESC – Enabling Product Data Exchange for Marine Industry", *Journal of Ship Production*, Vol.10, No.1, 1994, pp.24-30.

VENTURA, M. and GUEDES SOARES, C., "Hull Form Modelling using NURBS Curves and Surfaces", *Proceedings of the 7th Int. Symposium on Practical Design of Ships and Mobile Units*, M. W. C. Oosterveld and S. G. Tan (Eds), Elsevier Science, 1998, pp. 289-296

WELSH, M. and BRUN, P. "A Data Model for Integration of the Precomissioning Life-Cycle Stages of the Shipbuilding Product", *Journal of Ship Production*, Vol.8, No.4, 1992, pp.220-234.

Application of Information Technologies to the Maritime Industries, C. Guedes Soares, J. Brodda, (Eds.), Edições Salamandra, Lisbon, 1999, (ISBN: 972-689-157-4), pp. 163-176

MariSTEP - A Prototype of STEP for Shipbuilding

B. Gischner[1], J. Howell[2], B. Kassel[3], P. Lazo[4], C. Sabatini[5], and R. Wood[6]

[1] Electric Boat Corporation, 75 Eastern Point Rd, Groton CT, 06340-4989,
bgischne@ebmail.gdeb.com

[2] Intergraph Corporation, Huntsville AL, 35894-0001,
[2] jhowell@ingr.com, [5] csabatn@ingr.com

[3] Naval Surface Warfare Center Carderock Division, 9500 MacArthur Boulevard, West Bethesda, MD 20817-5700, kasselb@nswccd.navy.mil

[4] Newport News Shipbuilding, 4101 Washington Ave, Newport News VA, 23607,
lazo_pl@nns.com

[6] Ingalls Shipbuilding, 1000 Access Road, Pascagoula MS, 39568-0149,
woodrw@ingalls.com

Abstract

MariSTEP is a cooperative effort among several shipyards and their CAD vendors to prototype the exchange of shipbuilding data using the Standard for the Exchange of Product Model Data (STEP). The goal is to demonstrate data exchange by prototyping limited portions of the shipbuilding application protocols. The disciplines addressed by MariSTEP are ship moulded forms, arrangements, piping, and detailed structure. This paper describes the details of the data exchanges, the lessons learned will be reviewed, and the future of shipbuilding data exchange.

1. Introduction

The amount and diversity of data required to support the design and construction of a ship is staggering. Accessing, sharing, and archiving data is of great concern in the collaborative environment. In order to solve data exchange problems, organizations could agree to use the same Computer Aided Design (CAD) system, procedures, and synchronize the upgrade to new versions and enhancements. This approach would minimize exchange issues, but is impractical and ignores the business cases in which different companies select and integrate product modeling tools. Clearly, a neutral, platform and system-independent format is essential. The first attempt to solve this problem involved the Initial Graphics Exchange Specification (IGES). This led to the development of STEP to fulfill additional industry requirements for full product model data transfer. Data exchange quality depends on the information supported within the product modeling systems. In some instances the system may not support certain entities, and can therefore not import or export them. Some of the challenges to the shipbuilding industry are: define the schema for each application domain, accommodate the schemas data elements within each native environment, and extract the data from the native environment for exchange.

2. Evolution of Ship Product Model Technology

The U.S. marine industry has been using CAD systems for the design and construction of ships for the U.S. Navy since the early 1980's. Initially used to automate the creation of ship drawings, the technology evolved to allow creation of full-scale, 3-D ship models. These models now have sufficient detail for interference checking, advanced visualization, construction support and design approval. More recently, the shipyards have started to integrate the CAD system with the other IT based systems such as material management, purchasing, and robotic systems, paving the way for the integrated information infrastructure known as the 'Ship Product Model'. Unfortunately these improvements in computer technology and integration within the yards were accompanied by a drastic reduction in ship design and construction contracts. This resulted in some of the shipyards to establish teaming arrangements to capture at least some of the remaining work. Three examples are the establishment of the design/build teams by Electric Boat and Newport News for the Virginia class submarine, Bath Iron Works and Ingalls Shipbuilding for the DDG51 class, and Avondale Industry and Bath Iron Works for the San Antonio class.

3. Neutral file transfers

Data exchange involved a combination of direct translators and neutral mechanisms such as IGES, modified to meet the needs of an individual program. This was required in order to allow transfer of the program specific design and construction information. It was soon discovered that each new direct translator or project-specific IGES 'flavoring' was useful on only a single ship program. This was the impetus for the creation of a single, industry-wide neutral data transfer specification, developed by consensus. This would allow each organization to know in advance what data would or would not be available, increasing the efficiency of the development of data exchange programs. This led to the establishment of the Navy / Industry Digital Data Exchange Standards Committee (NIDDESC) in early 1987.

3.1. The NIDDESC Standards

NIDDESC was established to develop product model data exchange standards for the U. S. marine industry. The NIDDESC team was primarily composed of Navy and shipbuilding data exchange experts developing IGES and Product Data Exchange using STEP (PDES) exchange specifications within the U.S. IGES / PDES Organization. The product model was organized by discipline and teams were formed for the development of STEP exchange specifications. The disciplines are Ship Structure, Ship Piping, Ship HVAC, Ship Electrical & Cableway, and Ship Outfit & Furnishing. The goal was the development of Application Protocols (AP) that could be submitted to the International Organization for Standardization (ISO) for incorporation into STEP. The Configuration Management and Ship Library Parts models were also developed to be a common resource to the shipbuilding AP's. The process of development for each of the models was:

- Develop IDEF0 activity models to define the high-level ship design process and data flows that need to be supported by the models.

- Develop Nijssen Information Analysis Method (NIAM) information models to define shipbuilding objects and their relationships.

- Develop information models using the EXPRESS language to provide a computer interpretable version of objects and relationships in order to automate the development of translator software.

NSRP DOCUMENT	TITLE
0424	Ship Piping
0425	Ship Electrical Cabling
0426	Ship HVAC
0427	Ship Configuration Management
0428	Ship Outfit and Furnishings
0429	Ship Structure

Figure 1. Listing of NSRP DOCUMENTS

The NIDDESC models were issued April 1993 and were incorporated into the ISO STEP APs in cooperation with other members of the maritime industry through ISO TC184/SC4 (STEP) Shipbuilding Committee meetings. In 1995, the NIDDESC Application Protocols were issued as

National Shipbuilding Research Program (NSRP) reports and are being used to define the format for the delivery of LPD-17 product model data. The NSRP reports are listed in figure 1.

3.2. ISO Application Protocols

Separate, parallel efforts have been underway in Europe to outline the requirements of shipbuilding for STEP. The current Shipbuilding APs are listed in Figure 2. Initiatives such as NEUTRABAS, MARITIME, ShipSTEP, EMSA and SeaSprite view the problem from a different perspective than NIDDESC. Working together, five shipbuilding AP's are currently being developed and are planned to become international standards by 2001. Editing responsibilities for the ISO Application Protocols are divided between Europe and the U.S. The US subteam is responsible for APs 215 and 217, and the European subteam is responsible for APs 216, 218, and 226. The scope of the APs cover early stage design through the construction stage for any ship, with additional support for certain operational data and class society survey information. NIDDESC is developing a Business Plan and a Plan of Action and Milestones for completion of the entire suite of APs.

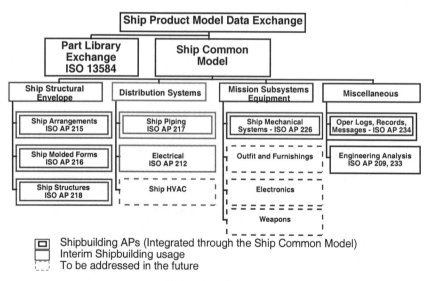

Figure 2. Application Protocols to Support the Ship Product Model

3.1.1. AP 215: Ship Arrangements

This AP supports the subdivision of ships into compartments and zones; definition of compartment geometric, functional, and operational properties; compartment connectivity, adjacency, and accessibility; tank capacities; cargo loadings for design and operations; ship product structuring by space; weight reporting; and damaged stability.

3.1.2. AP 216 Ship Moulded Forms

This AP supports the transfer of product model data to support the surface definition of hull shell and internal structural systems; station and spacing table definition; principle hull dimensions and characteristics; offset table and ship curve definition; and intact stability.

3.1.3. AP 217: Ship Piping

This AP supports the transfer of product model data to support piping flow; pipe sizing; pipe stress; piping connectivity checks; pipe system testing; interference detection; part fabrication; assembly and installation instructions.

3.1.4. AP 218: Ship Structures

This AP supports the transfer of product model data to support the design, manufacturing and approval of structural systems, plate parts, stiffeners, foundations, and welds. In addition it addresses the preliminary design of the ship structure and detailed design of all kinds of features including profile endcuts and interior, edge and corner cutouts.

3.1.5. AP 226: Ship Mechanical Systems

This AP supports the transfer of product model data to support the design and manufacturing of shipboard mechanical systems.

4. DARPA MariSTEP Project

The Defense Advanced Research Projects Agency (DARPA) is sponsoring a cooperative effort among several U.S. shipyards and their CAD vendors to develop prototype translators based on the ISO STEP Shipbuilding APs 215, 216, 217 and 218. It is a three year effort that began in August 1996 and

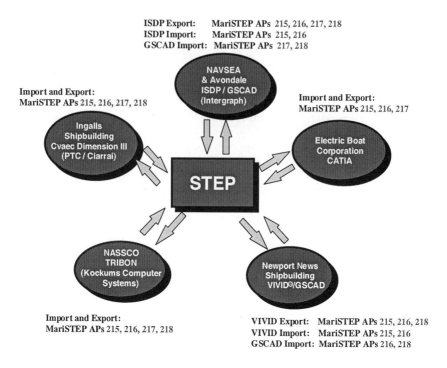

Figure 3. Five MariSTEP Shipbuilding / CAD Vendor Environments

was completed in December 1999. The MariSTEP consortium worked well together as a team, defining the steps to be performed, and using the consensus approach in making project decisions. The team was divided into "working groups", with each team member represented within each group. The five MariSTEP shipbuilding / CAD vendor environments are shown in figure 3 helped balance the workload required of each member, but also distributed modeling and shipbuilding knowledge among the participants. It also provided a "buy-in" mechanism at each project step. The MariSTEP implementation effort has provided valuable feedback to ISO community and given the U.S. shipbuilders an opportunity to influence the content of the ISO STEP Shipbuilding APs. Many significant improvements to the ISO product models were the direct result of the schema enhancements required for implementation within MariSTEP. And the effort identified Ship Product Model enhancements required at each participating shipyard. The steps followed by MariSTEP in the development of the prototype translators are outlined below:

- Identify ship life cycle processes.
- Select schemas which would best support those life cycle processes.
- Refine the schemas to support the MariSTEP implementation effort.

- Implement prototype translators.
- Provide periodic feedback to the ISO 10303 Technical Shipbuilding Committee (TC184/SC4/WG3/T23)

The MariSTEP team includes:

- Intergraph Federal System
- Newport News Shipbuilding
- Avondale Industries
- Parametric Technologies Corporation
- Ciarrai Computer Systems Ltd.
- University of Michigan
- Electric Boat Corporation
- American Bureau of Shipping (ABS)
- Ingalls Shipbuilding a Division of Litton Industries
- National Steel and Shipbuilding Company (NASSCO)
- Kockums Computer Systems
- Naval Surface Warfare Center Carderock Division (NSWCCD)

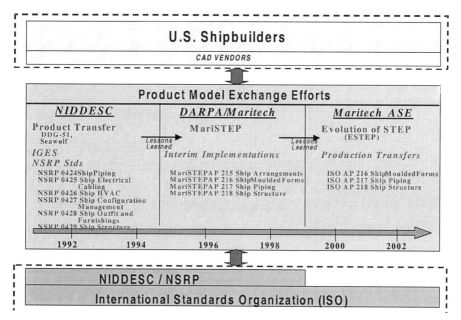

Figure 4. Evolution of U.S. Shipbuilding Product Data Exchange Effort

A new MARITECH Advanced Shipbuilding Enterprise (ASE) project called the Evolution of STEP (ESTEP) will continue these efforts as part of the Integrated Shipbuilding Enterprise Consortium (ISEC). The progress of development of international standards for the exchange of shipbuilding product model data is depicted in Figure 4.

5. Schema Selection and Development

A major goal of a prototype implementation is to validate the APs and discover problems, and MariSTEP was most successful in those undertakings. A major task of the MariSTEP team was to select and develop the schema. The MariSTEP schemas guided all the implementation efforts and although it led to the success of the project, it was a difficult and time-consuming process. One of the first tasks was to create a subset of the schemas in the ISO APs. The MariSTEP team encountered many difficulties developing these subsets when analyzing the various schemas to be implemented for the project. Each problem had to be resolved before translator development could begin. Some errors were the result of the ISO schemas having never being verified or implemented. While determining these schema enhancements was difficult for the MariSTEP team, the end result was that the MariSTEP implementations were successful, and the ISO APs have been significantly improved through these efforts. Since they have not yet been approved as international standards, this has allowed the identification and solution of problems. Systems Requirements Document (SRD). In order to provide consistent guidance to the team a Systems Requirements Document (SRD) was developed. The SRD was a dynamic document, in which all issues and their solutions were captured. Any change to the SRD required consensus by the MariSTEP team. In effect, the SRD is a mandatory implementers agreement allowing translator development to proceed using a static schema. The SRD is the most important document developed by the MariSTEP team. It provides guidance to the implementers, captures the solutions used to circumvent problems with the ISO schemas, and communicates program specific information to new participants.

6. Translator Testing

MariSTEP's success in identifying implementation problems with the ISO schemas was facilitated by the formal testing process followed for evaluation of the translators. A Product Model Database (PMDB) was developed which defines ships' systems and assemblies to support the prototype implementation in STEP format. The primary purpose of the database is to define STEP data used to evaluate translators. The database allows the Application Protocols using actual design and construction data.

6.1. PMDB Development

The first step in PMDB development was to determine the information to be included in the database. The goal was to define all of the types of data to satisfy the classes defined by MariSTEP, while minimizing the amount of data. For example, the product model contained pipes, components, equipment, etc. to define a portion of a system, but not all of the systems required for a complete engine room design were represented. The objective of the test cases was to exercise a broad range of information while minimizing the amount of data. In order for the data to be acceptable to the participants and non-proprietary in nature, it was culled from a Navy ship design project, the Engine Room Arrangement Model (ERAM). The PMDB was developed directly from the ERAM CAD data. Geometric data was provided using IGES and DXF. The attribute data was provided using text files and SQL statements. This allowed each of the participants to develop their native product model databases without having developed STEP translators. Each participant was responsible for developing specific types of data and translating it to the PMDB. Ultimately, a reduced set of test data was defined as a result of the combined effort. Extensive modeling of systems beyond the formal test data was done by some participants and will be available in STEP files to benefit future implementation testing and validation.

6.2. ERAM Data

The ERAM model is a slow speed diesel engine room designed to be commercially viable while satisfying the requirements of the U.S. Navy Sealift Program. The ERAM product model data consists of hullform, compartmentation, decks and bulkheads, structure, outfit and furnishings, piping, and HVAC. The hullform is defined for the whole ship. Theoretical surfaces are only defined for the decks, bulkheads, and compartments in the engine room and stack. Plates and stiffeners are placed on decks and major bulkheads.

7. MariSTEP Team Exchange Testing

The MariSTEP testing program was based on the Test Plan. The testing program was subdivided by implementation stage and track. During Stages 1 and 2, the MariSTEP shipbuilding environments exchanged data with members of the same track. Figure 5 below shows the three-stage schedule for this dual track effort. Two subteams were created, one addressing Ship Moulded Forms, Ship Arrangements and Compartmentation. The other subteam addressing Ship Piping. Implementation of AP218 was delayed until the first two phases were completed. Once these initial translators were developed, the two subteams switched tracks. Thus, at the conclusion of this second phase translators for APs 215, 216, and 217 were implemented by both subteams. At the conclusion of the project Pre and Postprocessors for all four of the ISO Shipbuilding APs being addressed (APs 215, 216, 217, and 218) in each shipbuilding environment.

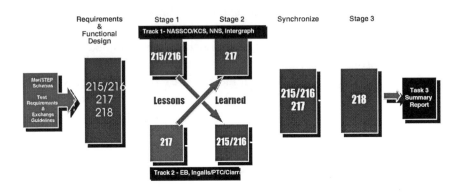

Figure 5. MariSTEP Staged Implementation

7.1. *Test Methods and Campaigns*

The MariSTEP project considered testing a very important phase of their translator implementations. A major portion of this project was planning and developing the test data and formal test procedures. The MariSTEP team exchange tests were organized by AP into "campaigns" which focused on testing a particular entity or group of related entities. The tests within each campaign progressed in complexity with each successive test. The idea was to start simple and "build" tests by adding different, but related entities. Test datasets were reused wherever possible to take maximum advantage of "proven" datasets in testing multiple exchange files and/or external references. Figure 6 shows three of the MariSTEP piping (AP217) test cases; pipe, pipe with fitting, and pipe assembly. Test cases progressed from simple to more complicated exchanges culminating with a complete piping system shown in figure 7. Every test was performed in every shipbuilding environment using the MariSTEP test worksheets and entity / attribute checklists specific to that test. For each test, there was a single MariSTEP template containing a test overview, a Preprocessor worksheet, a Postprocessor worksheet, and an entity / attribute checklist for that test. At the conclusion of each implementation stage in Task III, each shipbuilding environment summarized the test results and compiled a Data Transfer Report for delivery to the government.

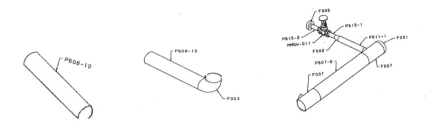

Figure 6. Typical piping test cases

7.2. Pre and Postprocessor Testing

In order to test the MariSTEP Preprocessors the ERAM product model data had to be modeled in each native system. Test case definition documents provided all information to ensure that the native models created by each partner were equivalent. Each environment produced a STEP Part 21 file which was analyzed to ensure that the native model was correctly represented and that a valid model was produced. The completed, validated STEP Part 21 file was published on the MariSTEP web site. The Part 21 file was then downloaded to each shipbuilding environment. Each dataset was processed separately and the entities / attributes in the Part 21 file were verified to ensure correct implementation in their system. This is the cornerstone of the prototype process and enabled the MariSTEP project to evaluate the ISO APs.

8. Lessons Learned

The lessons learned was one of the major reasons for the MariSTEP program. There were both negative as well as positive lessons which came out of this program. After all, one of the major purposes of a prototype is to identify promising areas in which to forge ahead, and problem areas to avoid.

8.1. Splitting the Tracks

The MariSTEP team divided its initial implementations into two tracks in order to enable demonstration of both structural and piping transfers earlier than would otherwise have been possible. Splitting of the tracks proved to be a double-edged sword. The advantage was to complete schema development and begin prototyping for all application protocols sooner. The problem was the number of implementations was too low. To further complicate things, the attention to detail by those who were not involved in the implementation was not sufficient to address issues they would later encounter during the crossover. And in the 217 track, the cardinal sin of data exchange testing was made, namely, having only two participants. On the other hand, this provided an interesting simulation of a real world data exchange problem. After the crossover, those who uncovered new issues had to take the extra step to convince others that a "released" standard needed to be modified, and in the event consensus could not be reached, that organization had to figure out how to deal with it. This, by the way, is a problem that will manifest itself through the entire life cycle of STEP.

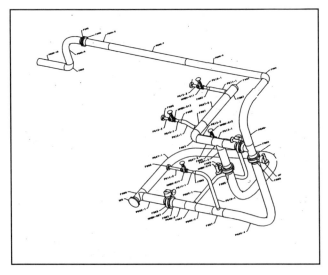

Figure 7. Complete Pipe System

8.2. *Schema Development Took Longer than Planned*

For various reasons, ranging from using unapproved schemas to finding ambiguities and redundancies in the schemas as a result of the consensus-making process, the development of suitable schemas took more time than originally scheduled. Delays were also caused by problems with STEP toolkits and because of the learning curve many participants had to overcome. It is important for the development team to start with the most complete and tested a schema possible. In the event the schema needs to be modified, documentation is critical. For MariSTEP this meant modifying and testing the schema, providing documentation in the SRD, and notifying ISO of the issues which resulted in the change.

8.3. Prototype implementations must maintain lines of communication with other similar prototype efforts

Since a snapshot of an emerging standard was used as the basis for the MariSTEP prototype translators, it is unrealistic to expect a successful data exchange between systems developed to support other prototypes, such as SeaSprite. The scope of the translator development only had limited overlap. For example, in SeaSprite, the emphasis of the data exchange is early stage design and classification, whereas the MariSTEP scope is detail design and construction. The schemas have diverged. As errors or ambiguities are corrected by separate organizations, the resulting schemas will be different, resulting in translators having different behaviors. This problem can be minimized through the effective use of memoranda of understanding between the organizations and an effective communication path. Whenever possible, other prototype efforts were informed of MariSTEP changes, and MariSTEP evaluated changes proposed by others.

8.4. Application Protocols should be Prototyped during Development

The development of a STEP application protocol should be prototyped before it becomes an international standard. This is not a requirement of the ISO process, and probably never will be. Meetings, discussions, and successful compilation, although critical elements, cannot find the deficiencies which can be found by a prototype implementation. If the prototype is not developed until the standard is released, it is too late to repair the schemas and to evaluate the affected relationships.

8.5. Parts Library Solution is Needed

The implementation of the MariSTEP AP's demonstrated the need for a library parts. Although, a standard is being developed to address parts and parts catalogs, the MariSTEP team could not come to consensus on it use. Therefore, the MariSTEP team developed its own parts library specification. However, even with this documented parts set, implementation discrepancies occurred among the team members. An international standard for the exchange of parts library data (ISO 13584) is under development by ISO, but it was not implemented for the MariSTEP prototype exchanges.

9. Summary

Today's Ship Product Model integrates CAD models with other models used in the corporate systems of the shipbuilding environment. It is a rich source of data for design, manufacturing and accounting data. Its exchange is useful throughout the life cycle of the ship, and that exchange can effectively reduce life cycle costs by enabling efforts such as collaborative design. The MariSTEP project encountered many challenges and difficulties in its efforts to develop the first implementations of STEP product model transfers for U.S. shipbuilding. Despite these problems, the project succeeded in implementing translators for four different STEP Shipbuilding APs in the five different shipbuilding / CAD system environments, as shown earlier in Figure 2. Through MariSTEP's feedback to ISO, the STEP Shipbuilding APs have been significantly enhanced, and are well on their way to adoption as international standards. The product model data captured at each participating shipyard has likewise been enhanced by the MariSTEP efforts, and the team members are significantly closer to their goal of full product model exchange using a neutral file transfer mechanism. MariSTEP is only one phase in the long, tortuous path to establish a product model data exchange capability for the shipbuilding industry, but it has been a success and will provide the foundation which future efforts will build upon. Further details on the MariSTEP project is available at the MariSTEP website: http://www.intergraph.com/federal2/project/step.

References

"Initial Graphics Exchange Specification, Version 5.3," *U.S. Product Data Association*, September, 1996.

"ISO TC184/SC4/WG3 N 531 (T12) Part: 215 Title: Application Protocol: Ship Arrangements," *International Organization for Standardization*, October, 1996.

"ISO TC184/SC4/WG3 N 538 (T12) Part: 216 Title: Application Protocol: Ship Moulded Forms," *International Organization for Standardization*, August, 1996.

"ISO TC184/SC4/WG3 N 593 Part: 217 Title: Application Protocol: Ship Piping," *International Organization for Standardization*, June, 1997.

"ISO TC184/SC4/WG3 N 532 Part: 218 Title: Application Protocol: Ship Structures," *International Organization for Standardization*, December, 1996.

"MariSTEP Vision for 2001," working paper of MariSTEP Project, August, 1996.

SHARING STRUCTURAL DESIGN MODELS USING STEP

Soon-Hung Han

Department of Mechanical Engineering
Korea Advanced Institute of Science & Technology (KAIST)
shhan@kaist.ac.kr

Abstract

In large Korean shipyards, different CAD, CAM, CAE systems are being used in different departments. Most of these automation systems are imported from USA or Europe and they use different internal formats for saving design models. These format differences create interface problems and the *islands of automation* phenomenon. STEP is an emerging international standard of which purpose is to solve the exchange problems. STEP has been applied to solve the problem inside the structural design department of Hyundai Heavy Industries. Starting from the midship section drawing, through FEM analysis, structural detail design, the product model or the design model should be transferred to different design tools. However direct translation of design models is not enough because of the nature of engineering design. The upstream design stage produce less data contents than down stream stages. There are gaps between production stages. The 2D midship section has been recognized by 2D feature recognition rules to reconstruct 3D models. The implementation has been applied to the structural approval system KR-TRAS of Korean Register.

1 Introduction

Computers have improved the shipbuilding productivity by the help of the technological development in engineering design, analysis, and production automation. But within each specialized domain or each department different computer systems are being used, because each system has own advantages and disadvantages.

While the functions of individual CAD system have been gradually improved, one CAD system cannot support every specialty function. Fig. 1 shows the situations in Korean shipyards where the two main design departments (hull and outfit design departments) use different CAD systems.

In the hull department, special purpose CAD systems developed only for shipbuilding industry are being used. While the outfit department uses general purpose CAD systems.

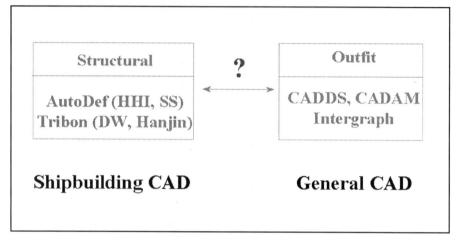

Fig. 1 Data exchange problem in Korean shipyards

Therefore the phenomenon called *Island of Automation* exists where diverse CAD systems are being used independently in each discipline. As a result engineering data management such as generation, storage, modification and exchange of ship design data has been a problem.

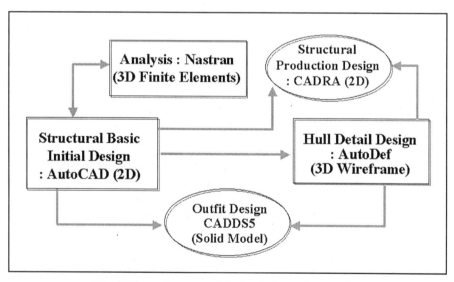

Fig. 2 Flow of structural design information in HHI

As shown in Fig. 2, different CAD/CAE systems are being used in the structural design office of Hyundai shipbuilders (www.hhi.co.kr). The data exchange between processes is neither harmonious nor automatic, and the data management becomes difficult.

The midship section prepared by AutoCAD is used by various downstream design activities; detailed structural design using AutoDef, structural analysis using NASTRAN, outfit design using ComputerVision's CADDS5, production drawings using CADRA. Internal formats of these systems are all different and the data exchange among them is difficult.

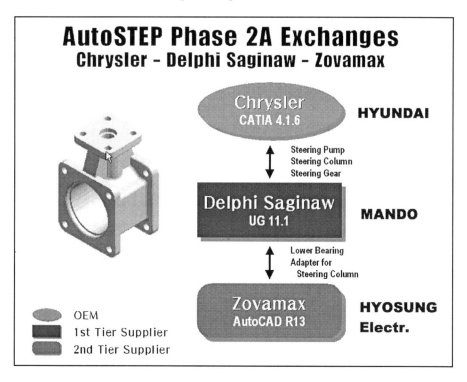

Fig. 3 Pilot implementation of AutoSTEP

2 Definition of the Midship Model Schema according to STEP

STEP (standard for the exchange of product model data) is an emerging international standard (www.nist.gov/sc24) intended to solve the data exchange problem among heterogeneous CAx systems.

In order to represent systematically a product model of a ship and to realize an open architecture framework, the STEP methodology has been utilized. A set of schema for the midship section of a bulk carrier has been defined according to the EXPRESS information modeling language.

It utilizes the shipbuilding BBs (Building Blocks) of EMSA (1996) that are the bases of the shipbuilding APs (Application Protocols) of STEP. Using the same schema throughout the lifecycle from design up to production and operation, engineering data can easily be integrated, exchanged, and shared.

Fig. 3 shows a pilot implementation in the automotive industry where parts supplied from a sub-contractor is assembled to a module and finally to a car. Because different CAD systems are being used in different companies, STEP has been used to exchange the model data. Because Korean automotive industry has the similar situation, names of equivalent companies in Korea are written together in the figure.

2.1 STEP methodology

The STEP methodology provides an efficient environment to represent product model because STEP is object-oriented and modularized.

The STEP standard consists of series of parts such as description methods (10s), implementation methods (20s), conformance testing methodology and framework (30s), integrated generic resources (40s), integrated application resources (100s), application protocols (200s), and abstract test suites (300s), and application interpreted constructs (500s), etc.

Fig. 4 summarizes all the parts of the STEP standards in several groups. Each part is a book of pages ranges from 20 to 3,000. APs are the main end products of STEP. Each industrial section has its own set of APs specialized to that domain. Other groups of STEP parts are to support each AP.

The STEP methodology separates the data structure from the data storage. The data structure (schema) is defined by the EXPRESS information modeling language. The real data can be stored either as the Part 21 format of ASCII file, or as a database management system using the Part 22 SDAI (standard data access interface).

The separation between the definition of data structure and the storage of data values helps to implement product models, and to extend or to customize the models. A schema is the definition of the product model structure of a specific domain and is written according to EXPRESS.

Within a schema other schemas can be referred using the import sentence. As it can refer to existing authenticated schema such as STEP AP203, a data model can be easily created.

2.2 Schema for the midship structural model

Fig. 5 shows the status of the shipbuilding APs (application protocols) (www.nsnet.com/NIDDESC/t23.html). Five AP projects are active; AP215 for general arrangement, AP216 for hull form, AP217 for piping, AP218 for hull structure, and AP226 for machinery.

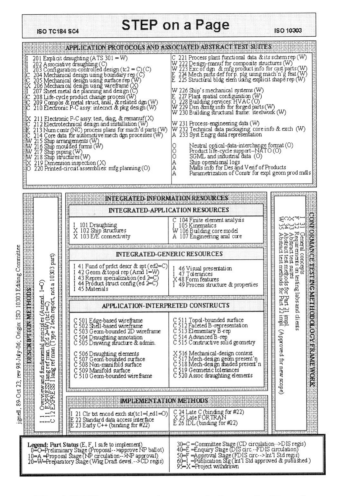

Fig. 4 STEP on a page (www.mel.nist.gov/sc5/soap)

Technical contents of these APs are expected to be completed within the year 1999. Three projects are leaded by European teams and two are by USA teams.

Fig. 6 shows a typical midship section drawing of a bulk carrier which has been drawn inside the structural design department of Hyundai shipyard. It is used for the detail design of hull structure, as the reference drawing for outfit design, and for the modeling of finite element analysis.

This is one of the key drawings the for shipbuilding process. Human designers can extract data of the intended ship from the drawing, although computers usually cannot reconstruct the intended 3D model of the ship for production.

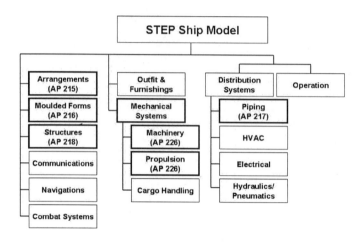

Fig. 5 Shipbuilding APs of STEP

Symbols and design conventions are used to deliver the design intention with a minimum set of information. Meanings of different line types and symbols should be interpreted properly.

The structural model schema defined in this paper consists of four BBs (Building Blocks) as Fig. 7. Each BB consists of three schemas called export, import, and model.

The BB methodology constructs a product model by collecting several independent BBs. Because a ship has tremendous data contents and different viewpoints, different people can construct a portion of ship product model in parallel. Building block approach can help to divide the big work into manageable sizes and to rejoin the blocks into single ship model.

Among above four BBs, *ship_mid_model* is newly defined in this research. *hull_cross_section_model* comes from the BBs of EMSA (European marine STEP association), which is modified to accommodate 2D midship cross section data. And the other two schemas, *support_resources_model* and *generic_product_structures_model* are borrowed from the 1996 version of EMSA BBs.

In *hull_cross_section_model*, there is *section_line* entity to represent 2D line entities. *feature_point* represents characteristic points of the midship cross section, *indexed_feature_points* defines midship cross sections for each type of ship, and *hull_cross_section* entity holds shipbuilding features such as deck, side shell, and girder.

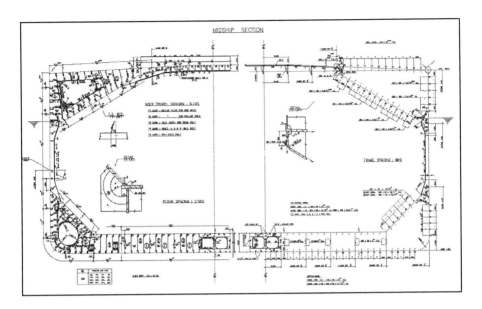

Fig. 6 Midship section drawing of a bulk carrier designed by AutoCAD

From *section_line* where line entities from 2D drawing are stored, *feature_point* which determines typical midship section is found, and then *indexed_feature_points* is constructed. From *indexed_feature_points*, shipbuilding feature is created and stored in *hull_cross_section*.

The recognized *hull_corss_section* entity creates 3D plate entities defined in the model schema of *ship_mid_model* BB and is transferred to the ACIS non-manifold model.

As the application protocol AP218 that standardizes the ship structure will be completed in the near future, it is more desirable to use the midship cross section schema of AP218 as the backbone schema.

3 Implementation of the System

3.1 Overview of the implemented system

Fig. 8 shows the architecture of the drawing recognition system. This system analyzes and enhances the 2D midship drawing and certifies the design according to the classification rules of KR (1998). The system is implemented in Windows 95/98 platform and uses the ACIS class library to handle geometric data.

The ACIS toolkit supports the non-manifold geometric modeling to process low-level geometric operations. The STEP toolkit *ST-Developer* and ROSE database is adopted to manipulate the ship design data instantiated from EXPRESS.

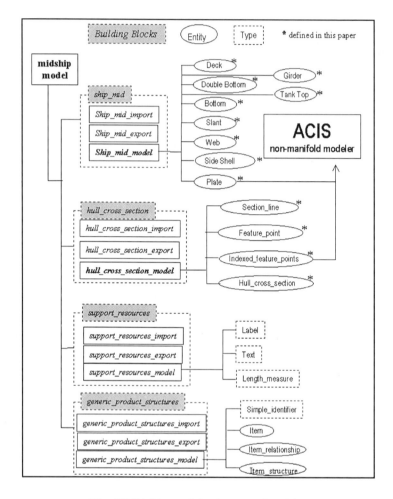

Fig. 7 Midship model schema and entities

The midship schema is constructed according to the STEP methodology. The non-manifold geometric modeling technology and the feature recognition methodology are utilized to manipulate the ship design data such as modification, mapping, and addition of data.

The input data required for the variables of KR-TRAS are extracted and passed into KR-TRAS, and so the structural design can be certified according to the rules of Korean Register of Shipping.

3.2 Recognition of midship section drawing

The midship section of Fig. 6 is stored as DXF ASCII formats of AutoCAD. A DXF file is composed of pairs of codes and associated values. The codes, known as group codes, indicate the type of value that follows.

Using these group codes and value pairs, a DXF file is organized of sections as follows. Sections are composed of records, which are further decomposed into group codes and data items.

- HEADER section: General information about the drawing can be found in this section. It consists of the AutoCAD database version number and a number of system variables. Each parameter contains a variable name and its associated value.

- TABLES section: This section represents the named objects and contains definitions for the symbol tables as follows. Line type table, Layer table, Style table, View table, User Coordinate System table, Viewport configuration table, Dimension Style table, Application Identification table.

- BLOCKS section: It contains block definition and drawing entities that make up each block reference in the drawing.

- ENTITIES section: This section contains the graphical objects (entities) in the drawing, including block references (insert entities).

- END section: tells the end of the file.

This file format has group codes and values for each entity, and the TABLE sections have been analyzed to extract attributes of LINE and ARC entities. For LINE entities the coordinate values of the start and the end points are extracted. For ARC entities, the coordinate values of the midpoint, the start angle, and the end angle are extracted.

Analysis of the DXF file is not enough to reconstruct the 3D shape of a hull because 2D drawing does not hold enough data contents. Fig. 9 shows a case where simple 2D sketch should be recognized into a real 3D model where thickness and rounding should be considered. Missing information should be added to complete the model. Direct translation cannot add any information. Methods of feature recognition should be borrowed.

Heuristic rules for the feature recognition have been applied to the extracted lines and arcs to construct a 3D model. According to the recognition rules of midship section (Table 1), deck, side shell, bottom, inner bottom, slant, and girder are extracted and recognized as the 3D elements. For example, the highest (upper), the longest, and the 10% inclined line among the extracted lines is recognized as the deck.

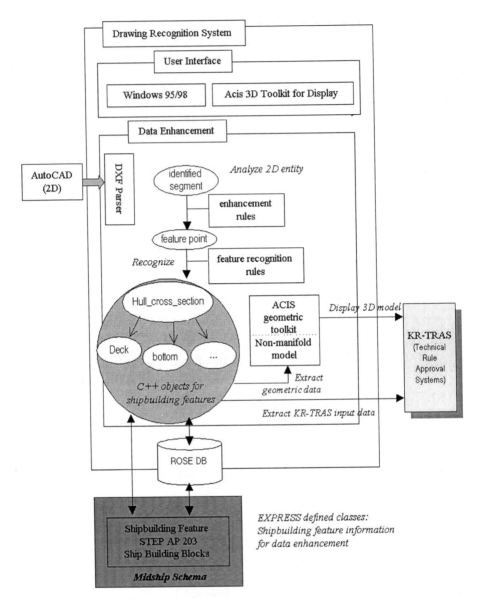

Fig. 8 Framework of the developed system

Using the recognized elements the hull assembly can be constructed. Fig. 10 illustrates the case for the corrugated bulkhead where plan, elevation, and side views are composed to get the 3D shape. More features can be recognized with the help of more sophisticated rules, but it is found that standardization of design conventions among designers is more effective in increasing the recognition rate.

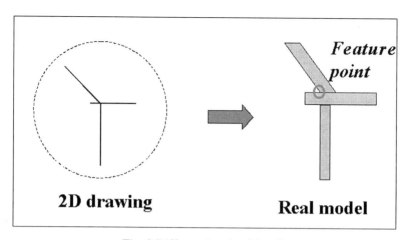

Fig. 9 Different levels of detail

Feature	H-Location	V-Location	Length	Direction
DECK	1ST UP	LEFT	LONGEST	10 % INCLINED
SSHELL		LEFT	LONGEST	VERTICAL
BOTTOM	1ST DOWN	LEFT	LONGEST	HORIZONTAL
IN-BOTTOM	2ND DOWN	LEFT	LONGEST	HORIZONTAL
GIRDER	DOWN	LEFT		VERTICAL
TTOP	2ND UP	LEFT		50% INCLINED
SLANT	DOWN	LEFT		50% INCLINED

Table 1 Feature recognition rules

The recognized feature model is visualized as a 3D model using the geometric modeling toolkit ACIS. The toolkit provides necessary functions to handle the ship geometry in 3D.

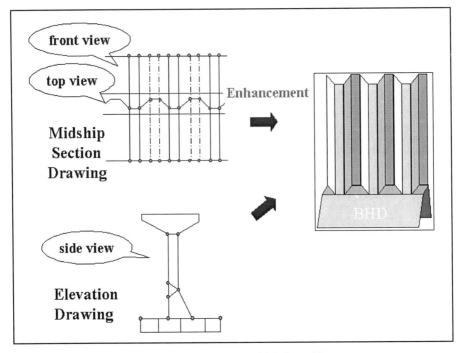

Fig. 10 Construction of 3D from 2D

Fig. 11 shows the recognized 3D model of the midship section. ACIS allows mixed dimensional (non-manifold) models including 2D, 3D, wireframe, and solid models. It has an advantage that both the wireframe model of the early design stage and the solid model of the production design stage can be saved and managed under one data structure.

Korean Register of Shipping has developed KR-TRAS (KR Technical Rule Approval System)[2], that is PC-based program for the review of ship structures and equipment according to the Rules of Korean Register of Shipping(1998). It offers information, which is used at each step of basic design, detail design, and outfit design in both shipyards and shipping companies.

Fig. 12 shows the overall structure of KR-TRAS. The *relevant Rules for Classification of Steel Ships* are applied according to the size and type of each ship, and KR-TRAS calculates individual part of the ship structure.

However the designer should type in every data into dialog boxes in order to perform these computations. In this study, the drawing recognition system based on the STEP methodology of Shin and Han (1997) and KR-TRAS is integrated to automate this data input process.

The whole process is; recognize features from 2D CAD drawing, build the 3D shape, extract input variables for KR-TRAS, and additional manual input into KR-TRAS for the calculation.

The problem is the mapping between the data structure of KR-TRAS and the data structure of midship schema which is based on the BB(building block) of STEP. The recognition of the shipbuilding features from 2D CAD drawings is also involved. Therefore techniques to increase recognition rate and to interface the drawing recognition system with KR-TRAS are required.

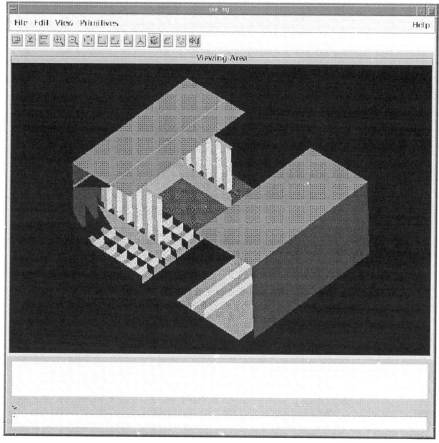

Fig. 11 Recognized 3D model of midship section

From the literature survey, the design data for the approval of ship structures has been exchanged using STEP in the European SEASPRITE project (Kendall 1998). The difference from this paper is that the European project has used the completed ship model after the detail design whereas this paper starts from the initial design stage.

After constructing a 3D model using the features recognized from the 2D drawings, we extracted the variables for KR-TRAS. The information of each plate is gathered from the drawing recognition system, then the input variables of KR-TRAS are found.

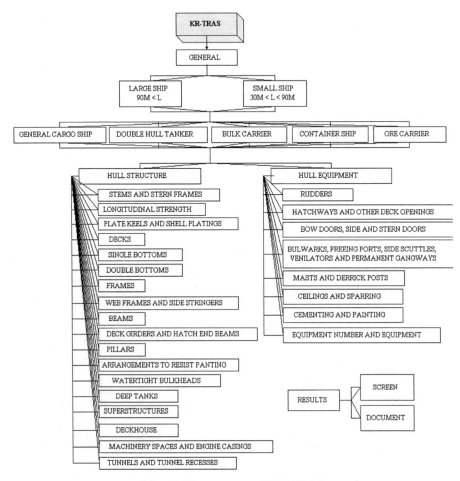

Fig. 12 The structure of KR-TRAS

Because a ship hull plate consists of many pieces, seam lines are represented on the drawing. To verify the design with KR-TRAS, we should find out the seam lines because we need not only the data of the whole plate but also the data of pieces. The recognized data is then transformed according to the variable types.

Among the input variables of KR-TRAS the coordinates, length, and thickness of the plate can be easily found. For the variables representing distances between horizontal and vertical diameters of the girder opening or the largest value among stiffener spaces of longitudinal frames which are attached on the girder, the information of these features should be parsed twice.

The system can recognize 36 variables (including arrays) from the midship section drawing among the 200 input variables of KR-TRAS. These recognized variables are mostly the coordinates and lengths of the plates.

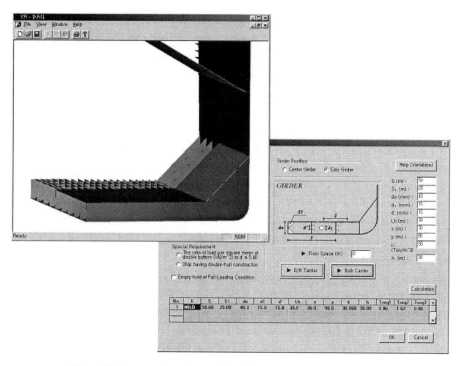

Fig. 13 The user interface of the drawing recognition system

3.3 Implementation results

The followings are implemented in this research.

(1) An EXPRESS schema for structural design model of midship section has been developed based on the STEP methodology. Information modeling with EXPRESS language enables systematic definition of data structure. The consistent data structure is maintained from the 2D drawing of initial design to the 3D solid model of detail design.

(2) 3D features have been extracted by applying the feature recognition rules to 2D design drawing data.

(3) The recognized features have been converted into a non-manifold model. The non-manifold model is used in order to process the geometric data

represented differently on each system. A standard neutral format such as STEP can solve the problem derived from functional differences among heterogeneous design systems.

(4) The variables have been extracted and delivered to KR-TRAS to check *the rules and guidance for classification of steel ships*. The menu import DXF has been added to an existing menu set of KR-TRAS so that 2D drawings of DXF format can be processed. As a set of drawing data is processed by the system, lines and arcs are extracted and saved in the database. According to the pre-defined feature recognition rules, the shipbuilding features such as deck, bottom, longitudinal, and seam line are recognized from the lines and arcs. Using the recognized features the 3D model can be generated and visualized. The data required for the calculation of KR-TRAS are provided to KR-TRAS. A designer should confirm whether the 2D drawing is properly converted into a 3D model. Fig. 13 shows the user interface of the drawing recognition system which is integrated with KR-TRAS system.

4 Conclusion

In this research the hull structural model based on the neutral format STEP has been constructed to share the data among CAD systems of functional differences.

We developed the system to analyze the 2D structural design data according to the feature recognition rules and convert them into 3D non-manifold models for downstream applications. This drawing recognition system has been interfaced with KR-TRAS (KR Technical Rule Approval System). It is a PC-based computer program for design scantling and review of ship structures and equipment according to the rules of KR (Korean Register of Shipping).

Because STEP methodology is utilized to define the model of this system, it is possible to share the data consistently and systematically when the 2D drawing data of initial design stage are transmitted to the downstream stages such as detail design, outfit design, or finite element analysis. Fig. 14 shows triangular meshes generated from the 3D model of Fig. 6.

In this research, only the length and the orientation of a 2D line are considered to define shipbuilding features. If more information can be added during the initial design stage, such as layer, line color, and line thickness, more design entities can be recognized systematically.

In order to recognize lines that represent scaled-down entities such as longitudinal stiffeners, pre-defined specifications of the entities have to be included as shipbuilding features. Texts such as alphanumeric dimensions are saved as ASCII formats in DXF drawings. Therefore, recognizing the texts together with graphic entities enables more complete recognition of design drawings.

If the recognition rate is high, a fair amount of work which should be repeated at the next stage can be reduced. Data mismatch between design stages or between design departments can be avoided. The more recognition from 2D drawings can be done, the more input variables of KR-TRAS can be extracted.

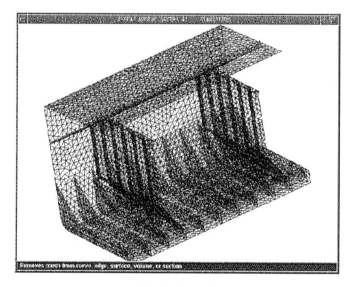

elements : 23,882
nodes : 12,733
file size : 2 Mbyte

Fig. 14 The 3D finite element mesh

References

AUTODESK, (1994) "AutoCAD Release 13 Customization Guide"

EMSA (European Marine STEP Association), (June 1996), "Building Blocks - Kobe version"

ISO TC184/SC4/WG3 N708, ISO/WD 10303-218 Ship Structures, April 1998

INT'L STANDARDS ORGANIZATION (ISO), (1995), "Industrial automation systems and integration - Product data representation and exchange - Part 21: Implementation methods : Clear text encoding of the exchange structure", ISO 10303-21

INT'L STANDARDS ORGANIZATION (ISO), (1998), "Industrial automation systems and integration - Product data representation and exchange - Part 22: Implementation methods: Standard data access interface specification", ISO 10303-2w

KENDALL, J. (Oct. 1998), "Ship product data integration and exchange to support ship design", SEASPRITE Report

FOWLER, J. (1995), "STEP for Data Management, Exchange and Sharing", Technology Appraisals

KR, (1998), "Rules for Classification of Steel Ships and Guidance Relating to Rules for Classification of Steel Ships", Korean Register of Shipping

KR, Homepage of Korean Register of Shipping, http://www.krs.co.kr/rnd/KR-TRAS.htm

GRAU, M. and KOCH, T. (June 1999), "Applying STEP Technology to Shipbuilding", ICCAS '99, 10th International Conference on Computer Application in Shipbuilding, Held in Boston USA

NIST, Composition of STEP, http://www.nist.gov/sc4/www/stepdocs.htm

RABIEN, U. and LANGBECKER, U., (June 1997), "Practical Use of STEP Data Models in Ship Design and Analysis", ICCAS '97, 9th International Conference on Computer Application in Shipbuilding, Japan,

SHIN Y. and HAN, S.-H., (Oct. 1997), "Data Enhancement for the Life-Cycle STEP Data Sharing", ICCAS'97, Japan, pp.543-552

SHIN Y. and HAN, S.-H., (Oct. 1998), "Data Enhancement for Sharing of Ship Design Models", Computer-Aided Design, 30(12):931-941

MODELING SHIPBOARD PIPING

Robert W. Schuler

Naval Surface Warfare Center-Carderock Division,
9500 MacArther Blvd. West Bethesda Maryland, 20817, USA
SchulerRW@nswccd.navy.mil

Abstract

This paper focuses on several aspects of modeling shipboard piping systems and discusses several data standards that are available to the shipbuilding community. Distributed systems in general and piping systems in particular present special requirements for computer models of ships. These systems are special because the physical arrangement of constituent components in space is designed to create a flow path for some medium. This implies connectivity constraints on the placement and alignment of component data within computer models of piping systems. Piping systems are also unique because they are currently modeled as one-dimensional objects for flow analysis, two-dimensional objects for schematic diagrams, three-dimensional objects for interference analysis, and as four-dimensional objects (three-dimensional objects changing in time) for simulation.

There are several data standards available to the shipbuilding community, that enable the exchange of piping system data in a format that is neutral of any particular modeling tool or computer environment. The "3D Piping IGES Application Protocol Version 1.2" has been available since 1994. ISO 10303-227 "Plant spatial configuration" is an Application Protocol that uses STEP (the Standard for The Exchange of Product model data) to describe process plant data including piping systems. ISO 10303-227 will be available as an international standard near the end of 1999. ISO 10303-217 "Ship Piping" is an Application Protocol that uses STEP to describe shipboard piping systems. ISO 10303-217 is currently a committee draft international standard and will most likely not be available until 2003.

1 Introduction

Distributed systems present special requirements for computer models of ships. These requirements stem from two sources. The first is that connectivity has a mathematical meaning based upon Kirchhoff's laws. The second is that references to ship's background require the whole ship rather than a single deck or compartment. Although this paper focuses on shipboard piping, many of the principles apply equally well to piping in buildings, electrical distribution, and HVAC (heating, ventilation, and air conditioning).

1.1 Connectivity

When modeling the placement of equipment like an engine, the relationship between the engine and its foundation can be considered a connection. The connection has some physical properties associated with it, but the primary attribute of interest is the physical location. Questions like, "Does the foundation match the footprint of the engine?" make sense. A similar connection idea exists when modeling shipboard piping. Pipes are physically connected to ship's structure by pipe hangers and bulkhead penetrations. Questions that make sense include, "Is the hole in the bulkhead big enough?", or "Can the pipe hanger be secured to the structure?". This sort of connectivity is referred to as physical connectivity throughout this paper.

In addition to the physical connectivity between a pipe, a pipe-hanger and a bit of ship's structure, pipe models must consider flow connections between piping components. Flow connections emphasize the fact that some medium (electricity, air, oil, water, etc.) shall be conveyed from one component to another. These connections are less oriented towards physical location and more oriented towards the mathematical effect resulting from the connection. Very often flow connections are emphasized on schematic diagrams, but it is equally valid to apply flow connections to 3D piping models.

Kirchhoff's laws conveniently summarize the mathematics of flow connections (for electricity and incompressible fluids):

1) the total volume of medium flowing into a flow connection is equal to the total volume of fluid flowing out of the flow connection, and

2) the sum of the pressure losses around any closed path (through two or more flow connections) is equal to zero.

When combined with the transfer function of each component, these laws allow engineers to predict the behavior of a piping system.

1.2 Dimensionality

The fundamental engineering problem of supplying the correct amount of fluid at the correct pressure and velocity is essentially a 1D problem called flow network analysis. Engineering questions that make sense from this perspective include, "Is component A connected to component B?", and "what is the pressure drop across component C?". These questions can be answered by computer models that do not carry any geometrical information.

A very common method for modeling piping systems is the schematic, which is a 2D representation that emphasizes flow connectivity. Computer models of piping networks can be further reduced into graphs, matrices and net lists. These are essentially 2D data structures that contain enough information to perform the flow network analysis.

Computer models that show the physical layout of a piping system make use of 3D representation. This has been the area of development that has advanced the furthest in the past two decades and seems to be the notion that most readers conjure up when they hear the term "computer model".

There are also 4D piping models that show 3D information changing in time. Models that show valve stems moving up and down in a simulation environment fall into this category. Visualization of vibration analysis also falls into the category of 4D pipe modeling.

1.3 Ship's Background

By their nature, shipboard piping systems are distributed systems; that is, they are routed throughout the ship, crossing several deck and bulkhead boundaries. This creates an interesting challenge for Computer Aided Design (CAD) tool authors. Specifically, piping system engineers and designers need to see the whole ship's background, but at a low level of detail. Higher levels of detail are required when routing pipe within a compartment. Software that is smart enough to switch between these levels of detail based upon the area of the ship being displayed are very difficult to write, and this author has not seen a CAD tool which does this well.

Views that are of interest to a pipe designer include:

1) Deck plan views that show major bulkheads and compartment boundaries and show how pipe runs traverse a deck.

2) Elevation views that show decks and major bulkheads and show how pipe runs traverse between levels of the ship.

3) Isometric views and exploded isometric views (views in which the distance between decks is exaggerated to make more room for piping detail to be shown) which combine information from the first two views.

4) Detail arrangements of spaces that are known to be densely packed with piping and other systems.

2 Data Structures for Modeling Piping Networks

2.1 Simple Example

Figure 1 shows a simplified schematic of the piping network that is used to regulate pressure in the 36-inch water tunnel at the Naval Surface Warfare Center-Carderock Division lab in Bethesda, Maryland. This arrangement of valves allows a sophisticated control system to keep the pressure in the water tunnel at the specified level.

This figure falls into the 2D category described above. This type of presentation is very useful in printed books like this one. The necessary connectivity is expressed at a level of detail sufficient to give most engineers a sense of how the system operates. The tank on the right-hand side of the figure is pressurized and has one inlet (node n) and one outlet (node g). The water tunnel on the left-hand side of the figure also has an inlet (node h) and an outlet (node a).

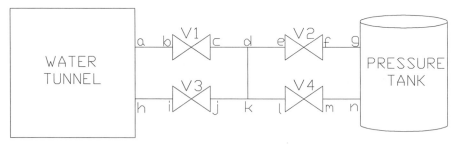

Figure 1 Simple Piping Schematic

By controlling the positions of valves V1 through V4, the control system regulates the pressure in the water tunnel. For example, closing valves V1 and V3 and opening valves V2 and V4, allows the system to circulate water through the path g,f,e,d,k,l,m,n. Closing valves V2 and V3 and opening valves V1 and V4 allows water to flow from the water tunnel into the pressure tank through the path a,b,c,d,k,l,m,n.

This figure is missing a lot of the information that is typically expressed in an engineering drawing. Specifically, the types of valves are not indicated, the pressure rating of the tank is not shown, nor is the elevation of any of the nodes shown. The figure is, however, detailed enough to highlight some of the methods available for storing piping data within a computer.

2.2 Graphs

One of the most powerful data structures for storing a flow network like the one shown in figure 1 is a graph. Graph theory is well established in computer science and there are many well-defined algorithms for manipulating data stored in graphs. "A graph $G = (V, E)$ consists of a set V of **vertices** (also called **nodes**), and a set E of **edges**. Each edge corresponds to a pair of distinct vertices. (Sometimes self-loops, which are edges from a vertex to itself are allowed; we will assume that they are not allowed.) A graph can be directed or undirected. The edges in a directed graph are ordered pairs; the order between the two vertices that the edge connects is important. In this case, we draw an edge as an arrow pointing from one vertex (the tail) to another (the head). The edges in an undirected graph are unordered pairs; we draw them as simple line segments." (MANBER, p. 186).

A graph of the flow network shown in figure 1 is shown here in figure 2. Notice how the schematic symbols for the valves, the tank, and the water channel have simply been replaced with straight lines. Furthermore, the nodes have been highlighted with shaded circles.

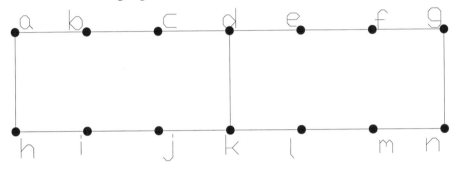

Figure 2 Graph of Flow Network

In effect, nodes d and k have changed the least. This is because in figure 1, these nodes where only connected to straight lines. All of the other nodes have had at least one of their edges replaced by a straight line.

2.2.1   Kirchhoff's Laws Illustrated

Each node in figure 2 is a flow node, as defined earlier in this paper. This makes figure 2 extremely useful for emphasizing Kirchhoff's laws. According to the first law, if five gallons per minute (5 gpm) are flowing from node c to node d, and six gallons per minute (6 gpm) are flowing from node e to node d, then eleven gallons per minute (11 gpm) must be flowing from node d to node k.

In the case where water is being pumped from the tank outlet at node g to the tank inlet at node n (path g,f,e,d,k,l,m,n,g), Kirchhoff's second law tells us that the sum of the pressure drops g-f, f-e, e-d, e-k, k-l, l-m, and m-n will equal the pressure difference between nodes g and n. In other words, the pressure drops around the loop sum to zero.

2.2.2 Representing the Graph as a Connection Matrix

One method for representing a graph in the computer is by use of a square matrix with the rows and columns labeled to match the nodes in the graph. If two nodes are connected by an edge then the corresponding cells in the matrix are set equal to one; otherwise, these cells are set equal to zero. The connection matrix in table 1 represents the graph in figure 2. Note that the zeros are omitted from the table to enhance legibility.

	a	b	c	d	e	f	g	h	i	j	k	l	m	n
a	X	1					1							
b	1	X	1											
c		1	X	1										
d			1	X	1						1			
e				1	X	1								
f					1	X	1							
g						1	X							1
h	1							X	1					
i								1	X	1				
j									1	X	1			
k				1						1	X	1		
l											1	X	1	
m												1	X	1
n							1						1	X

Table 1 Connection Matrix

There are two cells in the matrix for each edge in the graph. For example, the edge between nodes a and b is marked by a 1 in cell (a,b) and a 1 in cell (b,a). By removing this requirement for symetry, it is possible to represent directed graphs using a connection matrix. For example, if edge a-b in figure 2 was a directed edge, then cell (a,b) in the connection matrix would be set to 1, while cell (b,a) would be set to 0.

2.2.3 Representing the Graph with Linked Lists

Another popular method for storing graphs in the computer is with linked lists. A linked list for each node in the graph stores the name of all of the other nodes that are connected by an edge. This method has several advantages over the connection matrix, especially for sparse matrixes that are the norm for flow networks. The biggest advantage is that the linked list method uses much less memory for most flow networks. The heads of the lists may be themselves joined in a linked list, or they may be stored in a matrix. Table 2 shows a linked list representation of the graph in figure 2.

List	Connected Nodes
a	b, h
b	a, c
c	b, d
d	c, e, k
e	d, f
f	e, g
g	f, n
h	a, i
i	h, j
j	i, k
k	d, j, l
l	k, m
m	l, n
n	g, m

Table 2 Linked List Representation

2.2.4 Representing the Graph with a Net List

Another important method for storing flow network graphs is called a net list. This method focuses on the edges of the graph rather than the nodes. In this method, each edge is named along with the names of the nodes it connects. Many flow network analyses tools from the batch-processing era of computing use this method because it lends itself nicely to storage in well-formatted ASCII files. Table 3 shows the net list for the schematic in figure 1 (and the graph in figure 2).

Component	N1	N2
Pipe Segment	a	b
Valve	b	c
Pipe Segment	c	d
Pipe Segment	d	e
Valve	e	f
Pipe Segment	f	g
Pipe Segment	h	i
Valve	i	j
Pipe Segment	j	k
Pipe Segment	k	l
Valve	l	m
Pipe Segment	m	n
Pipe Segment	d	k
Water Tunnel	a	h
Pressure Tank	g	n

Table 3 Net List

2.2.5 Graphs for Shipboard Pipe Modeling

Graphs form the common denominator between all pipe models. It is possible to extract a graph from any pipe model no matter what dimension was used (1D, 2D, or 3D). Furthermore, the conversion between the methods for representing graphs is fairly well documented in computer science literature.

Graphs emphasize the connectivity that distinguishes piping system modeling from other branches of product modeling and simulation based design.

This author believes that it is possible to use "simple" algorithms to reduce the graphs extracted from two different pipe models and to compare them to determine if the models represent the same pipe network. At a minimum, graphs can be used to help keep disparate piping models of the same physical system synchronized.

The general problem of comparing two graphs is called isomorphism and is one of the few major problems whose status (either polynomial or NP-hard) is still unknown. (MANBER, p.248). In other words, computer scientists still don't know if an efficient algorithm can be found to solve the problem. The graphs extracted from piping models, however, are not random graphs. There is additional information that can be fed into algorithms designed to compare flow networks. By naming key nodes in graphs extracted from different sources, computer algorithms should be able to streamline the searches necessary to determine if two graphs are the same.

2.2.6 Visualizing Compiler Graphics (VCG)

The "VCG Visualization of Compiler Graphs" is a tool developed with support from ESPRIT project 5399 Compare. The software was available from ftp://ftp.cs.uni-sb.de/pub/graphics/vcg/ at the time this paper was written. VCG is a tool which assists in laying out graphs like the ones discussed earlier in this section of the paper. For input, VCG takes a simple ASCII file like the one shown in listing 1. VCG automatically generates a graph like the one shown in figure 3.

```
graph: { title: "Flow Network"
manhattan_edges:yes
orientation: left_to_right
node: { title:"a" label:"a"}
node: { title:"b" label:"b"}
node: { title:"c" label:"c"}
node: { title:"d" label:"d"}
node: { title:"e" label:"e"}
node: { title:"f" label:"f"}
node: { title:"g" label:"g"}
node: { title:"h" label:"h"}
node: { title:"i" label:"i"}
node: { title:"j" label:"j"}
node: { title:"k" label:"k"}
node: { title:"l" label:"l"}
node: { title:"m" label:"m"}
node: { title:"n" label:"n"}
edge:{source_name:"a" target_name:"b"arrowstyle:none}
edge:{source_name:"b" target_name:"c"arrowstyle:none}
edge:{source_name:"c" target_name:"d"arrowstyle:none}
edge:{source_name:"d" target_name:"e"arrowstyle:none}
edge:{source_name:"e" target_name:"f"arrowstyle:none}
edge:{source_name:"f" target_name:"g"arrowstyle:none}
```

```
        edge:{source_name:"d" target_name:"k"arrowstyle:none}
        edge:{source_name:"a" target_name:"h"arrowstyle:none}
        edge:{source_name:"g" target_name:"n"arrowstyle:none}
        edge:{source_name:"h" target_name:"i"arrowstyle:none}
        edge:{source_name:"i" target_name:"j"arrowstyle:none}
        edge:{source_name:"j" target_name:"k"arrowstyle:none}
        edge:{source_name:"k" target_name:"l"arrowstyle:none}
        edge:{source_name:"l" target_name:"m"arrowstyle:none}
        edge:{source_name:"m" target_name:"n"arrowstyle:none}
        }
```

Listing 1 VCG Input File

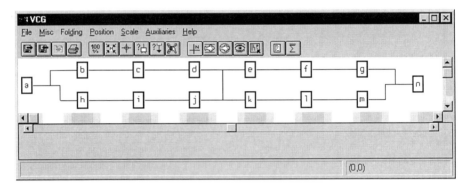

Figure 3 VCG Visualization

VCG can be used to "automatically" layout schematics by importing a graph extracted from a pipe model. The input grammar for VCG is very simple which makes the tool very easy to work with. Since the tool is distributed with its source code, it should be quite easy to extract the resulting graph layout for use in a CAD environment.

2.3 Computer Aided Design

Computer Aided Design (CAD) has become entrenched in all engineering disciplines and piping is no exception. The notion of CAD models is what pops into most readers minds when they read the words "piping model". In fact, the 2D and 3D models discussed in the "dimensionality" section of this paper are perhaps the most sophisticated method for engineers to communicate information about piping systems.

CAD tools store and manipulate collections of graphical primitives (lines and arcs) along with some formatting information in a manner similar to the way that word processors store and manipulate collections of alphanumeric characters along with formatting information. Just as a word processor collects characters into words, a CAD tool collects graphical primitives into symbols. The collection of graphics primitives, symbols, and the associated formatting information in a CAD tool is often referred to as an object space.

When evaluating CAD two questions are very useful in determining the power of each tool: "Is the tool parametric?", and "Is the tool associative?". These attributes apply equally well to 2D and 3D tools.

Parametric means that dimensions (length, width, and height) of objects drawn within a tool may be determined by variables (called parameters) that may be calculated based upon certain criteria. For example, a box may be drawn such that its width is equal to its height, and its length is twice its height. In this case, the CAD operator can change the height of the box, and the tool may automatically adjust the other two dimensions, and redraw the box.

Associative means that two objects in the tool's object space may be related. An example of a simple associative relationship is the requirement that two lines be perpendicular. If a CAD operator moves a line that is perpendicularly related to another, the tool may automatically move the second line. Sometimes, these types of associations are called constraints, and the algorithms responsible for updating the object space when the user makes a change are called the constraint solver.

2.3.1 Two Dimensional CAD Models

Two dimensional (2D) CAD models include schematics, deck plan views, elevation views, isometric projections, and exploded isometric diagrams. Common symbols for valves, pumps, heat exchangers, etc. allow diagrams like figure 1 to have well defined meaning to most engineers.

To specify the placement of a symbol in 2D CAD requires two points. For symmetrical symbols, like pipes, the order of the points is insignificant. For asymmetrical symbols, like check valves, the order is significant. Parametric symbols may require additional placement points and always require parameter values. Consider the case shown in figure 4.

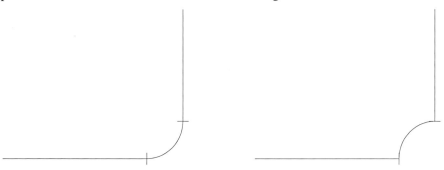

Figure 4 Placement of a Parametric Bend

In this case, it is not enough to specify the start and end of the pipe bend. The user must also specify the bend radius and at least one additional point to assist in orienting the bend. Without the third point, the computer cannot determine which way to draw the bend.

2.3.2 Three Dimensional CAD Models

Three dimensional (3D) CAD models generate the same output as 2D CAD models for deck plan views, elevation views, and isometric projections. The difference is that the 3D CAD model also has information about where symbols are in 3-space and how they are oriented. This additional information allows new projections (like a view looking aft) to be calculated by the computer rather than the draftsman (as is done in 2D modeling). Furthermore 3D CAD models enable the movement of a symbol in the plan view to be automatically reflected in the elevation view and the isometric view. Figure 5 shows a typical 3D CAD environment.

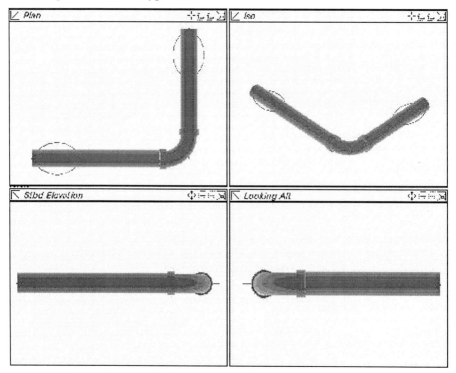

Figure 5 3D CAD Environment

To specify the placement of a symbol in 3D CAD requires three points, two end points and a third point for orientation. For symmetrical symbols, like valves, the order of the end points is insignificant. For asymmetrical symbols, like reducers, the order is significant. Parametric symbols require parameter values, but can generally be placed with only three points.

Three dimensional models are not generally used to express schematic information, and generally carry more connectivity data than their 2D counterparts. This is because every elbow, pipe bend, and reducer must be shown in the 3D model, while these symbols are generally suppressed into a single pipe symbol (a line) in 2D models.

3D CAD models are useful for interference checking. A simple algorithm for checking each symbol in the object space against every other object can be run in the order of n-squared time, where n is the number of objects. Most modeling tools use more sophisticated algorithms.

Current efforts in ISO and ANSI to standardize the exchange of piping data are focused on 3D data. The next section of this paper discusses three of these data standards.

3 Data Standards for Exchanging 3D Piping Models

There are several data standards available to the shipbuilding community, that enable the exchange of piping system data in a format that is neutral of any particular modeling tool or computer environment. The "3D Piping IGES Application Protocol Version 1.2" has been available since 1994. ISO 10303-227 "Plant spatial configuration" is an Application Protocol that uses STEP (the Standard for The Exchange of Product model data) to describe process plant data including piping systems. ISO 10303-227 will be available as an international standard near the end of the year 1999. ISO 10303-217 "Ship Piping" is an Application Protocol that uses STEP to describe shipboard piping systems. ISO 10303-217 is currently a committee draft international standard and will most likely not be available until the year 2003.

All three of these standards follow a three-tier approach to modeling:

1) A model is developed in the language of the application domain. This model is called the application reference model (ARM).

2) A model is developed which maps the ARM into a computer sensible language. This model is called the application interpreted model (AIM).

3) A data exchange format (physical file format) is specified for each construct in the AIM.

3.1 Initial Graphics Exchange Specification (IGES) version 5.3

The "Initial Graphics Exchange Specification Version 5.3" is published by the American National Standards Institute (ANSI) as ANS US PRO/IPO-100-1997. IGES (pronounced 'I guess' by the old timers) defines a collection of entities useful for exchanging data between CAD systems. There are two application protocols defined using IGES; one for 3D piping and the other for Layered Electrical Products.

3.1.1 IGES File Format

An IGES file contains 5 sections START, GLOBAL, DIRECTORY ENTRY, PARAMETER DATA, and TERMINATE. These sections are always in the order shown in table 4, each line in the IGES file is 80 columns wide and ends with a sequence number. The sequence starts over in each section of the file.

START	S0000001
GLOBAL	G0000001
	G0000002
	G0000003
DIRECTORY ENTRY	D0000001
	D0000002
	O
	O
	O
	D0000101
	D0000102
PARAMETER DATA	P0000001
	P0000002
	O
	O
	O
	P0000078
TERMINATE	T0000001

Table 4 IGES File Format

The START section comes first and contains arbitrary comments in human readable form.

The TERMINATE section comes last and contains a check-sum which tells how many lines each of the other sections contain.

The GLOBAL section contains information about tolerances, file names, and the version of IGES used. This section also contains date information that is not year 2000 compliant for IGES versions before 5.3. This is significant because the current version of the IGES piping application protocol requires version 5.2 of IGES, and is therefore not year 2000 compliant.

The DIRECTORY ENTRY section contains two lines for each entity in the file and each line is divided into ten 8-character fields. The Directory Entry fields are numbered from 1 to 20. Fields 1 and 11 contain the entity type number (110 means line, while 100 means circular arch). Fields 10 and 20 contain line numbers. Field 15 contains the form number of the entity. Each entity type may have multiple forms each with different parameter data.

The PARAMETER DATA section of the IGES file contains data unique to an instance of an IGES entity. This data is different for each type of entity. In the case of a circular arch (Entity 100):

- the first value ZT represents an offset from the XY-plane;
- the second and third values represent the X and Y-coordinates of the center of the arch;
- the fourth and fifth values represent the X and Y-coordinates of the start of the arch;
- and the sixth and seventh values represent the X and Y-coordinates of the termination point of the arch.

In the case of a line (Entity 110), the first three values represent the X, Y, and Z-coordinates for the start of the line and the last three values represent the X, Y, and Z-coordinates for the end of the line.

3.1.2 IGES Example

The correct pipe run in figure 4 (the image on the left) consists of 4 lines and one circular arc. Two of the lines represent pipes, while the other two lines show the interfaces between components. The IGES file that describes this image is shown in Listing 2.

This listing highlights one of the key problems with exchanging models from CAD systems. It is not really possible for the computer to distinguish between the two lines that represent pipes, and the two tick-marks used to show the flow connection between the pipes and the pipe bend. The elimination of this ambiguity is accomplished by adding extra information into the IGES file. This extra information is defined by the application protocol.

```
                                                                     S       1
,,12HA:\Elbow.dwg,12HA:\Elbow.igs,54HAutoCAD-14.01 (Microsoft Windows NTG     1
Version 4.0 (x86)),65HAutodesk IGES Translator R14.01 (Dec 9 1997) froG      2
m Autodesk, Inc.,32,38,6,99,15,12HA:\Elbow.dwg,1.0D0,1,2HIN,32767,    G      3
32.767D0,13H990525.112624,8.28869969028911D-9,8.28869969028911D0,,,10,0,G     4
13H990525.100947;                                                    G       5
       110      1      0       1       0      0      0    000010000D  1
       110      0      8       1       0                         0D   2
       406      2      0       0       0      0      0    000000000D  3
       406      0      0       1       3                         0D   4
       122      3      0       1       0      0      0    000000000D  5
       122      0      8       1       0                         0D   6
       100      4      0       1       0      0      0    000010000D  7
       100      0      8       1       0                         0D   8
       122      5      0       1       0      0      0    000000000D  9
       122      0      8       1       0                         0D  10
       110      6      0       1       0      0      0    000010000D 11
       110      0      8       1       0                         0D  12
       122      7      0       1       0      0      0    000000000D 13
       122      0      8       1       0                         0D  14
       110      8      0       1       0      0      0    000000000D 15
       110      0      8       2       0                         0D  16
       110     10      0       1       0      0      0    000000000D 17
       110      0      8       2       0                         0D  18
110,5.25D0,6.25D0,0.0D0,6.25D0,6.25D0,0.0D0;                         1P      1
406,2,0,1H0;                                                         3P      2
122,1,5.25D0,6.25D0,.5D0;                                            5P      3
100,0.0D0,6.25D0,6.5D0,6.25D0,6.25D0,6.5D0,6.5D0;                    7P      4
122,7,6.25D0,6.25D0,.5D0;                                            9P      5
110,6.5D0,6.5D0,0.0D0,6.5D0,7.25D0,0.0D0;                           11P      6
122,11,6.5D0,6.5D0,.5D0;                                            13P      7
110,6.25D0,6.21130030971089D0,0.0D0,6.25D0,6.28869969028911D0,      15P      8
0.0D0;                                                              15P      9
110,6.53869969028911D0,6.5D0,0.0D0,6.46130030971089D0,6.5D0,        17P     10
0.0D0;                                                              17P     11
S      1G      5D     18P      11                                    T       1
```

Listing 2 IGES File of 4 Lines and a Circular Arc

3.2 ISO 10303 STEP

ISO 10303 is informally referred to as the Standard for The Exchange of Product model data (STEP). STEP is a large international effort managed by the International Standards Organization (ISO) technical committee 184, sub-committee 4 "Industrial automation systems and integration". STEP defines a framework of related documents specifically aimed at the exchange of computer models.

Documents within STEP are numbered, but not sequentially. The number of a part tells something about the purpose of the part.

- Parts 1-10 are called Overview and fundamental principles and give general introductory information. Part 1 is the only part in this sequence.

- Parts 11-20 are called Description methods. These parts Define the EXPRESS language for describing schemas.

- Parts 21-30 are called Implementation methods. These parts define methods for exchanging and interacting with data that conforms to STEP.

- Parts 31-40 are called Conformance testing methodology and framework. These parts provide guidance on how to test for conformance to STEP.

- Parts 41-50 are called Integrated resources. These parts contain the basic building block entities used in the AIMs of STEP application protocols.

- Parts 100-199 are also called Integrated resources.

- Parts 201-300 are called Application protocols. These parts define the schemas which are actually used to exchange data using STEP. Part 227 and Part 217 are discussed in this paper.

- Parts 301-399 are called Abstract test suites. These parts contain rules and procedures for testing files and translator software for conformance to STEP application protocols. Part 301 is used to test part 201, part 302 is used to test part 202, and so on.

- Parts 501-599 are called Application interpreted constructs. These parts define application objects that are common to two or more application protocols, along with the mapping of these application objects onto the AIM level use of integrated resource entities.

Data conforming to ISO 10303 application protocols is exchanged using the file format defined in ISO 10303-21 "Clear text encoding of the exchange structure". It is common practice to refer to a file in this format as a "part 21 file."

3.2.1   ISO 10303 File Format

A part 21 file contains two sections: HEADER and DATA. The HEADER section always precedes the DATA section. The grammar for these files is defined using Wirth Syntax Notation which leverages many of the powerful techniques in computer science for lexically analyzing and parsing text files. Many people consider this a major improvement over the rigid column formatted (punch card oriented) file structure used by IGES.

Within the HEADER of a part 21 file is the name of a schema which defines the entities used in the DATA section of the part 21 file. This separates the syntactical rules for representing data from the semantic definitions of entities. This also means that a user must read the HEADER of the part 21 file to decide how to interpret the file contents.

Each application protocol within ISO 10303 defines its own schema.

Entities defined within a schema may be instantiated zero, one or more times in a part 21 file. The basic syntax is:

```
#29=ENTITY_NAME('value for first attribute', 'value for
second attribute', . . ., 'VALUE FOR LAST ATTRIBUTE');
```

ISO 10303-21 defines rules for associating the values in the list with the attributes defined for an entity defined in the EXPRESS language. EXPRESS is defined in ISO 10303-11.

```
ISO-10303-21;
HEADER;
FILE_DESCRIPTION((''),'2;1');
FILE_NAME('Elbow.stp','1999-05-26T07:57:48',(''),(''),'Autodesk STEP Translator
Release 14.01','AutoCAD Release 14.01',' , , ');
FILE_SCHEMA(('CONFIG_CONTROL_DESIGN'));
ENDSEC;
DATA;
#8=(NAMED_UNIT(*)PLANE_ANGLE_UNIT()SI_UNIT($,.RADIAN.));
#9=DIMENSIONAL_EXPONENTS(0.0,0.0,0.0,0.0,0.0,0.0,0.0);
#10=PLANE_ANGLE_MEASURE_WITH_UNIT(PLANE_ANGLE_MEASURE(0.017453292500000),#8);
o
o
o
#143=QUASI_UNIFORM_SURFACE('',1,1,((#139,#141),(#140,#142)),.SURF_OF_LINEAR_EXTRUS
ION.,.F.,.F.,.U.);
#144=CARTESIAN_POINT('',(6.250000000000000,6.250000000000000,0.0));
#145=CARTESIAN_POINT('',(6.500000000000000,6.249999999999999,0.0));
#146=CARTESIAN_POINT('',(6.500000000000000,6.500000000000000,0.0));
#147=CARTESIAN_POINT('',(6.250000000000000,6.250000000000000,0.500000000000000));
#148=CARTESIAN_POINT('',(6.500000000000000,6.249999999999999,0.500000000000000));
#149=CARTESIAN_POINT('',(6.500000000000000,6.500000000000000,0.500000000000000));
#157=(BOUNDED_SURFACE()B_SPLINE_SURFACE(2,1,((#144,#147),(#145,#148),(#146,#149)),
.SURF_OF_LINEAR_EXTRUSION.,.F.,.F.,.U.)GEOMETRIC_REPRESENTATION_ITEM()QUASI_UNIFOR
M_SURFACE()RATIONAL_B_SPLINE_SURFACE(((1.0,1.0),(0.707106781186547,0.7071067811865
47),(1.0,1.0)))REPRESENTATION_ITEM('')SURFACE());
#158=CARTESIAN_POINT('',(5.250000000000000,6.250000000000000,0.0));
#159=CARTESIAN_POINT('',(5.250000000000000,6.250000000000000,0.0));
#160=CARTESIAN_POINT('',(5.250000000000000,6.250000000000000,0.500000000000000));
#161=CARTESIAN_POINT('',(6.250000000000000,6.250000000000000,0.500000000000000));
#162=QUASI_UNIFORM_SURFACE('',1,1,((#158,#160),(#159,#161)),.SURF_OF_LINEAR_EXTRUS
ION.,.F.,.F.,.U.);
#163=GEOMETRIC_CURVE_SET('GCS1',(#132,#138,#143,#157,#162));
#164=GEOMETRICALLY_BOUNDED_WIREFRAME_SHAPE_REPRESENTATION('GBWSR1',(#163),#28);
#165=SHAPE_REPRESENTATION_RELATIONSHIP('SRRPL1',' ',#164,#124);
ENDSEC;
END-ISO-10303-21;
```

Listing 3 Partial Part 21 file of 4 Lines and an Arc

3.2.2   STEP Example

The correct pipe run in figure 4 (the image on the left) consists of 4 lines and one arc. The part 21 file that describes this image using ISO 10303-203 "Configuration-controlled design" is 147 lines long. A portion of this file is shown in Listing 3.

3.3   3D Piping IGES Application Protocol Version 1.2

The "3D Piping IGES Application Protocol Version 1.2" is published by the American National Standards Institute (ANSI) as ANS US PRO/IPO-110-1994. The ARM of this standard defines 18 application objects that may be used to define a piping system. The AIM of this standard defines how these 18 application objects may be represented using combinations of 35 IGES entities. Data conforming to this standard is exchanged using the IGES file format.

The IGES piping application protocol file generated from the 3D model shown in figure 5 is 175 lines long and contains 51 IGES entities. A portion of this file is shown in listing 4. The following Application Objects are present in the file:

- 2 Pipes
- 1 Unmodified Piping Component (the bend)
- 2 Piping Joints
- 1 Pipe Run
- 1 Pipeline
- 1 Piping System

3.4   ISO 10303-227 "Plant spatial configuration"

The ISO 10303-227 "Plant spatial configuration" application protocol is published by the International Standards Organization. The ARM of this standard defines 265 application objects that may be used to define a piping system and the process plant which houses the piping system. The AIM of this standard defines how these 265 application objects may be represented using combinations of 359 ISO 10303 integrated resource entities. Data conforming to this standard is exchanged using part 21 files.

Unfortunately, the author does not have access to a tool for generating a data file conforming to ISO 10303-227 at the time of this publication. This means that there are no statistics available for file size, entity count, or number of application objects. It is anticipated, however, that once ISO 10303-227 becomes an international standard, tools will become available.

```
This file was produced by Intergraph Corporation's Piping translator        S      1
1H,,1H;,8HINSTANCE,7Hmarexpo,35HINGR CPIGES 02.04.00.02 21-JUN-1996,         G      1
o
o
o
322,27HUNMODIFIED PIPING COMPONENT,4,2,17,3,1,19,3,1,0,0;                  53P     40
422,27HUNMODIFIED PIPING COMPONENT,18H9OELR371P1346P_1 1,0,0;               55P     41
420,47,0.,0.,0.,1.,1.,1.,2,,0,2,49,51,0,1,55;                              57P     42
132,65.,64.371999999999999,0.,0,2,2,,0,13HPIPE END PORT,0,0,0,             59P     43
0,0,0;                                                                     59P     44
110,65.,64.372,0.,65.,72.5,0.,0,0;                                         61P     45
132,65.,72.5,0.,0,2,2,,0,13HPIPE END PORT,0,0,0,0,0,0;                     63P     46
322,15HPIPE DEFINITION,4,14,1,2,1,18,3,1,57,3,1,2,3,1,50,3,1,4,            65P     47
2,1,28,3,1,5,3,1,23,3,1,36,3,1,85,2,1,86,3,1,98,2,1,99,3,1,0,0;            65P     48
422,1.000000,3HIPS,2HIN,9H90-10 CNA,,0.000000,,15HPIPE398Q1451F_            67P     49
1,7HCNA-200,6HPIPING,200.000000,3Hpsi,1.065000,2HIN,0,0;                    67P     50
322,4HPIPE,4,3,17,3,1,19,3,1,103,3,1,0,0;                                  69P     51
422,4HPIPE,17HPIPE398Q1451F_1 1,34H7D19010-PIPING-1.000000-1.000            71P     52
000-1,0,0;                                                                 71P     53
102,3,59,61,63,0,2,67,71;                                                  73P     54
322,8HPIPE RUN,4,4,17,3,1,19,3,1,37,3,1,55,3,1,0,0;                        75P     55
422,8HPIPE RUN,10HPIPE RUN 1,7H7D19010,10Hseq1_00336,0,0;                  77P     56
402,3,15,57,73,0,1,77;                                                     79P     57
322,8HPIPELINE,4,2,17,3,1,19,3,1,0,0;                                      81P     58
422,8HPIPELINE,10Hseq1_00336,0,0;                                          83P     59
402,1,79,0,1,83;                                                           85P     60
322,13HPIPING SYSTEM,4,2,17,3,1,19,3,1,0,0;                                87P     61
422,13HPIPING SYSTEM,4Hsys1,0,0;                                           89P     62
402,1,85,0,1,89;                                                           91P     63
322,12HPIPING JOINT,4,3,17,3,1,6,3,1,104,3,1,0,0;                          93P     64
422,12HPIPING JOINT,5H39-37,,0,0;                                          95P     65
102,2,49,5,0,1,95;                                                         97P     66
422,12HPIPING JOINT,5H38-44,,0,0;                                          99P     67
102,2,59,51,0,1,99;                                                       101P     68
S       1G       3D      102P      68                                       T      1
```

Listing 4 Partial 3D Piping IGES Application Protocol Version 1.2 File

3.5 ISO 10303-217 "Ship piping"

The ISO 10303-217 "Ship piping" application protocol is only a committee draft standard. It is currently available on the web at http://www.nist.gov/sc4/step/parts/part217/cdc/current/. The ARM of this standard defines 326 application objects that may be used to define a shipboard piping system. The AIM of this standard has not been published, so the number of ISO 10303 integrated resource entities that will be used is unknown. Data conforming to this standard will be exchanged using part 21 files.

Unfortunately, the author does not have access to a tool for generating a data file conforming to ISO 10303-217 at the time of this publication. This means that there are no statistics available for file size, entity count, or number of application objects. It is anticipated, however, that once ISO 10303-217 becomes an international standard, tools will become available.

Unlike ISO 10303-227, ISO 10303-217's ARM is documented using EXPRESS. This means that it is currently possible to generate part 21 files containing data defined in the ARM. This data is not really conformant to the application protocol, but it does provide a sense for how well ISO 10303-217 will support ship building needs.

4 Summary

4.1 Distributed Systems

Distributed systems present special requirements for computer models. These systems have an element of connectivity based upon Kirchhoff's laws that extends beyond the physical connectivity in other computer models. Distributed systems may be modeled in 1, 2, 3, or 4 dimensions. Distributed system models of shipboard systems require access to low detail level views of the entire ship and high detail level views of individual compartments; possibly at the same time.

4.2 Data Structures

The graph is a powerful tool for modeling flow connectivity and for synchronizing different models of the same physical system. The Visualizing Compiler Graphics (VCG) tool is under explored as a tool for accomplishing this type of synchronization. Computer Aided Design (CAD) tools primarily support 2D and 3D models of piping systems.

4.3 Data Standards

There are three data standards available for exchanging shipboard piping system data. The complexity and power of each standard is reflected in the number of application objects defined in the application reference model (ARM) and the number of data entities used in the application interpreted model (AIM). The standard to use depends on when you need to exchange data. Table 5 shows the relationship of these standards.

STANDARD	ARM SIZE	AIM SIZE	AVAILABLE
IGES 3D Piping	18 objects	31 entities	1994
ISO 10303-227	265 objects	359 entities	2000[*]
ISO 10303-217	326 objects	unknown	2003[*]
*Dates are based upon current ISO schedules and are subject to change.			

Table 5 Comparison of data standards

References

ANS US PRO/IPO-100-1997, (1997), "Initial Graphics Exchange Specification Version 5.3", U.S. Product Data Association.

ANS US PRO/IPO-110-1994, (1994), "3D Piping IGES Application Protocol Version 1.2", U.S. Product Data Association.

Douglas C. Giancoli, (1984), General Physics, Prentice-Hall, Inc., Englewood Cliffs, New Jersey 07632, pp.519-522.

ISO 10303-21, (1994), "Industrial automation systems and integration— Product data representation and exchange — Part 21: Implementation methods: Clear Text Encoding of the Exchange Structure(Physical File)".

ISO 10303-217/WG3/N593, (1997), "Industrial automation systems and integration—Product data representation and exchange — Part 217: Application protocol: Ship piping."

ISO 10303-227/WG3/N580, (1997), "Industrial automation systems and integration—Product data representation and exchange — Part 227: Application protocol: Plant spatial configuration."

Udi Manber, (1989), Introduction to Algorithms a Creative Approach, Addison-Wesley Publishing Company, New York.

Additional Reference Information

USPRO IGES ordering information https://www.uspro.org/

SC4 On-Line Information Service (SOLIS) information on all STEP APs http://www.nist.gov/sc4/

THE USE OF CAD IN THE DEVELOPMENT OF AN ENGINE ROOM ARRANGEMENT MODEL

Ben Kassel

Naval Surface Warfare Center Carderock Division,
9500 MacArthur Boulevard, West Bethesda, MD 20817-5700, USA
kasselb@nswccd.navy.mil

Abstract

The Engine Room Arrangement Model (ERAM) Project developed a specific set of design processes, using Integrated Product/Process Design (IPPD) techniques to reduce cost and schedule. One of the major tasks of this project was the generation of a 3D product model for visualization, verification, and to generate design documentation. The CAD subteam developed a product model using a commercial CAD system and general purpose relational databases to support the goals of the project. The program evolved from a paper based environment, in which the creation of drawings was the primary purpose of the CAD subteam to a model based environment in which in-process design reviews were performed in a virtual environment. This paper describes how the product model was defined and how the communication process changed the expectations and perspective of the CAD subteam as well as all of the ERAM team members.

1. Product Model Development Process

The primary function of the ERAM CAD subteam was the development of a 3D-product model that could be provided to the participating shipyards. The original task was to develop and maintain the product model as defined by the ERAM team. However, it soon became obvious the ERAM team required CAD support for system schematics, arrangement drawings, general design documentation, and side studies causing a shift in the CAD team schedule and workload. CAD resources were originally estimated as the minimum amount required to provide:

1. Preliminary design level of effort for modeling structure and equipment

2. Piping (> 75mm)
3. HVAC and cableways (> 150 x 150mm)
4. Structure weight estimates by block
5. List of piping components and length of pipe by system/level 4 unit
6. Drawings

The product model can be initiated from existing product models, CAD drawings, and paper sketches/drawings. During the conceptual phases, much of the 3-D layout is unknown so any of the three formats need to be accommodated. As the arrangements evolve, the CAD technician created the product model and generated reports and sketches as defined in the product model development procedures. The next step was the definition of pipe lanes. Once the piping lanes were identified the distributed systems were defined in more detail in the product model. As the model became more mature, the models were suitable for providing the documentation required for the design review. This more complete product model was used to optimize equipment arrangement and begin the grouping of equipment into units. As the units evolved, the foundations were modeled, and structural details designed. Notice that product model development lags slightly behind the optimal time in which data should be provided to the designer, however, the data can be delivered in time to have a positive influence on the design. This cycle was repeated until the end of the design phase.

Before a product model can be developed, an infrastructure must exist which includes configuration management, procedures, components/commodity items, and system support. The process of developing the product model requires the identification and modeling of equipment, outfit, and furnishings before it can be inserted into the product model. The product model is highly dependent upon the availability of commodity parts such as structural steel shapes, major equipment, outfit and furnishings, valves, fittings, etc. The first ship designed using the system is generally the hardest because in addition to design and construction, the infrastructure is under development.

2. Ideal Product Model Development Process

The ideal process for the development of a product model is shown in figure 1. The ideal process completely eliminates the requirement for explicitly created 2D drawings. The process begins with the definition of the hull, compartmentation, pipe lanes, and major structure in the 3D-product model and continues with the placement of equipment.

The model is then evaluated with respect to the "Illities" defined by the IPPD team. The arrangement is refined and the first attempt is made to define units. Evaluation of the product model is performed using the following techniques:

1) Interactively on the workstation
2) Screen plots and shaded images provided by the CAD subteam
3) 2D sketches generated from the model
4) Reports

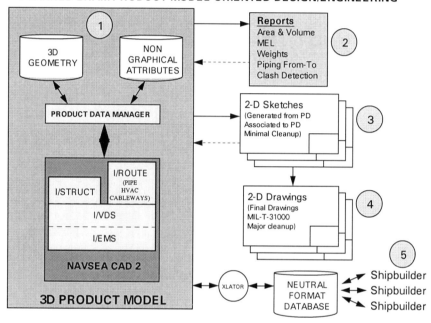

Figure 1 - ERAM Product Model Oriented Design/Engineering

After the arrangement and major structure is adequately defined, the major distributed systems can be modeled. The structure and equipment arrangements continue to be refined. The final step is the development of structural details and smaller distributed systems, time. The 3-D Product Model consists of a geometric model integrated with a database describing non-graphical attributes, including weight, CG, etc. Other attributes can be included in the CAD system, but a more efficient solution is an index, which allows data to be accessed from other databases.

Reports can be generated directly from the product model. This is usually limited to geometric intensive information such as weights, volumes, and from-to reports. However, the product model can also be used as a graphical user interface to access external databases. Hard copies of the reports are provided to the engineers who do not have direct access to the product model. Comments are provided to the CAD operators, who update the product model, regenerate the reports, which are distributed for review.

It is recognized that at this stage in the IPPD process, product model data may not be available or desired by all engineers and designers. 2-D output is still required to review the design and to convey information to external participants. These sketches can be extracted from the product model, and with a minimal amount of cleanup can be useful as a design tool. Marked up drawings are returned to the CAD operators. The product model is updated, and new 2-D drawings are generated. Hard copies of the sketches are provided to the engineers upon request. Comments are provided to the CAD operators, who update the product model, regenerate the sketches, which are distributed for review.

At the completion of the design, formal 2-D drawings (if required) can be generated from the product model, however, this requires a large cleanup effort. The product model is made available to the shipyards via a neutral file format or native data format at their request. In the near term, this data is provided as a combination of IGES files to represent geometry, and SQL files to represent non-graphical attributes. Long range plans include the conversion of the ERAM product model to SHIP STEP. SHIP STEP data will be segregated by structure, piping, HVAC, cableways, equipment, and configuration management data. Bi-directional transfer will be available.

3. Actual ERAM Product Model Development Process

The ERAM Team was composed of engineers from shipyards and equipment vendors from the US, Europe, and South America. The each brought with them the processes and practices of the their individual shipyards. The process for SSD#1, MSD, and SSD#2 depended on hand drawn sketches as the predominant method of communication. The intent was to use these sketches to develop the product model, which could be used for various analyses including volumes and clash detection as well as to generate documentation including drawings. The CAD team also had to develop the drawings for the design review. Models and drawings could not be developed concurrently, requiring the CAD team to temporarily suspend work on the product model. The workload was shifted entirely to the creation of 2-D drawings in support of design review. Subsequent drawing production was supported by modifying the product model, extracting the required views for the drawings, then adding minimal annotation required to support the engineer. This process is depicted in figure 2.

ACTUAL ERAM CAD / PRODUCT MODEL ORIENTED DESIGN/ENGINEERING

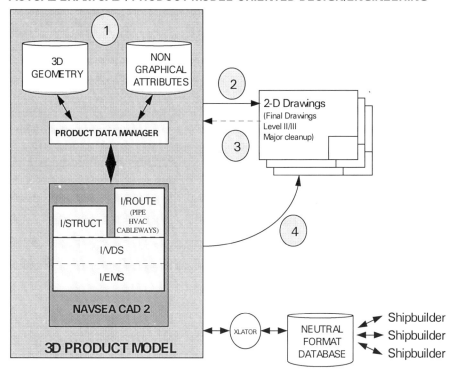

Figure 2 - ERAM Product Model Development (SSD#1, MSD & SSD#2)

The plan view deck arrangement drawings to support the design review were developed using a hybrid approach incorporating 3D geometry where it had already been defined. Equipment, structure, and major distributed systems, which were not defined, were drawn in 2-D. 3-D product model development continued using the 2-D drawings oriented correctly in the model and then used to place the 3-D equipment. 2-D output was still required to review the design and to convey information to external participants. These sketches were extracted from the product model, and with a minimal amount of cleanup were useful as a design tool. Marked up drawings were returned to the CAD operators. The product model was updated, and new 2-D drawings were generated. Hard copies of the sketches were provided to the engineers who did not have direct access to the product model. Comments were provided to the CAD operators, who updated the product model, regenerated the sketches, which were distributed for review. There was some evolution of the use of the product model by the engineers as the project progressed through these three designs, however, it was not focused or uniform and the results were mixed.

Maximizing the utilization of the 3-D product model was the focus of the Slow Speed Diesel #3 Product Model approach. For SSD#3 the product model was structured to support the design and construction of level 4 machinery units, which were standard modules similar to shipping containers. After the major structure (decks, major bulkheads, and shell) was adequately defined, primary structure was developed for a typical level 4 structural unit. Three initial designs were developed by subteams consisting of system engineers and a CAD subteam member. A common template was developed consisting of the outlines of the level 4 standard units. Functional grouping of equipment was carried out to identify the machinery units, which were multiples of the standard structural units. 3D equipment was placed in each unit and drawings were created in order to perform trade off studies. Equipment was then arranged in the appropriate level 4 machinery unit file using the primary structure as a reference. The routing of pipe was performed in parallel with the development of secondary structure. The structure and equipment arrangements continued to be refined. The final step was the development of structural details and smaller distributed systems.

The process begins with the definition of the hull, compartmentation, and major structure and continues with the placement of equipment and routing of distributed systems. The model is then evaluated with respect to the "Illities" defined by the IPPD team in the Strategic design Brief (SBD). Evaluation of the product model is performed using the same techniques defined for the ideal process with the addition of 3D walk through (Design Review).

In order for the product model to be integrated into the design, construction, and business practices employed at the shipyard it must have a sufficient level of detail to be useful in making design decisions. The type of data and level of detail available in the product model needs to be correlated to the various stages in the ERAM design process. The product model development scenario is based upon the following assumptions:

1. During the conceptual design stage, the product model is extremely dynamic but the level of detail is low.
2. Early stage design is concentrated on system diagrams.
3. During detail design, the product model is less dynamic, but the level of detail increases greatly, and configuration management becomes complicated.
4. During the construction phase, configuration management is most difficult due to the introduction of the many dissimilar systems required to support manufacturing processes.
5. The majority of engineers/designers do not have access to the CAD system.

6. Many engineers/designers supply data to one CAD technician.

The product model development process can be summarized as follows:

- Hull Definition
- Locate Decks / Major Bulkheads
- Define Major Structure
- Locate Major Equipment
- Locate Tanks
- Arrange remaining equipment
- Define Deck and Bulkhead structure
- Define distributed systems lanes
- Define library parts
- Locate major piping
- Optimize equipment location
- Organize equipment into units
- Structural details
- Optimize unit location
- Define foundations
- Arrange minor piping
- Optimize distributed system

In addition, for the product model to be useful it must support the development of the documentation required for periodic design reviews and the development of the traditional drawings at the completion of the design.

4. Library Parts and Commodity Parts

Since commercial CAD/CAM systems are used to develop arrangements, structural, and distributed systems models it is highly desirable that this data be provided in a digital format. This data would consist of the information required to represent the as-built geometric definition of the component as well as the attributes required to convey non-graphic information. The CAD subteam only accepted vendor furnished digital data for equipment that was used in the ERAM project. The vendor files were accessible to all CAD workstations for reviewing, printing and referencing as a "footprint" for modeling. A database was developed which provided information about the availability of the data and the developmental status of the library parts. It is highly recommended that a group be established to support the product model library consisting of CAD users and personnel who can obtain and document the data required to build the equipment. The best practice would be to receive the data formatted specifically for the product modeling system. This would require a partnership between the shipyard and suppliers. If this is not possible a hierarchy for the acquisition of library part data is as follows:

1) The first choice for digital data would be native format in conformance to product modeling library development guidelines. Basically, this data would consist of geometry for the various representations of the part (e.g. detail, 2-D symbolic, envelope, etc.) and the non-graphic attributes for the required level of intelligence.

2) In the event native data is not available the next choice would be to provide the geometry and attributes using the appropriate NSRP specification for the definition of STEP application protocol for shipbuilding.
3) In the event STEP data is not available the next choice would be to provide the geometry and attributes using the Initial Graphics Exchange Specification Version 5.2 or greater. Multiple formats are available within IGES to represent this data. The preferred method would be to use CSG and Brep solids to represent the geometry and the attribute table and instance entity to represent attributes. In the event the preprocessor is not robust enough to handle solids, then surfaces or wireframe geometry would be used. If the preprocessor is not robust enough to handle the attribute table and instance entities then a text file would be used.
4) In the event IGES data is not available the next choice would be to provide the geometry using DXF, and the attributes using a text file. The preferred DXF geometry type would be surfaces, however wireframe is acceptable if surfaces are not available.
5) In the event DXF data is not available, native format AutoCAD or Microstation is acceptable.
6) In the event vector data is not available, a scanned image of the applicable technical publication describing the component would be used and the attribute data would be provided in a text file. Regardless of the methodology used to represent the vendor data, it is highly desirable for a raster image of the technical documentation be provided.

If digital data is not available, the next choice would be to provide sufficient technical documentation to develop a CAD model of the exterior of the component, including the location and orientations of connections (structural, fluid, electrical).

5. Product Model Procedures

A set of procedures and guidelines must be established due to the complexity and the all encompassing scope of the product model. The product model is used in all aspects of the design and construction of the ship, and must be developed in a consistent fashion. There should be a general set of guidelines which pertain across all applications as well as application specific guidelines. For exampl onfiguration management, general model organization, PV'BS, and comp   it modeling procedures will probably be the same across pplications be ... they affect the product model globally. Value added modifications to the product model such as manufacturing data or engineering analysis data, which have a local effect between a limited number of groups requires unique procedures. The procedures need to consider not only how the product model will be used to perform a specific task, but the effects on other users as well.

6. Product Model Usage

In general it is best to have a single product model which can be accessed in a distributed environment by all 'electronic' design and construction processes (e.g. arrangements, distributed system layout, structural design, pipe flow analysis, structural analysis, naval architecture, plate nesting, pipe bending, etc.). This means the sophistication of the product model will vary among the shipyards. The definition of the product model should be based upon the NSRP specifications. The uses of the product model must be known in advance. For instance if the end product of the product model is the creation of drawings, a radically different approach is undertaken than if the product model is used to support ship construction. A process must also be developed for product model development. The definition of the product model as well as its development and implementation necessitates the involvement of all groups which will be creating as well as accessing product model data. The sequencing of access to the model must also be determined, including the output products required to facilitate communication of the information. Currently, access to the product model by others than CAD users is through annotated sketches generated from the product model. This is also the predominant methodology used for design review. Anyone who has input into the design must be trained and given access to the product model. Design reviews should be facilitated using electronic mockups wherever possible.

7. Product Model Output Products

Communication between applications as well as final deliverable are considered output products. They are used to provide information to downstream processes, documentation, and may be end products as well. For example, graphics files required by a visualization system for design reviews is an end product. Work packages generated from the product model in a paper format may be required on the waterfront by the trades. Final drawings are still a requirement in most applications. In-process output products include finite element models, equipment lists, and NC instructions. Sketches generated from the model may be required to convey information to the system engineer who does not have product model access.

1. Design Documents (released continuously)
   1.1. Sketches

1.2. Reports
1.3. Visualization files (shaded images, hidden line)
1.4. Manually created 2-D Schematics (provided upon request)
2. Design Review Documentation (released periodically)
   2.1. Annotated drawings required to communicate system diagrams and arrangements
3. Visualization files (Documentation (released semi-weekly)
   3.1. Product Model Review files downloaded
4. Product model neutral databases (as requested)
5. This data will initially be provided in the format as defined in digital data exchange procedures. Long term plans are to provide the data in STEP format conforming to the ship design and construction application protocols
   5.1. Arrangement
   5.2. Structure
   5.3. Distributed systems
   5.4. Library parts
6. Final Drawings (end of project)
7. This requires major rework of the latest design documentation. These drawings shall be developed explicitly from the product model and annotation added manually as required. Editing of line style shall be performed as required. This process is developed after the product model has been completed, and will be non-associative to the product model.
   7.1. Paper drawings
   7.2. Raster images (tif, gif, jpeg)
   7.3. DXF files (2-D)
   7.4. IGES files (2-D)

8. Product Model Organization

The CAD model is defined from the perspective of the design strategy. Beginning with SSD#3, the model was built up by units, which were reflected in the part and catalog structure. Parts were a combination of UNIX files that were organized in catalogs using PDM. Parts were organized by application, and further organized by unit. There were some exceptions; hull, subdivision, compartmentation, deck structure, and items not in a unit. The organization of the product model for SSD#3 is shown in figure 3 and 4. The primary workspace for equipment and distributed systems is the level 4 machinery unit file. The primary workspace for structure is the level 4 structure unit. Assembly files are created as required to facilitate visualization and to support spatial analysis.

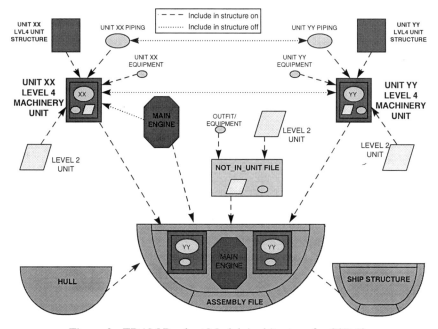

Figure 3 - ERAM Product Model Architecture for SSD#3

ERAM CAD FILE STRUCTURE

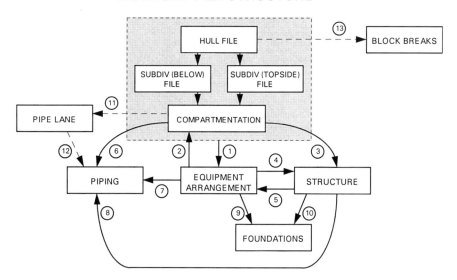

Figure 4 - ERAM Product Model File Structure and Relationships

0. The hull is used directly by the subdiv file. Compartmentation is defined from the subdiv file. The compartmentation file is used to provide the theoretical surfaces for all downstream applications.
1. Equipment is arranged based upon the theoretical surfaces in the compartmentation file. As compartmentation is revised, the equipment arrangement model owner is notified and an associative update can be performed. Theoretical surfaces for equipment arrangement shall only be defined in the compartmentation file.
2. It may be required for the compartmentation file to reference the equipment arrangement files in order to locate cutouts. The equipment file should be attached for reference purposes only.
3. Structure is placed on the theoretical surfaces defined in the compartmentation file. As compartmentation is revised, the structures model owner is notified and an associative update can be performed. Theoretical surfaces for structures models shall only be defined in the compartmentation file.
4. It may be required for the structure files to reference the equipment arrangement files. The equipment file should be attached for reference purposes only.
5. It may be required for the equipment arrangement file to reference structure. The structure file is attached for reference only.
6. Piping is contained in compartments defined in the compartmentation file. Pipe is also routed to/from tanks which are defined in the compartmentation file.
7. Piping is arranged between nozzles on equipment defined in the equipment arrangement file. The equipment arrangement file is placed in the relevant piping file as a placed part.
8. It may be required for the piping file to reference structure. The structure file is attached for reference only.
9. The equipment files are placed into the foundation files as a placed part.
10. Structure is placed into the foundations file as a placed part. A separate part is created for each foundation.
11. Pipe lanes define general areas in which piping, HVAC, and cableways should be run. They have been defined by the system engineers before the product model was developed.
12. The pipe lanes will be used to assist the CAD operators in routing distributed systems.
13. Block breaks are created directly from the hull file. They will be used to identify structure, distributed systems, and equipment which overlap block breaks.

9. Software Selection

Software has to be obtained to create and access the product model data. There are no commercial off the shelf systems that can adequately support ship design and construction within a specific business context without being customized. The development effort required to integrate the software, ease of use, and reliability, should be a major consideration in the selection process.

The crucial step in the selection of commercial software is the evaluation. Software must be evaluated in the context it will be used in the shipyard. The evaluation should include at least a prototype implementation in which interfaces are developed to all major shipyard processes. The implementation should be phased, based upon the requirements of existing and planned projects.

10. Personnel Selection and Training

The ideal CAD user is an experienced designer / engineer with an expert understanding of the application software. The user needs to be trained not only in the use of the system, but must be familiar with the design/construction processes as well. It is extremely important to integrate actual examples of shipyard processes into the training process in order to reinforce the theory as well as to prepare the user for actual tasks. The CAD team should consist of a core of application experts who can provide some guidance in addition to performing their own tasks. Initially, inexperienced users should develop library parts and assist the application experts. As they gain experience they will require less guidance and can be assigned more difficult tasks. Cross training should be performed where practical in order to provide awareness of the overall product model as well as to develop a reserve of users to accommodate a shifting workload. There are other resources that are required to support product model development. This includes system support, application programming, and library part development. The system support role does not really require knowledge or experience with the application software. The application programmers should have a great deal of knowledge and experience with the software. Experience and knowledge of the ship design / construction process although desirable is not necessary. Library part modelers should have an expert understanding of the CAD application and an understanding of the level of detail required to represent a component. Experience and knowledge of the ship design / construction process is not necessary. Notice the level of experience for the application programmers and library part modelers are opposite of the ideal CAD user. Additional training is required for non CAD users who require access to the product model. This training should consist of visualization and redlining techniques in order to review and comment on the work in progress. Application of IPPD process by the CAD sub team is critical due to the close interaction between all the roles involved in product model development.

11. Interaction between the CAD Subteam and the Core Team

Interaction between the CAD subteam and the Core team can be considered informal. The system engineers provide information using sketches, oral instructions, and/or by working with the CAD subteam member directly on the workstation. Information passes back to the Core team, in various forms, including screen plots, visualization files, and reports. The use of the visualization tool (DesignReview) increased as the project progressed. This enabled the system engineer to evaluate the 3D arrangement without depending on the CAD subteam and allowing the CAD subteam to concentrate on product model development. Additionally, the CAD team is responsible for providing a representative to the core team. The official representative is the CAD Subteam Leader, however, depending upon the subject of the core team meeting the person with primary responsibilities for the subject would attend. These responsibilities were divided as follows:

1. Drawings, sketches, schematics
2. Distributed systems
3. Equipment Arrangements
4. Library parts, VFI
5. Structures, Distributed systems lanes
6. Compartment Arrangements

A depiction of the flow of information between the CAD subteam and the ERAM team is provided in figure 5.

The ERAM engineers communicated the conceptual arrangements to the CAD sub team. The intent was to provide guidance to the CAD subteam in modeling arrangements and structure in the product model. Distributed systems were communicated using system diagrams. Continuous communications between the engineer and the CAD subteam ensured system requirements and producibility were incorporated in the product model. The product model was accessed by the engineers either interactively with assistance from the CAD sub team, or using plots of pictorial and orthogonal views for various analyses including volumes and interference detection as well as to generate documentation. The product model was continuously updated, and new plots were generated when required. Plots were provided to the engineers who did not have direct access to the product model. These plots were extracted from the product model with a minimal amount of cleanup and annotation that made them very useful as a design tool. Comments were returned to the CAD subteam for incorporation into the product model. The responsible engineer reviewed the changes at the CAD workstation, or plots were regenerated if a paper review was required. The CAD sub team developed drawings and other documentation as requested for the design review. The model and detail drawings could not be developed concurrently, therefore the core team directed the CAD subteam to temporarily suspend work on the product model, generate the drawings from the product model, and supply annotation as necessary. Product model walkthrough was performed external to the CAD system using Integraph's DesgnReview®.

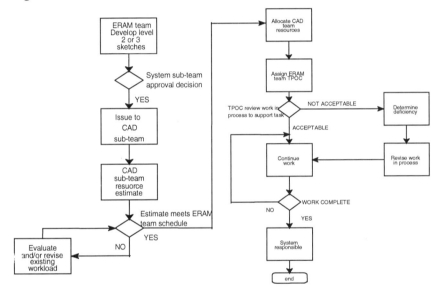

Figure 5 - System Engineer/CAD Team Information Flow

12. Lessons Learned

The time duration required for the development of the 3-D product model was extended because a baseline 3-D product model did not exist. The lack of commercial 3-D equipment models was an additional factor in increasing the duration. PD-337 hull lines were utilized as a starting point for creating the hull model and its associated structure, however, even this baseline required significant rework in order to be suitable for the product model. In addition, the 2D drawings required by the ERAM Requirements Document resulted in the cessation of all work on the 3-D product model for a significant period in order to support the design reviews.

The ERAM Team is composed of two separate skill types. The Core Team consists of engineers with system design experience with limited production design experience. The CAD Team consists of 3-D CAD operators also with limited production design experience. None of the system engineers are able to use the 3-D CAD system. Consequently, the product development consists of 2-D development by the system engineers which is then converted to the 3-D product model by the CAD operators. Concurrent development of the product model with the system engineer and the CAD operator viewing the product model on the terminal became the approached utilized in the final engine room design. Ultimately, it is desirable that the system engineer be capable of developing the product model.

13. Conclusion

Initially, ERAM appeared to be a radical departure from every perspective. Appearances however can be deceiving. All of the concepts used in this program were new to someone, but in reality ERAM was an evolutionary step forward. The ERAM program implemented a new design concept, a new social structure, and new techniques for developing and validating the design. But in the end, the program owed its successes to the dedication of the people who worked at the ERAM site and their ability to give these new techniques a chance regardless of their bias. The diversity and experience of the team truly provided a sum which was much greater than its parts. The actual technology used to develop the product model is not important. The actual processes used in daily operations is not important. The critical item was and always will be that every participant bought in to each of the processes, and these processes underwent continuous improvement. Hats off to the NAVY management which had the foresight and patience to allow this experiment to occur, and to the industry participants which supplied their most valuable resource, their people. All of the processes, and CAD models created to support this program are available at eramwww.dt.navy.mil.

References

ERAM TEAM, (1997), "ERAM Team slow Speed #3 Project Report", ERAM Team Carderock Division/Naval Surface Warfare Center.

ERAM TEAM, (1996), "Engine Room Arrangement Modelling (ERAM) Design Process Users Guide", Richard Devries and Kevin D Prince.

ERAM CAD TEAM, (1997), "ERAM CAD Standards", Rusty Dupont,, Chris Jones, Ben Kassel, Paul Rakow, Jake Robinson, and Nancy Russell.

NEW ICT TOOLS IN SHIPBUILDING

Marco Cremon and Andrea Favretto

EDP department, Technical Software Development, Fincantieri Italy
marco.cremon@fincantieri.it

Abstract

The paper presents an overview of the involvement of Fincantieri in European projects in the area of information and communication technologies. This includes an umbrella project that provided an overview of the ICT application in the shipbuilding industry and another one aimed at developing an automatic off-line robot programming.

1 Introduction

The European shipbuilding industry in general, and Fincantieri in particular, seeks to differentiate itself from its main competitors in Asia. While Korea and Japan go for the high-volume end of the market, delivering large quantities of relatively unsophisticated ships quickly, with cheap labour cost and big plants, the European shipyards are specialising in the construction of ships with relatively high added value.

In order to make the activity of building sophisticated vessels an economical success, the conditions that follow must be fulfilled.

- During design phase the concurrency of different engineering providers – i.e. technical department, design consultant, classification society etc. – must be well managed in order to maintain the coherence of the whole project.

- Procurement business chain, from tendering to warehousing, must follow the just in time concept, administrative work must be reduced and stocks must be optimised.

- The hull production phase must be very automated, mainly during the prefabrication, to reduce costs, but still very flexible.

- During the ship's outfitting good communication and co-operation with expert suppliers providing state-of-the-art technologies to maintain and improve production schedule are necessary.

Today's IT already provides some tools and techniques to help companies to improve mentioned processes. In same cases the available technology needs only to be known, accepted and widely spread to enable maritime industry to use it, but, in many others, research and development actions are needed to fill existing technology gaps.

Fincantieri management identified information technology as a key competitive factor to efficiently compete in the global market; following this strategy best practices were identified and their usage encouraged. To fill technology gap two main research and development actions were started. The first one, performed in an ESPRIT research project called MARVEL OUS leaded by Fincantieri as prime contractor, was devoted to the definition of a new, web-based, IT platform for the maritime community, to enable virtual enterprise and collaborative processes among different companies. The second one was related with workshop automation and hull fabrication cost reduction and had the goal to develop new tools to make robotics a success also for shipbuilding production.

As a consequence of that the contents of this paper are twofold. At first a description, extracted from the project public summary, of MARVEL OUS's approach and results is reported, then Fincantieri's results related with automatic off-line robot programming are presented.

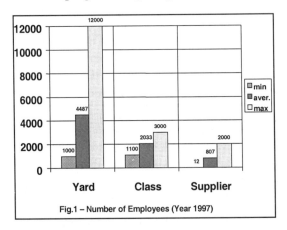

Fig.1 – Number of Employees (Year 1997)

2 New ICT Tools to Enable Virtual Enterprise in Maritime Community

2.1 IT State-of-the-Art

The first activity performed in Marvel Ous Project was the definition of partners IT related state-of-art through the answers given to a questionnaire. In the following of this chapter key points identified during this activity are reported.

Seven shipyards, three classification societies and four supplier companies were asked about (see figure 1), covering 37 different tasks and 110 related information elements participating in 31 communication processes, involving 29 applications.

The majority of European shipyards have less employees than the ones covered with our questionnaire, but those covered create more than 70% of the tonnage in Europe. The Classification societies are the three largest in Europe. The supplier companies are spread from very small to rather large. All of them deliver engineering services as well. Therefore the amount of trained engineers in the shipyards is comparatively small.

Due to the complexity of the product the most visible result is the necessity of co-ordinating many tasks and persons. In addition to that the support tools, techniques and skills are rather different.

Another interesting result is that almost all the tasks related to communication, goes beyond the borders of the building where the related information was created. In addition to that the co-ordination between co-operating companies is considered satisfying, but people believe that a significant improvement of communication tools is still possible.

E-mail is available at almost all companies and the personal access is very limited but increasing.

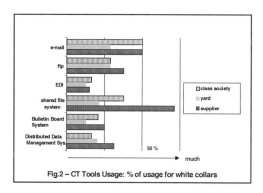

Fig.2 – CT Tools Usage: % of usage for white collars

Figure 2 shows how much communication techniques are used on a daily basis by most people in the companies.

It seems that the shipyards are less advanced than suppliers and classification societies in the usage of modern communication techniques, which is in fact dependent on the particular tasks considered. The production tasks are even more lacking than the design and engineering ones.

Looking at organisational models, big shipyards and classification societies organise significantly the work more through departments than according to projects, although the product under concern is of type one-of-a-kind. This might imply a more project orientated organisation. The supplier industry as well as the smaller shipyards are much more project orientated. Average for the entire maritime industry is 3.8 (minimum was 1 and maximum 5) which means slightly more department than project orientated.

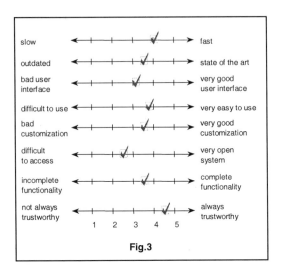

Fig.3

About hardware and software systems some important conclusions have been drawn. Most engineers (86%) as well as most white collar workers have a PC or workstation on their desk (73%). Many programmes used by engineers are either tailored to company specific needs or even especially developed. White collar workers work more often with standard packages.

Average quality and efficiency of software packages is reported in figure 3.

The last important result is regarding the number of people involved in a single task. A general statement is difficult, but it can be said that in most cases the amount of different departments involved is rather high. This might be another hint for the potential of structuring the companies more along the projects.

2.2 The MARVEL OUS Approach

The Marvel Ous technical annex provided a demonstration scenario for the specification and execution of a real-life demonstration of electronic data exchange.

The purpose was to show the short falls in existing practices and to highlight opportunities for virtual co-operative working. The demonstration has been applied to a ship already in service that involves some form of major hull or machinery modifications.

A ship operator, to perform a new service on a particular route, has purchased a container ship. In order to maximise the efficiency of the ship, it is intended to lengthen the ship by an integer number of container bays to increase its cargo carrying capacity. This lengthening is common in shipbuilding and is often referred to as jumboising.

In order to address all the interests of the participating members it was necessary to devise a scenario that involves as many as possible work package activities shown in the activity diagrams. These include for example, pre-design, steel design, outfitting design, steel and outfitting production, classification approval, trial-run and operation. The data exchanged between the various companies in the demonstration scenario should be typical of those encountered in everyday work. The problem of format conversion needs to be identified even if the project demo scenario does not suffer from any data translation problems. Marvel Ous is not a data exchange development project, it does not develop interfaces or interface specifications. However, it points out the business cases in which today technology and standard interfaces to a virtual enterprise are possible and identifies where additional developments are necessary to achieve business benefits.

The demo scenario covered a subset of the jumboising project. This kept the demo scenario simple, but nevertheless addressed all aspects of data exchange to be done in a real world project. The figure 4 and the list give an overview of the activities carried out by the scenario.

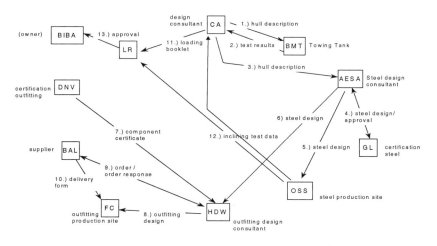

Fig. 4 – Actors and Data in MarvelOus Demo Scenario

Pre-design (Consultant)
- 1.) Transfer of hull data to the towing tank for detailed speed prediction
- 2.) Transfer of test results back to the consultant

Steel Design (Shipbuilder/ steel design consultant):
- 3.) Transfer of hull data to the steel design consultant
- 3.) Simulations of inclining test data
- 4.) Transfer of CAD data into scantling calculation tool and vice versa
- 4.) Transfer of inclining test datasheet for approval by the class society
- 4.) Obtain classification society approval

Outfitting design (Shipbuilder / outfitting design consultant)
- 6.) Transfer of hull data to the outfitting design consultant
- 7.) Obtain classification society approval
- 9.) Contact supplier / send order
- 9.) Receive order response
- 9.) Place orders

Steel Production (Shipbuilder and/or Sub-contractor)
- 5.) use of CAD data within robot simulation tool
- 5.) Feedback to steel designer

Outfitting assembly (Shipbuilder & Sub-contractor)
- 8.) transfer of hull data to the outfitting production site
- check produceability by 3D visualisation of piping arrangement
- 10.) receive material according to the orders made

Trial run and operation (Consultant, Shipbuilder and Class society)
- 12.) Shipbuilder makes inclining test results available to consultant and class
- 12.) Class society approves results of inclining test
- 11.) Class society approves final loading booklet
- 13.) Class society distributes approved information (class certificate)

2.3 The MARVEL OUS Demo

The demo has been implemented using available Internet technology. It was intended to have a common Marvel Ous demo scenario main page on each work package leader web server.

This demo scenario main page contains all links to specific work package pages where the information relevant for the demo scenario is available (see figure 5). The work package leader is responsible for his particular pages. These main pages are identically designed and allow the linkage to each other work package on the highest level. This way all partners are allowed to access the information they require for their role in the demo scenario. Partner actions such as modifying visible documents, trigger feedback actions. Those who have registered for a particular piece of information are automatically informed if updates of this piece of information are made available. The figure 6 illustrates the layout of the identical Marvel Ous demo scenario home pages.

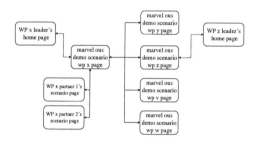

Fig. 5 – Marvel Ous Demo 1.0 and 2.0: Links between pages

The basic idea was to support navigation by a static list of push-buttons on the left hand side allowing to jump direct into each task. Once entered the task, a list (or IDEF 0 diagram) of subtasks is provided with their related output (documents). The entire structure is reflecting the Marvel Ous IDEF-0 activities model.

Once the user has arrived at a level of detail which matches his or her information requirement, one of the output documents can be selected and viewed. Registration is not meant as a security mechanism. Part of the Marvel Ous intranet is public (accessible via username and password) and only selected areas will be protected (IP address check, etc.). Once users are in the Marvel Ous net they can register for whatever information they might be interested in.

On both the client and the server side either PCs or UNIX workstations may be used. The only requirement is that they have to be powerful enough. For the PC platform this leads to a machine containing at least a Pentium 100, 32 MB of RAM and a graphics adapter supporting a resolution of 1024x768 pixels with 256 colours. The computers have to be connected to the Internet either directly by a network card or indirectly via Modem or ISDN. At least the server has to be permanently connected since it has to be accessed at any time by the partners. The browsers to be used are Microsoft Internet Explorer or Netscape Navigator. To visualise data formats (i.e. DXF graphic files) not directly supported by the browsers plug-ins are needed.

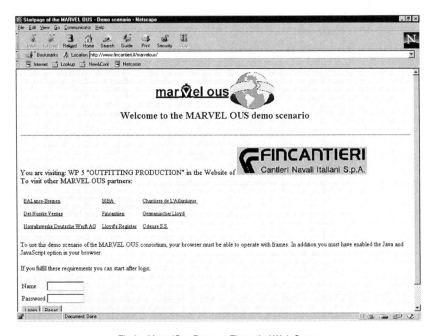

Fig.6 – MarvelOus Demo at Fincantieri Web Server

The demo scenario version 1 was the first implementation. It provided the functions reported on the following table.

- Navigation through the different Work Package
- Viewing of different document types
- Registration for specific documents
- Access control via logins

Although experimentation with this scenario was very successful, some weak points remained, raising the need for further development:

- Lack of a workflow system
- No central user administration

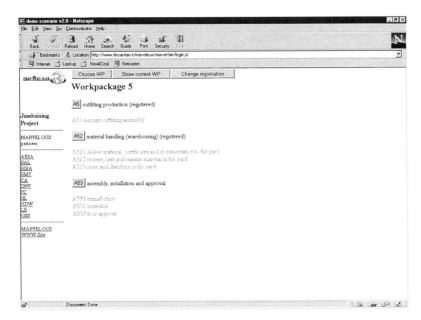

Fig.7 – A task Navigation Page

- Re-login after changes in the registration
- Partners without an own Work Package could not set up a document server
- Complicated installation and administration
- Viewing of non-standard document types did not work properly
- No notification
- No commenting
- System depended upon difficult to handle software packages (e.g. Perl)
- CGI-based system, therefore insufficient security

In the version 2 the following problems have been resolved:

- No re-login necessary
- No Work Package responsibility required for set-up of a document server
- Possibility to relocate single activities onto another server
- Much easier installation and administration
- Viewing of all document types works

Solving the remaining weaknesses would have caused a lot of additional effort to implement the system. Therefore, it was decided to develop a completely new, Java-based solution which is described in the following section. Nevertheless, version 2 has been finalised and installed at all partner's servers.

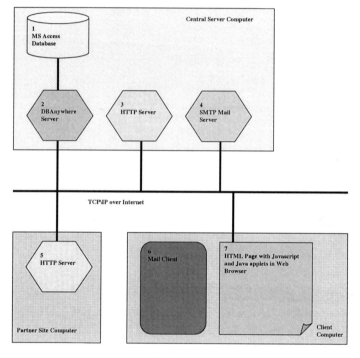

Figure 8

The third version of the demo scenario software was a new development using different technologies compared to the first two versions. For the users of the system it offers several advantages:

- Dynamic task structure (the tree of tasks can be altered from the browser).
- Status for tasks: Not Started, In Progress, Finished, In Revision.
- Task comments notice board: users can leave messages on task progress to be read by all.
- Detailed user and group permissions for the tasks and documents with write, read or no access settings in addition to special permissions for owners of tasks, documents and user groups.
- Central server approach means very simple installation at partner's sites.
- Real email notification for task and document changes.
- Consistent graphical user interface.

- History of notification events maintained.
- Extra data maintained on all documents including version, entry date, format, description and status.
- Simple system for adding and removing documents from the system.

In order to achieve these aims Microsoft Access was chosen as a database for this purpose. Symantec middle-ware products were used to allow the database to be accessed by Java clients over the Internet. Finally the Java client applets were developed to provide web based user interface for the database. The central system does not store the documents released on the system, these are still stored at the partners sites. To access the documents the Java program opens a new browser window that loads the document for viewing or downloading. Below diagram and description show the full architecture:

1) MS Access database – Runs at the central server site. It contains information on tasks, documents (not documents themselves), users, user groups, notifications, access permissions.

2) DBAnywhere server – Runs on NT as an interface to access to databases.

3) HTTP server – Is a standard piece of software responsible for sending out the HTML pages.

4) SMTP mail server – This is responsible for sending out notification e-mails to registered users of the system.

5) HTTP server – These HTTP servers at the partner sites are used to store and despatch the documents released by that partner.

6) Mail Client – An e-mail client program on the client to receive notification messages.

7) Web Browser – A Java 1.1 enabled web browser used to access the system.

Three different applets has been made available: the user manager, the document viewer and the task viewer.

The user manager can use used for adding new users and groups and defining attributes for users like password, e-mail address, company etc. It also allows assignment of users to groups.

The purpose of the document viewer is manipulation of documents and their properties. The user can view documents, comment them, register for the documents or insert links to new documents into the database. Access rights for different users and groups can be defined for each document.

The task viewer supports maintenance of the different tasks needed to carry out the project. In general, the same operations on tasks as on documents are possible. Dependencies between tasks and assignment of documents to tasks can be defined by means of this applet.

2.4 Special Aspects of Virtual Enterprises

The maritime industry is facing an important challenge: to compete in an world wide market. European maritime products are known for their high technology and high quality, but in order to be sold these products need to be produced at world price level. This requires availability of skills and resources as well as an enabling infrastructure.

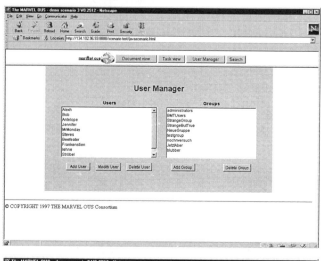

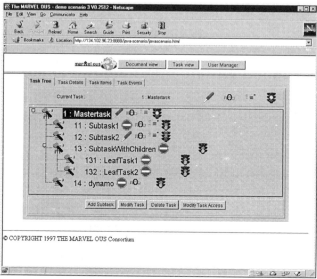

Figure 9

Over the last century the structure of shipyards have significantly changed. From fully autonomous islands covering every single aspect for the production of ships, with all required skills and resources under one roof, the shipyards have become much leaner and the trend seems to be that they become competence centres and final assembly places only. This trend is forced by the discontinuous market situation as well as the increasing complexity of modern maritime products. The outsourcing of departments and thus the concentration on the core business is a proofed strategy not only in the maritime industry. A community of highly efficient and competitive, specialist companies seems to be the right approach to face the challenges described above. Each new project will then be handled by a consortium tailored to the particular requirements of that particular project. To make the co-operation in such consortia most effective, Information Technology is seen as a key enabler. The vision to have standardised IT tools and systems ready to be configured to meet the specific requirement of such a consortium has to be made reality as soon as possible.

Marvel Ous has tried to define the requirements for such a system. In the Marvel Ous scenario version 1.0 and 2.0 described above the idea of independent companies without any leading company just linking them for their mutual benefit was followed. The lesson learned from this approach was that administration and set-up of such a decentralised environment was rather time consuming. The version 3.0 follows the concept of one trusted partner holding a central database and maintaining all the links to the documents, which themselves are still at the originators' computer. This approach supports also an workflow and planning opportunity which might be developed in the near future. Based on these implementations, user feedback was collected to evaluate the potential of the approach taken.

2.5 *Conclusion: General Potential Improvements*

One step towards the virtual enterprise would be to create a coalition between the parties involved in the development in order to produce an optimised result, rather than to compete against each other. Based on this type of business understanding, access to all relevant project information would shorten the development duration and thus improving each partners' process, which in turn would make the entire consortium more competitive. If Shipyards would succeed in making even the owner become part of this consortium, he would gain a better and more cost effective product in less time. Another critical point is the involvement of the classification societies because they partly present authorities and common interests and thus have to combine their technical competence and contributions with their control of rules and regulations.

Up to now the focus has been on concrete business processes which will be an integral part of tomorrow's virtual enterprises. The virtual enterprise to establish needs most probably much more than that. The education of next generation engineer is one of those topics that also need to be discuss.

The fact that quality in a distributed design and production scenario needs to have clear responsibilities, is another additional aspect to think about.

To define user requirements for both these areas additional effort is need.

The approach taken has shown its potential. While it is still too early to calculate the potential benefit, it can already be said that an implementation of this technology would improve European competitiveness and further more it would support and make advantage of the current situation of outsourcing and specialising as it can be monitored in maritime industry world-wide.

Last but not least it seems clear that in the same areas listed below, more development is required

- Tool support for project management of virtual enterprises
- Collaborative work
- Document management
- Document storage
- Security, privacy and legal issues

In conclusion the concept of virtual enterprise is becoming common within the maritime community, but industry has now to exploit it better and make it a business advantage toward a prosperous future.

3 New Tools for Robotics in shipbuilding

Until few years ago, the design phase of our ships was based on a CAD system that was developed within Fincantieri in 70s. The system was based on few initial core modules; then, considering the increasing needs of information, other modules have been added. Big drawback of final configuration was the low level of integration between the programs and the number of re-input needed in the different steps of design process.

Typically at the shop-floor level no information technology was available and only paper drawing and documents were available. The introduction of numerical control machinery involved new needs and blue collars became familiar with tapes, floppy disks and networks. So the design office had to be equipped with new tools to support the arising needs.

NuovoScafo is the Fincantieri project to satisfy the increasing need of integration and free flow of design data among the different design steps not only within offices but also into the yards until the area controllers, the robots and the numerical controlled machinery.

3.1 The Design System

NuovoScafo has been studied to take advantage of the new opportunities offered by current technologies and then produce a flexible software to better meet the needs arising from increasingly complex ships, shorten production cycles and larger number of robotised activities in the shipyard.

The system supports the design process starting from the functional phase up to the workshop documentation production to assure a competitive advantage to the company in which it has been introduced.

With reference to the past it is intended to assure greater design quality, shorter development cycles and quicker response to faster evolving product demands.

It allows the management of design data assuring consistency and exchange between different users and it also supports concurrent activities.

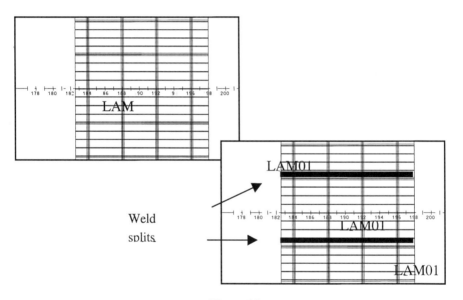

Figure 10

3.2 The Weld Object Module

The NuovoScafo kernel automatically creates weld information each time two components are connected.

But weld information, to be really useful for robotized application, have to consider the surrounding geometry. Therefore "theoretical welds" – that simply represent a connection line between two parts – are converted into "productive welds" to mach exactly the robot operations: any metal piece in the surrounding area is considered to split the theoretical weld and allow accessibility of arc-welding robots.

Within NuovoScafo each object is listed in the Bill of Materials that is linked to the Construction Bill of Materials. CBOM has the very important goal to determine which piece is processed where; not only simple pieces but also the different level of assembled pieces.

Specially developed module considers CBOM and the different production phase to get a list of ship components and extract their geometry data. Also, with only reference to the new aggregated components of that particular production phase, welds are considered: "theoretical welds" are converted into "productive welds", added to geometry data and sent to the arc-welding robot offline programming system.

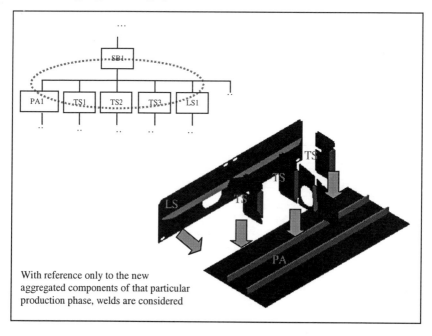

Figure 11

3.3 Historical Steps

Initially, robot instruction at Fincantieri was based on interactive graphic simulator software. On top of this standard software specific tools have been developed to speed up the process of robots instruction; in this way the global time need for the off-line programming was reduced and made equal or even less that the welding time and so acceptable.

The fundamental idea was that the majority of welds used for ship construction could be categorised into families (one family groups welds that connect objects with similar geometry). Each family can be programmed as a "primitive" or template, the parametrically mapped to each weld seam. In this way programming curved blocks – with highly individual and curved seams - is as easy as programming flat blocks having mainly flat and similar sections.

To program a certain area of the work-piece, the user only need to execute the correct primitive and select the weld zone with few mouse clicks on "most meaningful" surfaces.

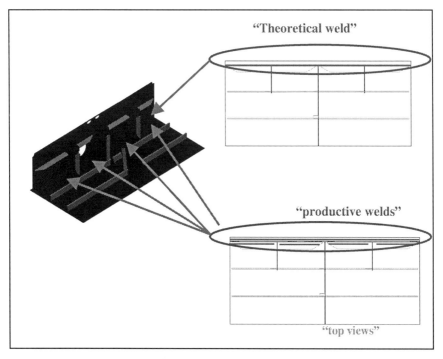

Figure 12 – "Theoretical welds" are converted into "productive welds"

The primitive capture years of welding experience and form a knowledge base for preserving vital information. Infact, the majority of robot programming is done by users that are not computer or robot experts. Therefore it is essential that the system is easy to use and smart enough to maintain important weld procedural information define by weld engineers. This is why primitive libraries are created before the programming is done. In this way robot and weld engineers can identify typical weld zones and structures and study appropriate primitives. One of these primitives is able to place paths with more that 50 points in just few mouse clicks. The end-user of the offline programming system is not requested to examine these single points. He will have to consider just the seam, and decide which seam configuration is better for a given geometry. Via points (additional points, with no particular functions in the robot program) to ensure collision free motion between weld joints are automatically generated. To minimise robot cycle times, weld paths are logically ordered and sequenced. The primitive also inserts complex camera sensors and robot master-slave configurations without any input required from the end user.

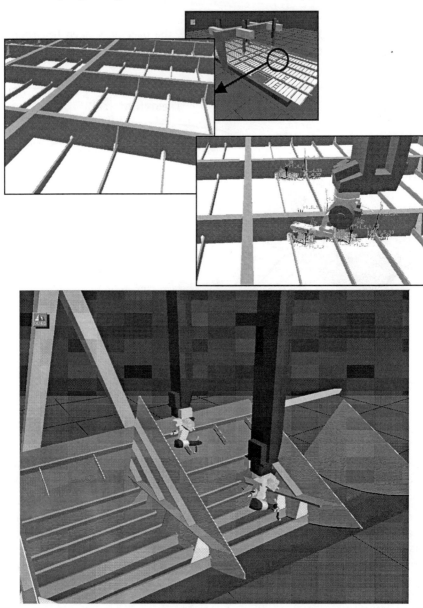

Figure 13 – Complex camera sensors and robot master-slave configuration are inserted by the primitive without any input required from the user

In addition to the automatic path generation, a mechanism able to detect errors and correct them is available to the weld and robot engineer that is developing primitives.

3.4 Automatic Generation of Robot Programs

To further speed up the generation of robot programs, the following areas of intervention have been identified within the interactive offline programming system above mentioned.

With the previous technique of weld primitives, the user had to select the different pieces to be welded together. For each weld it was necessary to choose a primitive that best fit the geometry involved, click on the two parts to be welded, select some "most meaningful" surfaces as required from the primitive, perform tests and where necessary make corrections.

Within this process some problems could arise:

- the user forgets some welds; at the end the robot program is generated without any apparent error; in the shop-floor robots will weld everything except what the user forgotten to consider;
- the user put a wrong interpretation on the geometry and choose a wrong primitive that does not fit that topology: after that robot paths have been created by that "wrong primitive", only with great effort the operator will be able to adjust the robots position – to avoid collisions, to guarantee reachability, to make joint values not exceed limits -; as a result the time spent will significantly increase;
- time spent to select geometry pieces, choose the correct primitive, perform checks and modifications depends very much on the user skill.

The solution found avoids any manual input: no more click on most meaningful surfaces. The new system gets the input from data that directly flow from NuovoScafo. In fact, each weld that comes from NuovoScafo stores the information necessary to run the old primitives to generate robot paths; in addition, greater precision and accuracy are guaranteed since weld information are automatically generated within the design system and then processed by a software procedure that will never forget to consider one single item.

Also the "human factor" is no more a variable of the robot programming process. In this way programming time not only will be reduced, but also will be made constant and not variable with the worker's humour and skill: in fact programming time will be produced by a procedure that automatically consider the welds and generate robot paths. In addition it can be evaluated in advance for better scheduling of activities.

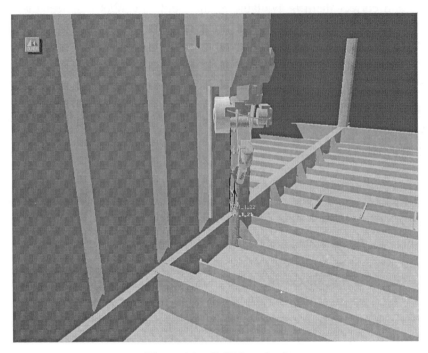

Figure 14 – Collision checks

Although robot programs are generated into simulation environment where it is possible to perform a complete test of robot movements and operations, sometimes errors appear when the robot performs the real welding. The automatic robot programming system performs and automatic test on the robot paths just generated and, if any error or problem is detected, will make corrections. Specific developed algorithms (called methods) will have to test each robot positions and, in case of errors, try different robot configurations, different external axes values, different torch orientations and positions so that the robot program at the end results free of errors. Only if none of the algorithms is able to correct the situations, the system will decide to skip that particular weld: this will be reported and the user may try to perform a manual programming with "classic tools" or give up to make the shop workers do the job by hand.

3.5 Recognizing Geometry

After geometry and weld data are available within the simulation environment the user has to perform a key operation. He must recognise the geometry belong to a specific category of a list of possibility. Like in the previous system, primitives are referred to specific classes of geometry since the algorithms of the primitives start from geometric considerations.

The user have to run selection rules (each primitive has its own selection rules) to define sets of welds and link them with one primitive (one primitive of each set of welds). These rules require to select few surfaces to create subsets of work-piece geometry: welds contained in that portion of geometry are grouped in one set, related to a specific primitive and completed with all necessary information needed for the automatic generation of robot paths.

4 Conclusions

Cost reduction and better quality in ship prefabrication processes are a key factor for European shipbuilders to improve their competitiveness. The goal is reachable trough the introduction of really flexible automation in hull production workshop. Investment to do that are quite huge and to payback an automated off-line programming tool, with the mentioned characteristics, must be available.

In conclusion the approach taken by Fincantieri has shown its potential, but the implementation of this technology must be monitored in the next future. The exploitation of the new system is not only a technical matter, but also something connected with the organisation of the workshops and of the work preparation department; now the new system must be tested and industrialised to make it a business advantage.

PLANNING AND SCHEDULING OF SHIPYARD PROCESSES

G. Chryssolouris[1], N. Papakostas[2], S. Makris[3], D. Mourtzis[4]

University of Patras, Laboratory for Manufacturing Systems, Department of Mechanical Engineering and Aeronautics, Rio, 26110 Patras, Greece
[1]gchrys@hol.gr; [2]papakost@lms.mech.upatras.gr; [3]makris@lms.mech.upatras.gr; [4]mourtzis@lms.mech.upatras.gr

Abstract

This chapter provides an overview of the planning and scheduling of the shipyards' processes, focusing on the short-term dispatching, the job shop and the resource constrained project scheduling problems. The industrial and commercial perspectives are presented, and a new planning method is discussed. The method includes an hierarchical model of the shipyard's resources and their workload. The model including an assignment logic of the workload to the shipyard's resources has been implemented in a software system. The proposed system simulates the operation of the shipyard and produces a schedule for the resources and a set of performance measures, which enable the user to evaluate the created schedule. A set of scheduling experiments with data coming from a shiprepair yard have been conducted in order to validate and test the approach under different conditions.

1. Introduction

A major difficulty of planning the operation of shipyards is that between the start and the completion time of the work there are typically many work changes which include added, cancelled work and priority changes. Ship repair jobs, in particular, are often done to a fixed budget and is therefore a "Fixed Cost" exercise. In the shipbuilding yards, poor scheduling keeps workers waiting for the pre-requisite sub-assemblies, causes fluctuation of workloads resulting in expensive overtime works, and may cause delay in delivery, Lee et al. (1997).

Modern software systems often fail to grasp the whole picture of complicated and interrelated scheduling activities as well as the dynamic spatial layout, i.e. spatial resources with material handling equipment like cranes, Lee et al. (1997).

Therefore the major requirement for the planning of a shipbuilding/shiprepair yard is the ability to produce quickly a good schedule with a system that is flexible and adaptive to changes of production data.

The most commonly adopted approaches to the planning of shipyards, is modelling the problem as a job-shop scheduling problem, Stidsen et al. (1996), or a resource constraint project scheduling problem-RCPSP, de Boer et al. (1997), which is a generalisation of the job-shop problem, Herroelen et al. (1998). These methods will be discussed in the following sections.

2. Academic and Commercial Perspective

The decision making activity of generating lower-level commands is called short-term dispatching. Dispatching is concerned with the detailed assignment of operations to production resources, Chryssolouris (1992). Multi-criteria decision making methods for allocating manufacturing resources to production tasks, utilising decision theory in tandem with randomised search methods have been reported, Chryssolouris et al. (1991), Chryssolouris et al. (1992), Chryssolouris et al. (1994). Other recent approaches include decentralised agent-based techniques, Papakostas et al. (1999). The shipyard scheduling is often addressed as a job-shop scheduling problem, Stidsen et al. (1996), which is a subset of the short-term dispatching problem. In a job shop, resources with the same or similar functionality or material processing capabilities are grouped together. In this structure, the part or lot of parts moves through the system by visiting the different work centres according to the part's process plan, Chryssolouris (1992).

The job-shop scheduling problem, Jain and Meeran (1999), also referred to as $\bullet_j$ consists of a finite set J of n jobs $\{J_i\}_{i=1}^{n}$ to be processed in a finite set M of m machines $\{M_k\}_{k=1}^{m}$. Each job J_i must be processed on every machine and consists of a chain or complex of m_i operations $O_{i1}, O_{i2}, ..., O_{imi}$, which have to be scheduled in a predetermined given order(precedence constraint). There are N operations in total, $N = \sum_{i=1}^{n} m_i$. O_{ik} is the operation of job J_i which has to be processed on machine M_k for an uninterrupted processing time period $\bullet_{ik}$ and no operation may be preempted.[1] Each job has its own individual flow pattern through the machines which is independent of the other jobs. Each machine can process only one job and each job can be processed by only one machine at a time (capacity constraints). The duration in which all operations for all jobs are completed is referred to as makespan C_{max}. The objective usually considered is to determine starting times for each operation, $t_{ik} \geq 0$, in order to minimise the makespan while satisfying all the precedence and capacity constraints:

$$C^*_{max} = \min(C_{max}) = \min_{feasible-schedules} (\max(t_{ik} + \tau_{ik}) : \forall J_t \in J, m_k \in M) \quad (1)$$

In a more general statement of the job-shop problem, machine repetitions (or machine absence) are allowed in the given order of the job $J_i \in J$, and thus m_i may be greater (or smaller) than m. Jain and Meeran (1999) provide a number of references that address the deterministic job-shop scheduling problem.

In Stidsen et al. (1996), a shipbuilding yard is modelled as a workshop consisting of one large assembly line divided into 12 different sections, called stations. At the first three stations the large steel plates are placed on the assembly line. These three stations are not addressed by their proposed scheduling methodology. At stations 4-8 the different parts of the blocks are mounted and point-welded by workers called shipbuilders. Station 7 acts as a gate where new blocks can be injected into the line; no work is performed at this station. Station 9 is a robot station where welding robots perform the welding. At the three remaining stations, welding is done by handwelders, since not all welding can be performed by robots and additionally, the welding performed by robots need to be checked and occasionally repaired by human welders. In the proposed scheduling approach, two types of constraints are taken into account:

a) geometrical constraints - the parts (called also blocks) should fit in the available area of a station, in order to be dispatched in the station; the blocks that are placed together at each station are called packages

b) time constraints - starting and finishing dates for each block, which are defined by a long-term scheduling plan; these constraints are weaker, i.e. they might be violated

---

[1] In this analysis each operation is given a unique number from 1 to $(m*n)$. If M is the ith machine required by O_{ik}, with respect to precedence constraints, then its operation number is $n(i-1) + i$.

The scheduling mechanism used is based on genetic algorithms (GA) and the parameters that optimises are:

a) definition of the packages
b) the order in which the packages are to be produced
c) the number of human resources assigned to each station for each week and each shift

In the DAS project, Lee et al. (1997), which lasted for 3 years (1991-1993), operations research (OR) and artificial intelligence (AI) methods were jointly used for developing a set of integrated scheduling systems for a shipbuilding company. These systems were able to perform:

a) Constraint-directed graph search for erection scheduling considering the work loads at the preceding indoor shops
b) Spatial scheduling
c) Line balancing with flexible process planning and dynamic cycle time
d) Processing time estimation using neural networks
e) Interface and co-ordination among multiple expert systems and databases

The combined spatial block scheduling problem for a shipyard is also addressed in Kyungchul et al. (1996), where partial enumeration and decomposition is used.

In de Boer et al (1997), the problem of planning and execution of maintenance projects is addressed. Specifically, procedures are defined for both aggregate capacity planning and detailed capacity scheduling of large maintenance projects, where information is generated through the use of a process planning database. In this paper, the finite capacity scheduling of the ship maintenance activities in a dockyard is addressed as a RCPSP. The RCPSP is the problem of scheduling activities of one project subject to precedence relations between activities where each activity may need capacity from various resource groups simultaneously and the capacity of each resource group is limited. There are K resource groups $R_1, R_2,..., R_K$ available to process the activities. Resource group R_k $(k = 1, 2, ..., K)$ consists of Q_k identical servers (e.g. machines or men) which are continuously available from time 0 onwards. Each server can process at most one activity at a time.

The project consists of N activities which are denoted by $A_1, A_2, ..., A_N$. Each activity A_j $(j = 1, 2, ..., N)$ requires $q_{jk} \leq Q_k$ servers of resource R_k $(k = 1,$

2, ..., K) during a non-interrupted interval of p_j time units. The set P_j denoted the predecessors of activity A_j. Each activity in P_j must be completed before A_j can start. A *schedule* • specifies for each activity A_j a completion time $C_j(\bullet)$. It is *feasible* if both the capacity and the precedence constraints are met. The objective is to find a feasible schedule in which the time to complete all activities, $C_{max}(\bullet)$, is minimised, where $C_{max}(\bullet) = max_{j=1, 2, ..., N} C_j(\bullet)$, also called the *makespan* of schedule • . In de Boer et al. (1997), the adaptive search method proposed by Kolish and Drexl (1996) is proposed. A survey of recent developments on RCPSP is included in Herroelen et. al (1998).

There are some European R&D projects relative to scheduling of shipyards such as the ESPRIT project EP26924 SYRIOS – "Small shiprepair yard related integrated operation systems – business synchronisation for contract driven small shipyards." The objective of this European R&D project is to produce an Integrated framework for dealing with the processes of small shiprepair yards supporting the major functions such as the tendering, the information management and production planning process and the communication with external suppliers and Subcontractors. The development will include the integration of the operations systems of the yards streamlining manufacture and repair functions. It will also embrace business functions such as sales, marketing, distribution, purchasing and engineering.

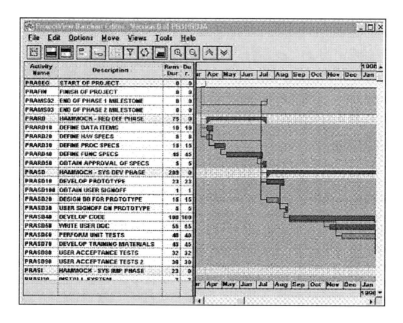

Figure 1. Artemis ProjectView BarChart Editor

Various commercially available software products are claimed to perform scheduling of complex operations. Commercial products available for planning are described in the following.

Artemis ProjectView is a project management application, which combines project planning, resource scheduling, cost control, and graphical reporting. It helps to plan and schedule the activities and resources of the project (Figure 1). In addition, ProjectView uses a graphical planning structure to organise and navigate projects by hierarchy (Figure 2). ProjectView provides capabilities for resource and cost management in project environments. The major features of ProjectView planning and scheduling are:

- Build and update project schedules using graphical Gantt or spreadsheet style interfaces
- Assign a number of resources per activity or project
- Schedule using resource and time constraints
- Prioritise activities during scheduling
- Display resource usage for selected resources or skill groups
- Establish and navigate project relationships

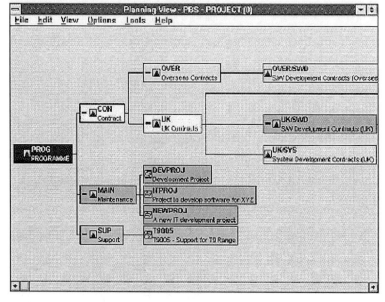

Figure 2. Artemis ProjectView Multiple Projects' Navigation

As part of the Views family of integrated, role-based applications, ProjectView can be combined with other Views applications to create a complete solution for enterprise project planning & scheduling, activity & resource tracking, cost control & earned value management, and executive reporting & analysis. Plus, because all Views applications are based on a centralized, industry standard SQL database, changes to project schedules, deadlines and resources in ProjectView are visible in other Views applications.

Welcom Software Technology Open Plan provides Decision Support allowing scheduling and reporting the aspects of single and multiple projects. It is feasible to produce charts and graphs, and provide support for informed decision making.

It also helps assessing, planning, scheduling, managing, and reporting project elements. In addition Open Plan helps to solve the problem of managing limited resources across multiple projects by allowing managing and reporting on resources, costs, and schedules for multiple projects. Open Plan allows displaying information in bar charts, spreadsheets, histograms, S-curves, cross tabulations, and semi-time phased network diagrams. (Figure 3, Figure 4). Moreover it offers a range of options to manage resources on one or more projects.

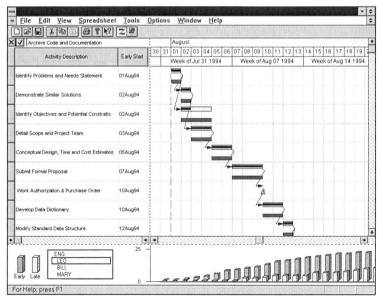

Figure 3. Open Plan Bar Chart Results

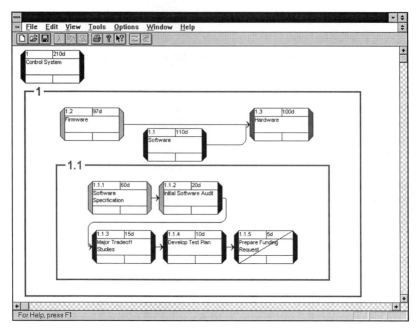

Figure 4. Open Plan Time phased network

PRIMAVERA Project Planner supports Planning and Scheduling and provides the means for:

- Building the schedule for the project
- Visualising the schedule results
- Perform Resources analysis
- Scheduling generation and print out of reports relative to the schedule (Figure 5)

MARINOR RASTwin is a computer-based system that covers the requirements for planning and follow-up of plant operation and maintenance, including material management and purchasing.

In addition to planning of preventive, corrective and condition based maintenance; the system will also be an efficient tool for use in the company's quality control.

The RASTwin covers the functions that are normally provided in a program for planning and control of operation and maintenance.

RASTwin may communicate with other programs in the market.

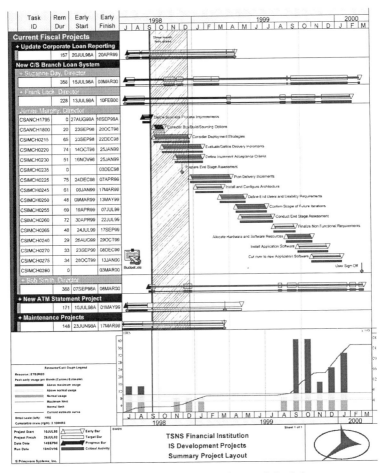

Figure 5. Primavera Project Planner Schedules

A module for administration of documents and drawings is integrated in RASTwin. This module may accept most documents on electronic format. When using the facilities available in RASTwin the user may select to work in a graphic interface for drawings or in the program menus (Figure 6). The results of Rastwin are saved in files, which can be imported, to MS Project, producing a Gantt Chart.

3. An Hierarchical Method for Planning and Scheduling

The work described in this section is based on the operation of an actual repair shipyard. The Production System of the shipyard to be modelled consists of six sections: the Supervisor Engineers, the Mechanical, the Naval

Works, the Riggers & Painters, the Technical Support and the Quality Management Section (Figure 7). The Supervisor Engineers supervise the shiprepair activities. The Mechanical Section involves two groups of fitters with different responsibilities, one group responsible for the interior of the ship and one responsible for the exterior of the ship. This section also includes a group of workers specialised in chemical cleaning, and the two floating docks. The Naval Works section consists of five groups: the platers, the welders, the pipers, the boilers and the carpenters. The Riggers & Painters Section includes three groups: the riggers, the painters and the vehicle drivers and operators. The Technical Support Section includes the electricians, the firemen and the people working on the piers of the dockyard and the tugboats. Finally, the Quality Management Section includes the chemist, the foundry of the shipyard and the Quality Control section.

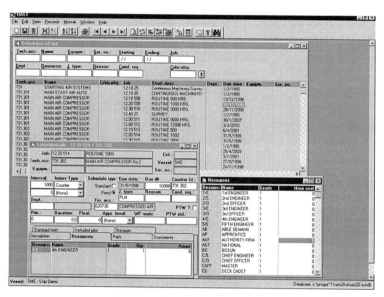

Figure 6. Marinor RastWin Schedule Results

From a planning point of view the important parts of the sections of the shipyard are the docks, the fitters, the platers, the welders, the pipers the riggers, the painters and the electricians. Therefore the modelling and planning approach has been concentrated on these parts which are shown in boldface characters in Figure 1.

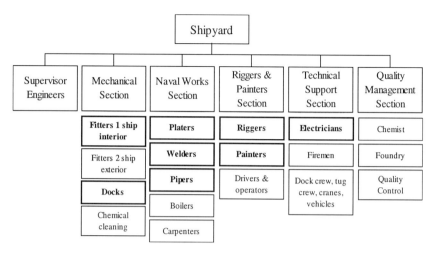

Figure 7. The sections of the repair shipyard

In this work an hierarchical model with four levels has been adapted to the repair shipyard's planning problem (Figure 8).

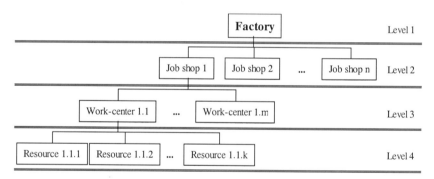

Figure 8. The four-level hierarchical model

The Factory corresponds to the entire shipyard and includes a number of Job Shops. Each Job Shop consists of a number of Work Centers, which in turn consist of a number of Resources. Job Shops correspond roughly to the sections of the shipyard, while Work Centers correspond, to some extend, to departments of the sections. The Resources included in each Work Center are a sort of "parallel processors", namely they can "process" identical Tasks. Depending upon the assignment logic or dispatching rules, a Task is assigned to one of the Work Center's Resources. In this particular application the term Resource is used for a group of workers who are typically working, according to the shipyard's rules, to a particular Task, from the beginning to the end of the Task.

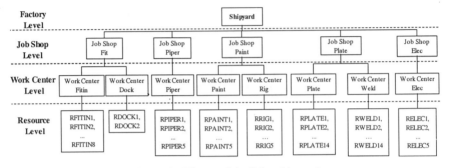

Figure 9. The model of the shipyard

Job shop	Process Description	Work Centers	Resources
Fitters	Fitting Jobs (interior of the ship)	Fitting	8 (each of these 8 resources includes 5 workers)
		Docks	2 docks
Pipers	Piping Jobs	Piping	5 (each of these 5 resources includes 4 workers)
Painters - Riggers	Blasting-Painting-Rigging Jobs	Blasting-Painting	5 (each of these 5 resources includes 6 workers)
		Rigging	5 (each of these 5 resources includes 12 workers)
Platers - Welders	Plating-Welding Jobs	Plating	14 (each of these 14 resources includes 6 workers)
		Welding	9 (each of these 9 resources includes 4 workers)
Electricians	Electrical Jobs	Electrical	5 (each of these 5 resources includes 5 workers)
5 Job Shops		**8 Work Centers**	**53 Resources**

Table 1. Elements of the shipyard model

3.1. Work Release and Assignment

Corresponding to the facilities' hierarchy there is also the workload's hierarchical breakdown. The Orders consist of Jobs which in turn consist of Tasks. The Orders correspond to the Factory and they are divided into Jobs which are released to Job Shops. A Job, based on its specification, can be processed only by one Job Shop and is thus released to the proper Job Shop. The Tasks that are included in a Job can be again processed only by one Work Center and are therefore released to the corresponding Work Centers. However, the Tasks can be processed by more than one of the Work Center's Resources and the assignment of a Task to a Resource is done with the help either of a complex decision making logic Chryssolouris and Dicke (1991), Chryssolouris (1992), Chryssolouris et al. (1992), Chryssolouris, and Lee (1994), or a simple dispatching rule.

An Order corresponds to the entire work that has to be done for the repair of a ship. The release of Jobs to Job Shops is based on the Job specifications. Similarly Tasks are released to the Work Centers (Figure 10).

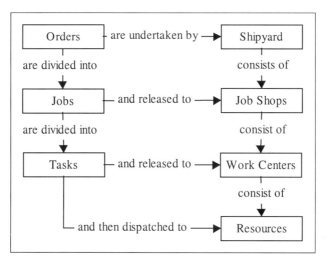

Figure 10. Work release and assignment

For example, all the plating and welding work on the ship is one Job which is assigned to the plating-welding Job Shop. The Job consists of a number of specific plating and welding Tasks, such as Deck Plating work, Cargo Control Room Plating work, Vent Risers & Ladders welding etc. The plating Tasks are assigned to the plating Work Center, whereas the welding Tasks are assigned to the welding Work Center. In each Work Center there are Resources which could perform the same Tasks. Therefore the Tasks have to be dispatched to the Resources according to an assignment logic, using dispatching heuristics or a multi-criteria planning mechanism that formulates and evaluates resource allocation alternatives, Chryssolouris and Dicke (1991), Chryssolouris (1992), Chryssolouris et al. (1992),

Chryssolouris and Lee (1994). An important constraint in releasing and dispatching of Jobs and Tasks is the precedence relationships among them.

The assignment of the shiprepair tasks to the shipyard's resources results in a schedule for each resource of the shipyard and thus a detailed plan and schedule for the critical parts of the entire shipyard is produced.

4. Implementation and Results

4.1. Software Implementation

The approach discussed above has been implemented in a software system with the help of Visual C++ version 5.0 (Win32 API) and it operates under Microsoft Windows 95 and Windows NT on a PC.

The system allows the user to construct an hierarchical model of the shipyard's facilities and their workload. The facilities model includes the definition of the Factory, the Job Shops, the Work Centers and the Resources. The user "fits" the workload model to the factory model, by specifying the Orders, the Jobs and the Tasks. Furthermore, the system allows the user to specify which Resources are suitable for performing each Task, the precedence relationships, the processing times and the set-up times. The system could include information on the cost for performing each Task and the processing quality. The graphic user interface is menu-driven, with win32 dialogues for guiding the user through the modelling process (Figures 11 and 12).

A simple coding scheme could be used (based on the practice of the yard) for specifying the elements of the facilities and the workload model. As an example for the purpose of this work, the *Pipers* section is modelled as a Job Shop named *JSPIPER*, including one Work Center named *WCPIPER* which includes five Resources named *RPIPER-xx* where *xx* takes values from one to five. The workload for the Pipers' Job Shop consists of one Job named *JBPIPER* which includes three Tasks: *TP3110, TP3800,* and *TP3801.* The four-digit numbers in the task codes are the actual codes used by the shipyard modelled in this work.

The system uses event driven simulation to simulate the operation of the shipyard and the execution of the workload by the shipyard's resources. The simulation mechanism releases the workload to the Job Shops and Work Centers, respecting the precedence relationships which are defined by the user. In each Work Center an assignment mechanism decides which Task is going to be assigned to which Resource. Consequently, a dispatching decision is required when a Resource becomes available for processing. The assignment mechanism allocates the available Resource to a pending Task. The system simulates the operation of the production facilities either for a certain period of time (user specified) or until all the Tasks have been processed by the Resources. In either case, a detailed schedule for each Resource is produced in graphic or alphanumeric format (Figure 13).

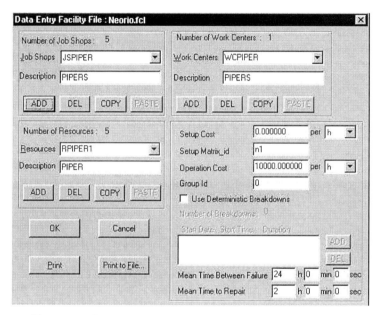

Figure 11. System's user interface: Facility data input screen.

The user has the option to select among a set of dispatching rules (Figure 12) and a multiple criteria decision making method. Furthermore, the system has the ability to consider planned maintenance in the production schedule and unexpected interrupts such as resource failures, which are statistically simulated. The schedule produced can be used for the planning of the activities of the shipyard.

In case of a change on the workload or on the status of the facilities of the shipyard, the user can feed the system with the new data and reproduce an updated schedule and plan. Since a simulation run for a planning horizon of a few months takes a few minutes, it is very easy for the user any time that something unpredicted occurs, to reproduce efficiently an updated plan for the entire shipyard.

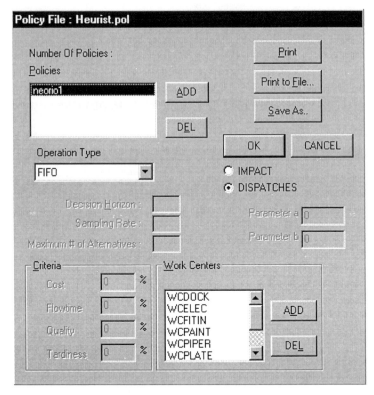

Figure 12. System's user interface: Selection of dispatching rule.

Resource Name	Work Center	Name of Task	Start Time	End Time
RPAINT1	WCPAINT	TN8010\1/1	10800.000	1134000.000
RPAINT1	WCPAINT	TN8491\2/2	3909600.000	5032800.000
RPAINT2	WCPAINT	TN8010\2/1	2613600.000	3736800.000
RPAINT3	WCPAINT	TN8491\1/1	10800.000	1134000.000
RPAINT3	WCPAINT	TN8010\1/3	3304800.000	4428000.000
RPAINT4	WCPAINT	TN8010\1/2	183600.000	1306800.000
RPAINT4	WCPAINT	TN8491\2/1	2613600.000	3736800.000
RPAINT4	WCPAINT	TN8010\2/2	3909600.000	5032800.000
RPAINT5	WCPAINT	TN8491\1/2	183600.000	1306800.000
RPAINT5	WCPAINT	TN8491\1/3	3304800.000	4428000.000
RRIG1	WCRIG	TN9030\1/3	432000.000	1123200.000
RRIG1	WCRIG	TN8020\2/2	3909600.000	5032800.000
RRIG2	WCRIG	TN9030\1/1	0.000	691200.000
RRIG2	WCRIG	TN9030\2/1	691200.000	1382400.000
RRIG2	WCRIG	TN8020\2/1	2613600.000	3736800.000

Figure 13a. Schedule produced by the system - Alphanumeric format

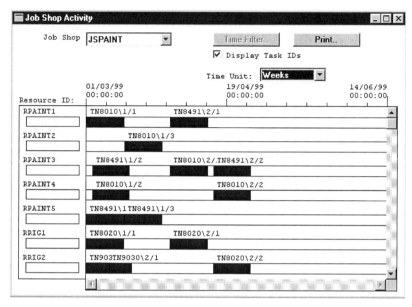

Figure 13b. Schedule produced by the system - Gantt Chart format

4.2. Experiments and Results

A set of experiments have been conducted in order to check the model's feasibility and produce realistic schedules for the repair shipyard. The quality of the schedule can be evaluated by the user via a set of performance measures, which are calculated by the system based on the produced schedule. The performance measures include job flow time, job tardiness, number of tardy jobs, capacity utilisation etc. The job-related performance measures are calculated for each job and as mean values for all the jobs included in the entire workload. The capacity utilisation is calculated for each Resource and as a mean value for each Work Center, Job Shop and the entire Factory.

For the experimentation a set of orders with different arrival times has been defined. The job due dates for the experiments have been calculated as follows:

$$DD = A.T + k*P.T \qquad (2)$$

Where DD = Due Dates

A.T = Arrival Time

k = Constant

P.T = Processing Time of the Job

The constant k equals to k=1.3. This value of the constant results in a set of relative tight due date for the jobs. For the processing times, work and facilities related data were received from the shipyard.

A number of dispatching rules have been used for the experimentation with the model. The rules were applied for the allocation of Resources to pending Tasks for each Work Center. Each experiment includes one simulation run with the same facilities and workload data but with a different dispatching rule. Each simulation run produces a particular schedule and a set of performance measures specific to this run (Figure 14).

As was expected the EDD rule produces very good results for the mean tardiness, but performs poorly with respect to the capacity utilisation. The SPT rule on the other hand, performs well with regard to the utilisation. An interesting observation is that the EDD and FONPR rules produce similar results for most of the performance measures. This can be explained, considering that most of the jobs have comparable processing times and, since their due dates are calculated as functions of their processing times, the jobs with the fewer operations are the ones with the tighter due dates. Therefore the two rules result in similar assignment patterns.

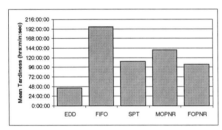 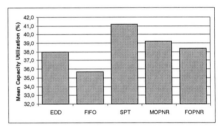

Dispatching Rules

EDD: Task from the Job with the earliest due date is selected.
FIFO: Task from the Job which first arrives at the factory is selected.
SPT: Task from the Job with the shortest processing time is selected.
MOPNR: Task from the Job is selected which has the most operations remaining to be performed.
FOPNR: Task from the Job is selected which has the fewest operations remaining to be performed.

Performance measures

MEANTARDINESS: $$MT = \frac{1}{N^{comp}} \cdot \sum_{j=1}^{N^{comp}} \max_i \left[0; T_j^{comp} - T_j^{dd} \right]$$

MEAN CAPACITY UTILIZATION: $MCP = \dfrac{\sum_{J=1}^{N^{comp}}\left(T_j^{comp} - T_j^{start}\right) + \sum^{N^{proc}}\left(T - T_{n_p}^{start}\right)}{I \cdot T}$

where
- N^{comp} : the number of completed Tasks
- T_j^{comp} : the completion time of Task j
- T_j^{dd} : the due date of Task j
- T_j^{start} : the start time of Task j
- N^{proc} : the number of in-process Tasks at time (T)
- $T_{n_p}^{start}$: the start time of the in-process Task n_p at time (T)
- T : the time at which the performance measure's value is calculated
- I : the total number of Resources

Figure 14. Experimental results: Mean Tardiness and Capacity Utilisation vs dispatching rules

References

CHRYSSOLOURIS, G. (1992), "Manufacturing Systems – Theory and Practice", *Springer – Verlag*.

CHRYSSOLOURIS, G., PIERCE, J. and DICKE, K., (1991), "An Approach for Allocating Manufacturing Resources to Production Tasks." *Journal of Manufacturing Systems*, Vol. 10, No. 5, pp368-382.

CHRYSSOLOURIS, G., DICKE, K. and LEE, M., (1992) "On the resources allocation problem", *International Journal of Production Research*, Vol. 30, 12, pp2773-2795

CHRYSSOLOURIS, G. and LEE, M., (1994), "An Approach to Real-Time Flexible Scheduling.", *International Journal of Flexible Manufacturing Systems*, Vol. 6, pp 235-253

de BOER, R., SCHUTTEN, J. M. J. and ZIJM, W. H. M. (1997), "A Decision support System for Ship Maintenance Capacity Planning", *Annals of CIRP,* Vol. 46, pp391 – 396

HERROELEN, W., de REYCK B. and DEMEULEMEESTER, E. (1998), "Resource-Constrained Project Scheduling: A Survey of Recent Developments", *Computers Ops Res.,* Vol. 25, No. 4, pp279-302.

KOLISCH, R. and SPRECHER A., (1996), "PSPLIB – A Project Scheduling Problem Library", *European Journal of Operational Research* 96, pp205 – 216.

KOLISCH, R. and DREXL, A., (1996), "Adaptive Search for Solving Hard Project Scheduling Problems", *Naval Research Logistics 43*, pp23 – 40.

KYUNGCHUL,, P., KYUNGSIK, L., SUNGSOO, P. and SUNGHWAN, K., (1996), "Modeling and solving the spatial block scheduling problem in a shipbuilding company", *Computers and Industrial Engineering*, Vol 30, Issue 3, pp357-364

LEE, J. K., LEE, K. J., PARK, J. K., HONG, J. S. and LEE, J. S., (1997), "Developing scheduling systems for DAEWOO Shipbuilding: DAS project", *European Journal of Operational Research*, pp380-395

LI, K. Y. and WILLIS R. J., (1992), "An iterative scheduling technique for resource-constrained project scheduling", *European Journal of Operarional Research 56,* pp370-379.

MORI, M. and TSENG, Ch. Ch., (1997), "A Genetic Algorithm for Multi – Mode Resource Constrained Project Scheduling Problem", *European Journal of Operational Research 100,* pp134 – 141.

PAPAKOSTAS, N., MOURTZIS, D., BECHRAKIS, K., CHRYSSOLOURIS, G., et al., (1999), "A Flexible Agent Based Framework for Manufacturing Decision Making", *Proceedings of the 9th International Conference on Flexible Automation and Intelligent Manufacturing, June 23 - 25, Tilburg, Netherlands, published by Begell House Inc. Publishers*

STIDSEN, T., KRAGELUND L. B. and MATEESCU, O., (1996), "Jobshop scheduling in a shipyard", *Proceedings of the 12th European Conference on Artificial Intelligence, Published by John Wiley & Sons, Ltd.*

IMPROVING THE COMPETITIVENESS OF SMEs IN THE EUROPEAN SHIPREPAIR SECTOR BY THE USE OF INFORMATION TECHNOLOGY

G. Bruce and A. McDowall

Department of Marine Technology, University of Newcastle upon Tyne, UK
George.Bruce@newcastle.ac.uk

Abstract

Shiprepair is a volatile business, in which planning is inhibited and management is made difficult by the inevitable, short-term changes in work scope as contracts are carried out. This paper outlines the main characteristics of shiprepair, and the information and management requirements of the business. These include the need to deal with a forward workload often of only a few weeks, to manage constant re-scheduling and to manage the flexible use of resources. These include sub-contractors and casual labour, as the resource levels and skills mix vary with workload.

Information technology is increasingly seen as critical to the effective management of shiprepair in a very competitive market. In particular many companies have identified the need for integrated systems, to manage the flow of information within (and outside with suppliers and clients) their businesses. Secondly, the need to improve the business processes which use the information is also seen as an important development by the SMEs in the repair sector.

Some initial uses of IT in this manner are described, and further aspects of the business, including planning, scheduling and management accounting are identified. Some of the IT tools which are applicable are also outlined.

1 The Shiprepair Business

Shiprepair is a business, which differs in many respects from ship construction. Although the two sectors both deal with ships, and use very much the same sets of facilities, equipment and skills, they also have crucial differences.

Shiprepair differs from new construction in several important characteristics

- The timescales are much shorter
- The predictability of the workload is lower
- The proportion of labour costs is much higher

It is however, very similar to new construction in other important ways

- The market is very competitive
- Price and delivery are critical

Shiprepair timescales are much shorter than for new construction. For a new ship, the time from contract to completion is typically two years, though for a small ship it may be only twelve months or less. On the other hand, for a warship the time for contract to delivery may well be five or more years. A typical shiprepair timescale would be:

- Enquiry to contract,   - two to four weeks
- Contract to ship arrival,   - one to three weeks
- Ship time in repair yard,   - one to two weeks

Annual refits for cruise vessels or ferries may require three weeks in the repair yard, unless there is a major overhaul or replacement of machinery. Even a major refit or ship conversion is usually completed in three to six months.

The basis of a contract is the Owner's Specification. This will vary in size and content, but typically describes each individual work item to be carried out. However, in many cases, the work which actually requires to be done will depend on findings and agreement after inspection of the ship equipment concerned. Using the specification, the shipyard estimates the cost of each work item and bids accordingly. If successful, a contract will be placed.

The agreed arrival date may change, depending on the Owner's use of the ship, and a lucrative cargo may result in the ship being late, or even in cancellation of the contract as the ship is diverted elsewhere. On the ship's arrival, the Owner's representative may delete items, and/or include additional work.

Labour costs are a significant proportion of the total costs and in most cases, the labour force has a small core and up to three times as many temporary workers. Therefore labour cost control is of major importance. This includes,

- Identifying all labour on site, from day to day
- Allocating all time to ships
- Allocating all time to specific work items
- Collating the information at least daily
- Preparing running accounts for agreement with the owner's representative.

The Labour Force is differently structured, as compared to new construction, where stability of workload is usually an important goal. This permits a steady labour force, which can be both highly trained and specialist. Some new construction companies, particularly smaller companies, do use flexible labour to manage variations in their workload. Shiprepair, on the other hand, usually has a constantly varying labour force, with casual labour used for a single ship contract, or part contract and sub-contract companies used for large elements of the work.

Shiprepair is a significant sector in the maritime industries, which is vital to the continued operation of the many tens of thousands of ocean going and local vessels. Over one third of the world's ocean going ships trade into European waters, and there are many thousands of smaller ships operating locally both at sea and on inland waterways. The sector therefore has particular importance for Europe because competitiveness with other regions of the world is possible. (DTI, 1995). It also is a major provider of employment and supports a large and growing ship conversion and major refitting business.

The work carried out in shiprepair is very varied, from dealing with the most minor items to major conversions which create virtually a new ship. There are a number of generally recognised categories of shiprepair and conversion operations. These vary in duration from a few hours, to days, weeks or months. These may be briefly summarised as:

- Voyage repairs, where minor repairs are carried out with a ship in service, often during a stay in port.
- Routine docking, where the ship is docked for underwater work to be carried out and the opportunity is taken to make other repairs.
- Major refits, where the ship is substantially re-equipped, including work arising from special surveys.
- Conversion, where a ship is refitted for a different use.

There are also damage repairs, where extensive work, particularly to the ship's structure, may be required.

During the course of these repairs, different classes of work are carried out, reflecting the diversity of ship types and of the equipment installed in them The work typically includes some or all of the following:

- Cleaning and painting, underwater fittings.
- Steelwork, replacement of corroded or damaged material.
- Overhauls and repairs to main and auxiliary machinery .
- Miscellaneous work, on deck equipment, accommodation and other systems.

2 Shiprepair Activities

The basic set of activities which shiprepairers carry out when they undertake a contract has similarities with most other businesses. That is, there is a need to obtain a contract, to plan its execution, to obtain the necessary resources and materials, to complete the work then finally to secure payment.

To present these activities specifically for the shiprepair business, an activity map is a convenient format. This shows the stages of a shiprepair contract, from the marketing and sales required to obtain the work, through to the presentation of a final invoice. The functions which are needed to complete all these stages are also shown, giving a matrix format. Where a function needs to carry out some process at a stage of a contract, there is an activity box.

Each stage of the contract, from marketing to presentation of the final invoice, results in specific outputs, which are also included in the activity map. These outputs provide a basis for performance measures.

The functional, rather than departmental, definition is used because many smaller shiprepair yards do not have distinctive departments for many of the functions, but instead the small number of managers carry out the activities as required. Others adopt a project management approach, where an individual is responsible for all stages of a contract, from the initial estimate to the final invoice, including the production management. Basically clerical assistance is available in some cases for the routine elements of the activities.

Functions such as quality assurance and purchasing are frequently performed by managers in a addition to other duties.

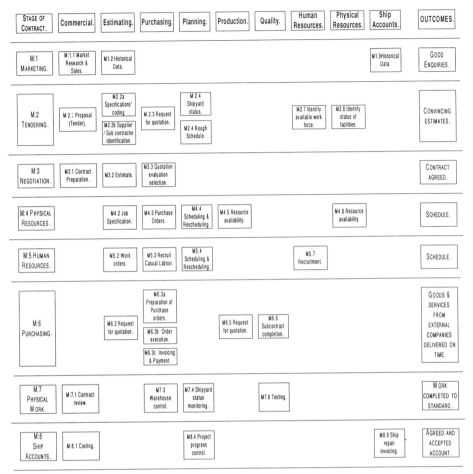

Figure 1. Activity map of shiprepairing.

3 Management Problems

Most authorities are agreed that shiprepair is a difficult business to manage. Variously described as "complex", "dynamic", "fast-moving", "chaotic", the business of shiprepair is undoubtedly difficult to plan and then manage. Many practitioners are firmly convinced that the processes of shiprepair cannot be planned in the conventional sense, and that any control is limited to short term, often reactive management of resources. The nature of the work involved does make this a difficult argument to refute, at least with respect to some categories of work which fall under the heading of shiprepair and conversion.

The planning and management needs vary according to the category of work and vessel type. Major conversions and refits can be considered to be closer in organisational terms to new construction, and can use related systems in some cases. But there remains a need for improved management information, planning and scheduling systems to support the routine and emergency repairs. This is a particular problem for the smaller companies in the industry, which have limited management resources.

The general response of the shiprepair industry in Europe has generally been to develop a highly effective infrastructure of sub-contractors, suppliers and casual labour. In other areas, where labour costs are lower, the pressure on managing resources may be less and some under-utilisation of resources, particularly people, may be acceptable.

This use of sub-contract and casual labour creates additional management problems. The effect is that the workforce can increase and decrease very rapidly, to match a fluctuating workload. It is therefore essential to maintain real time information on the status not only of the existing permanent workforce, but also the potential additional temporary workforce. This requirement to manage resources also results in a demand for more effective IT systems.

Another characteristic of the shiprepair business, one that is shared with other service businesses, is the perishable nature of the "product". That is, where the objective is in part to sell time in a dry dock, that can only be done today, and if the dock is empty there is no way the lost time can be recovered. It is not possible to make and store products, or interim products, or have inventory. Basically, the shipyard tries to fill its dry dock(s) with ships, and the occupancy rate for the docks is often seen as a useful measure of performance.

4 Planning and Management of Shiprepair

The planning and scheduling problem in shiprepair differs significantly from ship construction, or even from major refit and conversion projects. First, the forward workload is not certain. A ship construction project, once the design is sufficiently advanced and assuming there is a well-organised system in place, can be planned in detail with a high degree of certainty. A conversion, despite initial uncertainty about the condition of existing ship structure and systems, can be planned in advance, and re-planned after the initial stages. On the other hand, a repair contract, even where a relatively detailed specification is in place, and has been quoted against, is subject to change. Often the specification for the contract will actually be relatively sparse in terms of the work requirements, and the detailed requirements will only emerge once the repair work is underway.

Second, in almost all cases, whether highly specified or not, there will be emerging work, as the contract progresses. This is because in many cases the specification will call for an item of equipment to be inspected and then repaired or replaced as necessary. If the work required is substantial, then additional jobs must be done. These in turn may lead to the cancellation of other, less urgent work, to allow the total cost of the repairs to remain within a budget total. Inspection of hull structure may lead to significant replacement requirements for corroded material in older ships, again the extent of the work being unknown until the contract is underway. (Bruce et al, 1999)

There is another complication for the shiprepairer. In the case of ship construction, there is an estimate for the contract which is then the basis for the contract price (almost certainly fixed). The estimate is based on specific measures of productivity for typical shipbuilding activities, based on past work, which the shipyard can use with some confidence. These may be modified to take account of variations in the ship or planned improvements based on new investment or methods. In general, however, the shipbuilder has a budget for man-hours, broken down by tasks, and can plan, resource and monitor the contract against these. If the work is completed within, or under budget, the result is at least potentially profitable. If the work is over budget then there is likely to be a loss. (Braiden et al, 1992)

In the shiprepair case, the position is more complex. In the first instance, there are few routine jobs which can be used as a basis for productivity measurement. Such items as hull cleaning or painting, planning can be based on the specification and square metres to be covered, but for many items the workload associated with the task is variable. Even in the case of hull cleaning, the work required will depend to some extent on the pre-existing condition of the hull, and any fouling or corrosion. This can be very difficult to assess prior to the ship docking. Then, once work commences, there may be variations in the tasks, which result in variations in the man-hours.

However, whereas in ship construction, with fixed tasks and a fixed price, any unforeseen variation results in additional cost with probably no redress, the situation in shiprepair is more complex. There is a clear need to try and manage each task within the initial budget, provided there is no variation in the work content of the task. This will apply primarily to tasks such as painting and dealing with underwater fittings, and the basics of docking and undocking. Such items as the supply of power to the ship in dock can be based on a tariff and measured. However, many of the shiprepair tasks do vary, and once they do so, then a number of different conditions may be found (Filipic, 1994).

More work may be necessary within a fixed price, resulting in a loss. This is avoided as far as possible, by not fixing prices where there is much uncertainty in the scope of the task. Once a fixed element is agreed, the situation in terms of the need to maintain a budget is similar to ship construction. (Stewart, 1997)

More work may be necessary, but to be paid for against an estimate and agreed price. The problem is now still to manage within the (revised) budget. From a planning viewpoint, the enhanced task will still require to be completed within a fixed overall timescale. If there is a large amount of emergent work, then the timescale may be re-negotiated. If the work is not completed within the agreed timescale, then there may be financial penalties.

More work may be necessary, to be paid for as incurred. There is in this case no problem for the shiprepairer, except to monitor expenditure accurately.

Other characteristics of shiprepair planning are similar to those of new construction, particularly with respect to maintaining the end date. The ship under repair has been taken out of service to enter the shiprepair yard, and is almost certainly scheduled for another voyage immediately afterwards. The completion date is therefore rigid. Even if there are changes to the workload, as outlined above, the end date must be maintained.

The planning of a repair contract is therefore a mixture of maintaining an end date - which requires some form of critical path analysis, and frequently updating variable workload and resources. Managing the contract is a case of maintaining the end date against that background of continual variation in work content and therefore resource requirements. In this situation, there is little available software. Conventional planning software is based on a network, but assumes in general that once a plan has been developed, and as far as possible optimised, every effort will be made to maintain it. Much work on ship construction planning is based on the sub-division of the contract into very small tasks (or work packages), of short duration, and then avoiding any variation in time or work content.

In order to manage the work as the contract progresses, the ability to collect accurate progress information, and to transmit this rapidly to those responsible for maintaining the contract status is essential. The information is also needed allow assessment of the forecast to completion for the contract, and therefore underpins any re-scheduling as the emerging work is identified. Almost real-time data collection is desirable to be able to manage the rapid changes of scope which are experienced.

The critical difference between ship construction and shiprepair is that in ship construction any change in work or schedule is avoided if at all possible, whereas in shiprepair the expectation is that there will be change.

5   How Shiprepair differs from other Industries

There are many thousands of SMEs in Europe, and many of these face problems which are also identifiable in the shiprepair industry. It therefore seems reasonable to try to identify existing information technology and software systems, which might reasonably be expected to meet the needs of shiprepairers. A number of basic solutions have been reviewed.

A selection of those industry sectors which might be seen as having similar projects and operating environments to shiprepair are considered in this section of the paper.

Building and civil contracting

The basis of the software systems was predominantly financial, giving good historical information but limited capability for project control. There is some need to deal with a varying labour force, but in a relatively limited range of skills and over long periods compared to shiprepairing. Most importantly, the extent of contract change is relatively small and slow, and its impact on purchasing and other resources in most cases is also small. Materials are largely standard, and can be used for stock in many cases, whereas in shiprepairing there is a vast range of materials and parts which may be required, and they have to be bought against the specific needs of a particular ship.

Hotels and related services

These share a perishable commodity with shiprepairing, that is if a room in a hotel is not occupied for a night then the opportunity to sell that commodity is lost permanently. The need to maximise occupancy is also present. On the other hand, there is a limited set of transactions that can take place with a customer. The forward workload is more predictable in seasonal and other cyclical terms, so pricing policy can be set to attract a sufficient number of a large population of potential clients. The task is a simpler one to manage than shiprepair, where a series of highly individual and customised transactions is required.

Vehicle maintenance

There is a variable workload, within a relatively standard maintenance schedule. The repair work is not date driven, in that if a vehicle has more repair work than was initially anticipated, its completion late is not an issue.

The vehicle can be substituted by another of identical, or near identical, specification. In most cases, the geographical location of vehicles is close and they are often based at a depot. This contrasts with ships, where in many cases the ship could be anywhere world-wide, and even where similar ships are available, their location is such that replacement is impractical.

General manufacturing

In general small companies make a relatively straightforward product, where the future workload is reasonably predictable, and stocks (both of input materials and finished products) can be used to balance variability. Relatively, or very, large volumes of production, of semi-standard products are undertaken, and the products generally have a small number of components. The emphasis is generally on as much stability of production as possible, and the planning, scheduling and other operating systems reflect this situation.

There are procedures designed for job shop environments which allow variations to be managed. However, these are primarily intended to allow re-scheduling of job sequences within a resource constraint, whereas shiprepairers use flexibility of resources to maintain the contract schedule. Most job shops aim to maximise efficiency of fixed resources, whereas the shiprepairer has to use resources efficiently, but must meanwhile also allow them to fluctuate in accordance with current contract requirements.

6   Background to Current IT Research

Many European shipyards have taken a keen interest in finding a solution to the problems posed by planning and management of shiprepair. These solutions have generally been based on the use of computers which provide the basic requirement of a means of handling and manipulating large quantities of data in a short time. (Lindahl, 1994)

A UK survey of computer use in smaller repair companies, carried out in the early 1990s, identified a large gap between their use in large companies and the situation in smaller companies. Reviews of a similar nature in the USA and other evidence from Europe all indicated that the smaller companies were not at that time making any significant or systematic use of computers. (Hills et al, 1995)

The survey also identified a number of opportunities to exploit computing in the management of the smaller shiprepair companies, and small, pilot programmes were initiated. The first of these set out to develop a computer based information system that would replicate an effective paper system, but would permit much faster transmission of data. Other benefits which were sought were the reduction of errors inherent in a paper system, including transcription errors as information was copied from department to department on different formats. The ability to maintain an up to date picture of the status of any contract, and to ensure that no costs were "lost" through the slowness of paper systems would be a further benefit. Finally, the company planned to use the programme of work as a means of developing an awareness of IT in its staff, to be able to exploit the new technology effectively (Brewster et al, 1997).

The first project lasted three years, which gave a lengthy timescale, but this met a need to achieve a significant cultural change, and to do so within a very busy company operation with limited management and staff resources. The shipyard also had to continue in operation during the period, maintaining its existing systems in parallel with the development. The project also had a research element, in that very little information was available about shiprepair operations, with few if any formal studies having been carried out previously.

The primary objective of the company was re-confirmed as managing the transactions between the different departments, that is ensuring a rapid and accurate flow of information. In principle, as soon as a piece of information was created, it should be available to any authorised system user.

A formal model was created of the relevant elements of the shipyard operating systems. The flow of information was analysed and a detailed flow chart - a "brown paper" model - of the shipyard in the form of a large wall chart was produced. This was then translated into a system specification, which apart from an outline written description was primarily in the form of a prototype, dummy database. This allowed the users to see what the finished system would look like, and allowed them also to have an input into the screen formats which would replace their existing paper forms.

It was decided to restrict the system quite severely to managing the routine aspects of the business, with a focus on the transmission of data, leaving a lot of the planning and other internal, departmental processing, and exceptions to the routine, to be managed separately. Although this reduced the functionality of the system, it made the development faster and resulted in a simpler and more robust output.

The benefits which the company gained from the system are primarily those which were agreed at the outset, in the increased accessibility and reliability of information on the status of the company, and its contracts. The processes in the individual departments - estimating, purchasing, labour cost control and ship accounts - also have some modest improvement to their efficiency, giving the ability to process more information for the same resources as previously available.

However, during the course of the work, it became apparent that the initial brief - basically to computerise an existing and effective paper system - could be greatly extended. The introduction of the computer system improved the processing and flow of information within the company. At the same time, once in operation, as each module of the system came on stream, numerous potential additional benefits were identified. As a result, some improvements were made to the processes, as opposed to purely the transmission of information. These improvements were essentially restricted to the use of spreadsheets to replace manual calculations. However, the potential for a fully integrated management information system appeared to be enormous.

The initial computer experience which the staff in the company had been given through a parallel training programme had proved to be necessary, in fact essential, to ensure that the most effective use could be made of the computers. The outcome of the project was therefore both a basic, but effective, information management system, and a reasonably computer-literate staff who were in a position to use the system well. In addition, the staff were now in a position to identify where the information technology could be further applied to enhance the system. The opportunity was now seen to create a management information system which could be far more integrated and effective.

7 Further Developments

Effectively, it became clear that a two-stage approach to the development of the use of IT in a shiprepair SME was required. In the first stage, the need was to improve the flow of information. Using the paper-based system, there had often been up to two days required to write, transcribe, and send information internally. The introduction of the information management system allowed this to be reduced to a matter of minutes, using a central database. The more or less instant access to information which the computer provided speeded up operations considerably. It also reduced transcription, and error rates, which provided additional benefits. Staff time was re-deployed to more useful tasks, principally aimed at securing more business and improving financial control through better billing of clients.

The second stage which was identified during the course of the development, was the improvement of the processes themselves. The opportunity was taken to do this, in particular the use of spreadsheets to create and manipulate estimates and to produce tender offers for the shipowners. The same information was then available as a master form against which to track progress, extras and to maintain a running total of costs for a shiprepair contract.

However, the focus of the work programme was on the transfer of information around the company, not on its creation or effective use.

The work was used as part of the basis for the feasibility study which preceded the SYRIOS project. The wider review which was subsequently undertaken of the requirements and status of this industry sector, in the US and elsewhere as well as in Europe, revealed that there is still a need for effective, integrated IT systems for shiprepairers. This is particularly the case for the SMEs, where there are limited resources and the most volatile operating environment.

There is a need for some form of hybrid system which is specific to the shiprepair problem. The characteristics of such a system can be specified, based on the factors which are critical to the successful management - in planning terms - of a shiprepair contract. These factors are:

The total elapsed time available for the contract. The time to be spent in the repair yard, and hence the delivery date, is in nearly all cases an absolute requirement, and is dependent on a critical path comprising the work items which take the longest times.

The dock time is a major element of the time for most shiprepair contracts. Ships may spend time afloat at a quay prior to and after docking, but the dock is the key facility, and maximising the numbers of ships through the dock is one measure of efficiency for a shiprepair yard. Again, there is a critical path for this segment of the repair, involving the main underwater items.

The activities which combine to set a critical path for a shiprepair contract are:

- Any major engine repairs, afloat or in dock and contributing to total time.
- Any major equipment installations, afloat or in dock.
- Any major refitting activities.
- Steelwork repairs, particularly underwater, affecting dock time.
- Cleaning, painting and any other underwater work affecting dock time.

The first requirement in planning a shiprepair contract is to create a preliminary schedule, based on several elements, including.

- The proposed arrival and departure dates required by and specified by the shipowner,
- The expected dock and quay times, using past contract data,
- The total estimated man-hours and the numbers to be employed on the ship,
- The tasks to be completed, particularly those which require sub-contractors and external services.

Of the tasks only a few will be critical, and a simple network can use these to establish the critical path for the contract. This will be developed without considering resources in the first instance. Provided the times which are identified, and the associated resource levels are realistic (that is, the numbers required can be obtained and deployed) then an appropriate combination of sub-contract and in-house resources can be used. The use of sub contractors, and casual labour in many cases, allows the planning to be done without resource constraints as a major issue.

Once the critical tasks are determined and the overall timescale agreed, the remaining tasks can be scheduled. Again, these may need external (sub-contract or casual) resources as well as internal resources. Account needs to be taken of interferences and dependencies between different trades and contractors, but in most cases, work can be scheduled as required.

There is a further need to look across all the contracts which are current in the shiprepair yard, and to take into account any enquiries which may be converted in the period covered by the shipyard planning horizon. The rapidly changing contract situation, and the possibility of a damaged ship requiring immediate attention, also contribute to the volatility of the planning situation.

Overall, the complexity of the shiprepair industry, the rapid changes in requirements, typically across several contracts and the use of external resources have combined to make planning a neglected aspect of the business processes. In recent years, changes in IT and related areas have produced some opportunities to re-visit planning, with some prospect of success in managing this complex environment. Other areas of operations which have potential for improvement using IT include the estimating of work content, labour cost control, purchasing and the management of the flow of information through and outside the companies.

8   IT and software trends supporting the planning and management process

Previous experience of the industry, and the partial development of an integrated Management Information System (MIS), referred to above demonstrated that it is a pre-requisite that any estimating, planning and other processes used in ship repair should be part of a MIS. This is so as to ensure rapid transmission of information as conditions change. Consequently those responsible for selecting an appropriate system will almost certainly need to be aware of the characteristics of the I T environment in which the planning function is to operate. Some important aspects are outlined below:

Because of the varied nature of the shiprepair business the development of a software framework for an integrated MIS within companies using a variety of business methods and perhaps operating in a variety of countries requires careful consideration. Although some IT trends are reducing differences between software used in different countries, potential requirements can differ due to different cultural practices and the rate of adoption of new technology. For many shiprepair yards the sophistication and affordability of the IT systems available will be a key issue in any decision to adopt a particular product. The probability of successful implementation will also depend on the level of sophistication built into the system.

The nature of the shiprepair business requires rapid response, the ability to handle and co-ordinate many tasks simultaneously, collate data very rapidly and handle many different projects and customers during a typical day. Thus the solutions needed to facilitate concurrent engineering practice require a clear understanding of the product model, the technical and business processes and support documentation.

The industry has problems with an ageing workforce and potential personnel shortages in areas which are important for the key success factors in the industry. Many of these factors concern experience and knowledge and therefore the use of artificial intelligence, or at least rule-based decision making methods, may offer significant benefits for the industry (Bruce et al, 1998).

Due to the time pressures the industry will be very interested in any technology which can collate information quickly, reduce data input, improve the accuracy of information and improve productivity.

The software framework should be multi-tiered and provide the link between the application tools, the underlying business process logic, and the persistent storage medium. There should be a comprehensive ability to communicate electronically over the Internet, through company intranets and other systems.

The product should be built in modules and in such a way that individual sites can chose what functionality to implement and in which order. This aspect should also allow the degree of sophistication of the underlying IT systems to be flexible. Thus a site should be able to add functionality and levels of sophistication over time. For example the estimating modules may have two levels of functionality (i.e. one based on standard values and one based on formulae).

The application should remain open with regard to transfer and access of information i.e. not be tied to specific proprietary databases, Internet providers, browsers or viewers.

There will typically be a Business Process Service Layer which contains the logic that glues the management, design, cost estimation information etc. together. This represents the business processes of a shiprepair yard.

The Data Service Layer is a persistent data store for the information used by the application service layer, and should be structured to facilitate access to and updating of the various contracts which are undertaken.

The cost/performance trends in hardware create opportunities to provide secure systems with back-up and duplication of storage at reduced cost. The cost of storage is also falling, thus allowing the use of the latest database technology on readily available and affordable hardware. This trend will continue. Client-server technology is now maturing and readily available although there are still problems with platform interoperability. The various flavours of UNIX are as diffuse as ever and show no signs of reduction. Lack of binary compatibility is a problem, with some UNIX systems using 64 bit technology giving ready access to large storage devices. UNIX systems will continue to be purchased in large numbers for five plus years specially for servers. This operating system will be supported for many years to come due to the large number of existing users. Most UNIX based systems are robust and stable, can access large storage devices and can provide adequate security. They are suitable for on-line real time systems. UNIX based systems also have scaleability beyond that currently available using Windows and Intel based systems.

The choice of Operating Systems is important, and MS Windows 95, 98 or 3.1 clients will have almost certainly have to be supported by any IT system, due to the probable high installed user base in shiprepair yards. This could pose some fundamental problems, since these systems will not support some of the technologies which may be required and can be unstable compared to Windows NT and the requirements of an on-line real time system.

Client server systems using UNIX servers and Windows for clients are commonplace but carry the overhead of systems administration on at least two platforms and possibly an additional network system. Knowledge of IT systems, both hardware and operating systems is spreading but the successful implementation of IT systems will require training, updating or some recruitment of new personnel. This is also a potential problem for the smaller SMEs in the shiprepair sector.

Documentation Storage includes, in addition to the documentation generated in support of the normal business operations, many documents sent in by customers, prospective customers, approval authorities and suppliers etc. Whilst many of these may be communicated in electronic format in the future, most documents will be sent in hard copy format for some time to come.

Document management as a technology and a discipline has traditionally augmented the capabilities of a computer filing system. By enabling users to characterise documents from many sources document management systems allow users to store, retrieve, and use their documents more easily and powerfully than they can do within the computer file system.

Data exchange continues to be a major problem for technical and particularly graphical information. This arises in part from the underlying mathematical libraries used in CAD systems which have different representations of surfaces and use different tolerances. A basis is needed for transfer of data between equipment suppliers and the shiprepair yards.

One of the principal uses of structured information is to enable Electronic Data Interchange (EDI). Unfortunately different industries create consortia to specify the content model on which they all agree, and which they use to mark up their information so that they can share it with each other easily and efficiently.

The World Wide Web is an ideal venue for electronic data interchange. The Internet will be needed for mobile users such as salesmen, project managers and riding crews, as well as for communicating with customer and with suppliers. Thus many users will have regular access to or use of the Internet. Internet technology will impact on standards used to transfer, view and store data.

The use of the Internet is cheaper than direct point to point solutions although it can suffer from slow response at certain times of the day. The use of e-mail also overcomes the problems of communicating across time zones.

The World Wide Web (WWW) will play a part in the marketing activities of a yard. A web-page-editor should form part of a management system.

The above topics have been incorporated into this paper with the aim of making the reader more aware of those developments in IT which are available to managers and planners. The use of appropriate electronic / IT tools can considerably enhance the management and planning capability of a shiprepair organisation.

9 Conclusions

It is now common practice for a shipowner to request a planning schedule for repairs which are to be carried out. This may well form part of the formal contract documentation. The ability of a ship repair yard to produce a well-documented programme of work, and a schedule is seen by the customer as an indication of a well-managed organisation. The confidence in the shiprepair yard's ability to manage projects effectively is further enhanced by supporting documentation which is readily available and produced in an accurate and consistent manner. The provision of the information is consistent with, and if properly managed supported by, certification to ISO 9000 or other appropriate standard.

For a large shiprepair, and particularly conversion, contract the requirements to demonstrate pre-planning and sound organisation will be equivalent to the "Build Strategy" routinely prepared for new ship construction contracts

The use of information technology in this context is now an expectation of the customer, not an option which a shiprepair yard can exercise if it chooses. These developments will also increasingly apply to sub-contractors, and the ability to electronically access and share information is now a key element of supply chain management. For a shiprepair yard to remain competitive, effective planning and management of contracts, supported by information technology, is a pre-requisite for success.

10 The SYRIOS project

Using the observations above as a start point, the project has been developed and is in progress. The objective of SYRIOS is to develop an innovative IT framework to increase the competitiveness of the operation of small project / contract-oriented shiprepair yards in the European Union. The development will include the integration of the operations systems of the yards: thus streamlining manufacture and repair functions and embracing all the business functions such as sales, marketing, technical and distribution / purchasing.

The results will be of direct relevance to the small shiprepair yard industry sector at a collective level, where individually this would not have been possible. The research will extend the current state-of-the-art, through innovative techniques, and develop new solutions for practical application, leading to increased yard (predominantly SMEs) competitiveness thus securing the future of this sustained market. The SYRIOS consortium has been built to optimise industrial skills, experience and markets, backed by creative concepts and technologies from academia and IT specialists, and supported by specialist project management, dissemination and exploitation resources, including the appropriate trade association.

The research aims to complete a number of key tasks:

- Business modelling as a set of Networked Resources, identified by the ability to process material and information, characterised by specific timescale and resource profiles - Networked Resources are input / output systems which interact and are controlled by certain constraints;

- The establishment of dependable and efficient communication channels among the Networked Resources (shipyards, shipowners, suppliers) - the communication will be facilitated using Electronic Data Interchange techniques;

- Design and implementation of innovative decision support components that will be encapsulated in *Networked Business Objects (NBO)*; these components will enable the shipyard enterprise to make decisions based on accurate, consistent and up-to-date information; the processes that will be addressed include commercial, technical, purchasing, production planning / scheduling, and management information; decision making methods will be utilised in order to provide the user with a sufficient range of operational alternatives.

The IT framework that is proposed will encapsulate business knowledge, will be component i.e. business object based and not transaction based, and will not rely on expensive resources or know-how. It will be firmly based on the models of the business, which are summarised in the activity map. Moreover, the system will be easily configured (assembly based configuration) by the enterprise, it will recognise the Network nature of the interconnections (internal and external to the enterprise), and will take into account the fact that the shop-floor personnel may not be computer literate.

References

BRAIDEN, P., BRUCE, G., HILLS, W. and SNAITH, G.R., (1992), "Computer-aided Engineering in Shipbuilding and Repair", Final Report, Department of Trade and Industry, Contract Report, October 1992

BREWSTER, A., BRUCE, G., EVANS, M. and HILLS, B. (1997), "Development of cost-effective computer management information systems for small shipyards", Journal of Ship Production, May 1997 Vol. 13, No. 2, pp. 125-137, Published by The Society of Naval Architects & marine Engineers, Jersey City, NJ, USA.

BRUCE, G., GRANGER, N. and HILLS, W., "The skills crisis in the UK shipbuilding & shiprepair industry", RINA paper presented at Newcastle upon Tyne University, 19th November 1998

BRUCE, G., HILLS, W. and MCDOWALL, A., "Planning and Managing Shiprepair and Conversion", RINA Conference, May 1999.

DEPARTMENT OF TRADE AND INDUSTRY, (1995), "Study of UK Ship Repair and its International Competitiveness", Contract Reference: EC/4913 First Marine International Limited. August 1995

FILIPIC, B. (1994), "Task Scheduling and Resource Management in Ship Repair Using a Genetic Algorithm", 8th International Conference on Computer Applications in Shipbuilding, Sept 5-9 1994 in Bremen, Germany. (Volume 2). Publisher : Berry Rasmusson Reklam AB, Sweden. ISBN : 91-630-2762-3

HILLS, B and STORCH, R.L, (1995), "Computer Aided Manufacturing in Small Shipyards: a U.S. and U.K. Comparative Study", Journal of Ship Production May 1995. Vol. 11, No. 1, pp. 81-89

LINDAHL, I. (1994), "The Computerisation of the Information Flow in Ship Repair", 8th International Conference on Computer Applications in Shipbuilding, Sept 5-9 1994 in Bremen, Germany. (Volume 2). Published by Berry Rasmusson Reklam AB, Sweden. ISBN: 91-630-2762-3

STEWART, H.P., (April 1997), "Successful Production of a Competitive fixed-price Ship Repair Job", Journal : Marine Technology. April 1997, Vol. 34, No. 2, pp. 96-108, Publisher by The Society of Naval Architects & marine Engineers, Jersey City, NJ, USA.

IMPACT OF INFORMATION TECHNOLOGIES ON THE SHIP CLASSIFICATION PROCEDURE

M. Huther and MF. Renard

Bureau Veritas - Marine Division
17 bis Place des Reflets, 92077 Paris La Defense Cedex, France
mhuther@bureauveritas.com

Abstract

First a short recall of the evolution and progress observed during the last twenty years in hardware and software and of the changes in the classification philosophy is presented. Then the consequences of the IT evolution on the classification rules development are analysed, starting by the review of the possibilities offered by the new IT tools for hull girder, local loads and rules calibration. The use of software for design approval, structure design and management are detailed, pointing out the gains in time and efficiency. Finally, the IT application for ship in-service management is presented dealing with hull state survey, real time monitoring at sea and machinery state survey, and showing the provided help to the owner with respect to the ship efficiency and safety. The conclusion points out the ineluctable evolution toward a network of the whole actors of the maritime world and the importance that standards for data exchanges will have to ensure the necessary efficiency and safety all along the ship life cycle.

1. Background

To obtain a better understanding of the impact of the computing progresses on the Classification Society activities, it could be useful to give a historical view of the use of software and computation in ship classification.

In France, as an example, the first ship structure computation took place in 1968. The reason has been a problem of shear buckling of the transverse rings of the first world built 300 000 tdw tanker. The phenomenon was new and quite impossible to handle by formula and hand calculations. This first exercise allowing to understood what happened and to find a solution, the ship has been at sea without any troubles during a normal life time, marked an important change in ship design. Naval architects and engineers in design offices were discovering that computation was no more something for university R&D centres, and could help them in their design tasks.

Classification Societies also at this same time discovered the capacity of the computation. We shall not say computer capacity as, for example, Bureau Veritas first computer at that period was an IBM 1130 with 8 Ko memory, rapidly extended to 32 Ko.

However such computer, with help of disks and tapes, allows to start calculations which were non practicable by hand or calculators. The first applications in classification were intact and damage stabilities, still water bending moment, static wave bending moments, calculation which were representing a large progress with respect to the existing approximate formula.

The first results has been, from Classification Society point of view, a big change by accepting the introduction in classification rules of direct calculations and physical criteria of acceptance, and for the shipyards better distributed scantlings and hull steel weight reductions.

In parallel to classification activities, Classification Societies entered in the R&D process, making the link between university R&D centres and marine industries. The R&D programmes were concerning Finite Element modelling and practical ship structure calculations (static and vibrations), ship motions and dynamic bending moments on wave computations. Doing so the Classification Societies obtained means to improve existing rules and develop new rules.

They also modified totally their rules and regulation philosophy by introducing the possibility offered to designers to use direct approaches when duly justified. That lead to change rules from non explained formula to scantling processes with definition of the loads, modelling conditions, result criteria of acceptance.

2. Rules developments

In spite of the extended use of computation in ship design, the deletion of all formula and replacement by only direct calculation procedures in classification rules is not yet acceptable. Although the direct computations allow to assess and optimise a yet defined structure scantling, they do not allow to design from the owner specification. Formula based on experience are always necessary to determine the first version of the structure and to fix domains of acceptable scantling variations. Direct calculations, although the progresses during the past years imply a large number of hypothesis and simplifications and the resulting structures must be assessed versus experience, which allows the classification rule formula.

Therefore the Classification Societies make an extensive use of the computers to improve existing rules and develop new rules to cover shipbuilding innovations.

Three areas are the predilection of software applications: hull girder strength which fixes the midship section modulus and has an important impact on the hull steel weight, local loads induced by the sea loads and liquid or bulk internal cargoes which fix the local element scantlings, rules formula safety factors calibrations.

2.1. Hull girder

Referring hull girder strength, the target is to optimise the minimum modulus requirement versus ultimate and fatigue strength. To reach this target it is necessary to obtain the more precise possible values of the long term vertical, transversal bending and torsional moments along the ship.

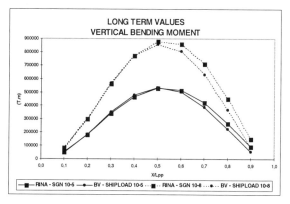

Bulk carrier   L = 85 m

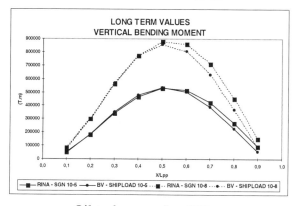

Oil tanker   L = 336 m

Figure 1: Computed wave bending moment curves

Such parameters require the ship motion on wave and resulting loads calculation, which can only done by mean of software. The more commonly used software are based on the strip and spectral theories, although some imprecision exit with respect to quartering following seas and non linear large ship motions. As an example, to determine the bending moment rule formula, a Classification Society may compute and analyse the results of more than a dozen typical ships with their different loading conditions.

To gain in precision, software based on time step integration are also applied, but they cannot be so easily used for systematic calculations and analysis as necessary for rule development. The reason is the difficulty of representation of the time histories of the sea states required to represent the long term scatter diagram encounter by the ship during her life.

2.2. *Local loads*

The local elements scantling require the knowledge of the water and cargo pressures on the hull plates.

The internal pressures, for liquid or bulk, are computed from the resulting gravity and ship motion accelerations. Due to the internal complex tank or hold shape, software are necessary for a good accuracy.

When liquid motions are expected, the liquid dynamic response has to be calculated, which requires to solve the fluid dynamic equations under forced excitations (ship motions). Such calculations are only possible through fluid dynamic software. The latest developments apply finite volume theory with time step integration and allow to compute the exact liquid behaviour and velocity field.

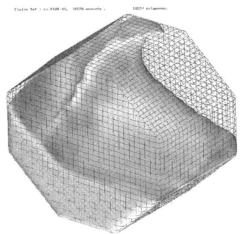

Figure 2: DIVA 3D results illustration for a high filling

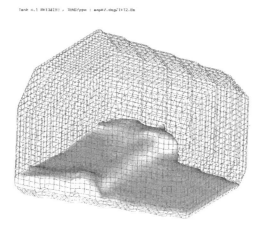

Figure 3: DIVA 3D results illustration for a low fillings

Referring the external hull pressure, the problem is not yet correctly solved. Some methods apply approximations from diffraction, radiation theories and ship motion strip theory computations, but the more promising is the CFD methods, although they are not yet able to handle the ship speed, parameter which is fundamental for ship behaviour correct computations.

2.3. *Safety factors calibration*

The computation offers another alternative to the Classification Societies, the possibility of developing full semi-probabilistic rules. In a semi-probabilistic rule, at the opposite to a classical formulation where few global safety coefficients are introduced, each parameter in a formula is affected by its own partial safety factor.

In such format, the problem faced by the rule developer is to define correctly and coherently each factor, process which is called calibration of the code.

The calibration of a semi-probabilistic code requires three steps:

1) Code safety target definition (safety level to be ensured, acceptable minimum scantling from experience) which is defined versus the application area of the code.
2) Calibration of the partial safety factors $\{\gamma\}$ of each rule considered alone, after verification of the semi-probabilistic format coherence.
3) Code calibration as a whole system for scantling by adjusting the $\{\gamma\}$ of the rules so that the coherence between them is ensured.

The calibration process imply the determination of the reliability of the elements and of the global structure from a detailed reliability analysis in which the mechanical models used for the strength and load calculations (FEM) in the limit state function are more sophisticated than those used in the code verification rule.

The $\{\gamma\}$ are determined from a process based on optimisation methods including a penalty function and constrains followed by a reliability index calculation using FORM/SORM modelling.

Such calibrations are complemented by analysis, with extensive computations, of return experience on ships in-service after damages observations, normal or unexpected, recorded during classification periodical visits.

3. Design approval

The used software by the Classification Societies for rules improvement or development generally require work-station or large computers which are not at the disposal of many engineering, shipyard design offices or owner's technical offices.

The development of powerful personal computers and the general development of this type of equipment's has allowed to develop software for the assessment of the compliance with classification rules and international regulations.

3.1. Drawing approval and certificates

A first step in using the offered possibilities by the personal computers has been the development of a series of dedicated software to design rules. These software are based on very user-friendly platforms and cover classification areas as reviewed in the following.

A series deals with the hull strength and concern longitudinal strength of hull girder, scantlings of plates and longitudinals in any transverse section including buckling verification, optimisation of longitudinal structure scantlings by successive runs of programs.

Support for direct calculations, as specified by rules, can also be performed through software using 3-D beam analysis for primary members with interactive modelling including plane modelling, duplication of 2-D rings in space, creation of symmetrical model by mirror effect, use of graphics for input checking and results outputs. In addition exits software for torsion and shear analysis of open deck ships with calculation of shear stresses induced by vertical and horizontal shear force, longitudinal stresses induced by an external torque all over the hold area and displacement due to torsion.

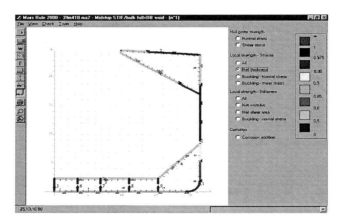

Figure 4: Midship section verification output

Not only structural calculations are concerned. Software exist, for example for automation, allowing an accurate electronic checklist to be drawn up and fulfilled versus the requested automation notation.

To these software of general application, more specialised ones has been developed such as, longitudinal scantling of High Speed Craft, marine fibre-reinforced plastic material properties (skin and sandwich laminates), container lashing strength assessment.

3.2. *International regulations*

But the applications does not only cover the Classification Society rules. Classification Societies has developed software for international regulation application, in particular intact and damage stabilities, probabilistic damage stability for dry cargo according to SOLAS 1997,chapter II-1, part B, IACS unified requirements for bulk carrier safety according to UR S19 & S22 for existing ships or UR S18 & S20 for new buildings. These software helps designers and owners to assess the compliance with the applicable regulations.

For chemical carriers programs allow optimum ship operation and design by generation of chemical cargo lists appended to Statutory and Class Certificates, identifying the carriage capacities of tankers according to ship's characteristics, tank materials, coating and equipment.

Software supports do not only concern sea going ships but also inland navigation. In particular, for inland product vessels PC programs provide the list of products allowed to be carried in accordance with ADNR requirements. The list is based on the table of products in Appendix 4 to the Annex B.2 to the ADNR and includes the transitory arrangements.

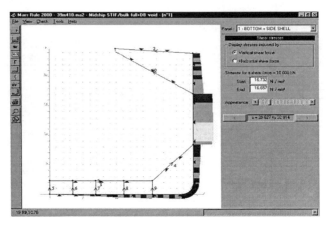

Figure 5: Results of torsion and shear analysis output

4. Structure design and management

The personal computer capacity increases associated with the development data base management systems and of user friendly environments lead to the development of integrated software for design analysis, class rules compliance assessment and feedback surveys. The European Classification Societies systems, on which the following is based are: BV (Bureau Veritas): VeriSTAR, DNV (Det Norske Veritas): Nauticus LR (Llyod's Register): ShipRigth, GL (Germanisher Llyod): Poseidon.

Unlike previous paper-based empirical calculations, the integrated systems provide the Maritime Community with invaluable technical information in a readily usable form.

4.1. Software system functionality

Each vessel has its own dedicated database starting from the design stage. It can be installed at any time during an existing ship's life. Each database is divided into two constituent parts containing different types of information necessary for the hull structure management.

The first section allows the users to examine Classification Society calculations using the same graphical interface. If the user wants to know, for example, which loads have been considered for the structural calculation, clicking on the 'load' icon highlights the corresponding compartments and illustrates their contents. Through simple manipulation of the ship's three-dimensional views, the user can also examine calculation results in a very simple and safe way, without fear of destroying protected Classification Society information. All rule criteria is automatically checked and displayed using unique and powerful, colour-coded stress ratios for immediate visual confirmation.

The system allow calculation following limited modelling as specified in the Classification Society rules but also full ship, mainly necessary for container ships. These vessels, with their wide hatch openings, have required specific developments, in order to account for the torsional moments on the ship's structure.

The second section allow users to store and handle their own data and is mainly use for in-service ship management. More details will be given in the following chapters.

The database always begins in the as-built state, even if the vessel enters the system during its service life. This state represents the start of a ship's history. All events entered into the database will always be compared to this initial state. For each survey, the updated hull condition is analysed and stored in the database. Steel renewal and repairs are therefore easy to forecast and optimise.

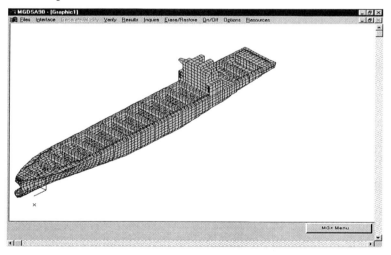

Figure 6: A full 3-D container ship finite element model

The graphical interface allows users to select, by clicking, several plates of the ships structure and determine instantly, the corresponding steel weight. Documented survey photos can also be stored in the database, allowing a pictorial history of the ship to be followed at any time.

4.2. Ship structure assessment

The Microsoft Windows based system can be used to quickly build a new model of the hull from transverse cross-sections. In addition, the finite-element model thus created can be exported to other systems via the incorporated NASTRAN interface. The structural model includes the complete hull and a rough arrangement of the superstructures, in order to obtain a good weight distribution.

For all these elements, and particularly for smaller ships in the range 100-150m in length, only a complete finite-element ship model has sufficient accuracy to study complicated stress combinations induced by local, overall vertical and transverse bending and torsion components.

A complete set of loads has been developed to define a realistic representation of the dynamic load components and combinations suffered by the vessel while at sea. The considered load components are as follows:

- external static and hydrodynamic pressure over the ship length induced by a regular wave of any relative heading and length. These loads are calculated in a transparent manner by the system, using the well-proven hydrodynamic tools used for a very large number of ship types.
- internal static and dynamic pressure loads due to partially or totally filled tanks. The ship model used includes the notion of tank volume, that the user can load inputting only the filling percentage and the density of the fluid.
- concentrated mass loads, like loads due to container stacks stowed in holds or on the deck or any mass where the precise location of the centre of gravity is needed for a proper calculation of the inertia forces. The corresponding user interface is very user friendly and has been developed on the model of modern loading instruments intended for onboard use.
- structural weight of the structure is calculated with high accuracy by the program from the scantlings defined by the user. The remaining items of the shipyard defined lightship weight distribution can be entered in the usual way by entering tabulated values.

The software solves the dynamic system for displacements and stresses, using a time step method, where the different loads, both static and inertial components, are computed for the instantaneous relative position of the waves train and the moving ship. For a complete strength assessment, seven basic load cases are defined , potentially for each analysed loading condition, each of the these load case reaching the Classification Society rules prescribed value of a dominant load effect. The considered effects are the following:

1. vertical wave bending moment amidships (hogging)
2. vertical wave bending moment amidships (sagging)
3. vertical wave shear force at user's defined distance from aft perpendicular,
4. wave induced torsion and horizontal bending at user's defined distance from aft perpendicular,
5. rolling angle and transverse acceleration,
6. relative vertical motion at sides amidships,
7. vertical acceleration at forward perpendicular,

Strength criteria analysed by the system are those defined in the Class Rules, including yielding, buckling and fatigue. Like its predecessors, the system uses the widely acclaimed colour plots of the Element Work Ratios (EWR), displaying the percentage of rules permissible value for every structural element and each load case, taking into consideration all the strength criteria. This considerably simplifies the analysis work on the structure, allowing notably to see in one colour plot a synthesis of the hot spot areas of the whole ship, all load cases being considered.

In addition, and specific to this version, the various moments and torques, including still water values, are calculated internally and displayed. This allow a very quick and really complete analysis of additional loading cases when the structural model is available.

5. In-service ship management

In addition to the personal computers supports, Classification Societies have considered the opportunities offered by the world network development.

Implemented in adequate platforms, the systems can give on-line details of the Ship condition at any time. Such tools facilitate the safer operation of ships able to operate at lower maintenance costs within the envelope of continually updated design regulations. Such application are mainly adapted to owners and Classification uses.

5.1. Hull structure status

The same technical software as reviewed for design are now used for in-service ship operation and survey all along her life. At each Class survey, the Classification Society expert up-date the ship data bank by the observation and measurement results.

The systems can file reports and pictures under various headings ranging from coatings, steel renewal, corrosion, to measured scantlings, damages, and inspections. These headings are not exhaustive, and new customised titles can be added by the owner.

The system divides the ship into compartments, and can recall data under all headings for each particular space. This means that when looking for any information, the user only has to click on the compartment he is interested in. The corresponding data will appear in a preview window, sorted by date or by name as preferred. The information stored can easily be retrieved.

This makes it easier for the ship's operator to track corrosion, and forecast structural reconditioning for shorter, less costly drydockings.

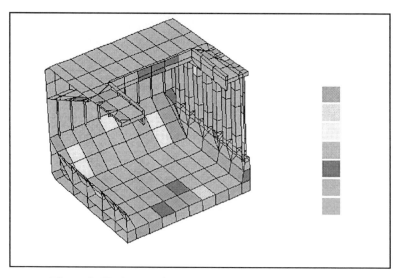

Figure 7: Veristar tank space view, computed stress levels

Another area dealing with the safer ship operation, and now possible due to the IT progresses, concern the ship hull monitoring. The systems, based on PC software provide ship's personnel with 'real time' ship motion and hull stress monitoring information. It helps ensure that the ship operates within design and operational limits, reducing the probability of damage to ship or cargo during loading or unloading and in heavy weather conditions. The system also allow for data recorder to be used for analysis purposes.

The installation enables:

- stresses in the ship to be monitored during loading and unloading
- stresses in the deck while at sea to be monitored and appropriate action taken by the ship's personnel in the event of adverse conditions
- damage due to unfavourable seas to be avoided or reduced

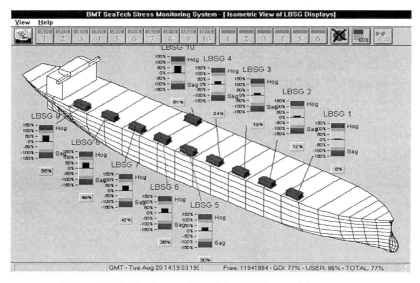

Figure 8: Monitoring on-board installation and limitations

5.2. Certificates status

If private networks are used for the technical activities, ship data are also now available through Internet, so from any phone connecting plug.

Classification Society Internet ship management systems provide two different levels of information: the public information, accessible to anyone having an Internet connection, and the confidential information, accessible only to the Classification Society clients who have applied to obtain the necessary access rights.

The public information correspond to the previously published ones, Register of ships, Society directory, Recognitions and Authorisations, Statutory News.

The confidential information provides Classification Society clients with a unique management tool, allowing shipowners and managers to access, on-line, information entered in the central database, as soon as the surveyor's report has been processed.

The functionality covers:

- Ship's Status: class and statutory position of the different certificates issued by the Classification Society
- Survey reports and certificates: available on-line for viewing and/or printing
- Emulation of future surveys: provides the check-lists that will actually be used by the surveyors during forthcoming surveys.

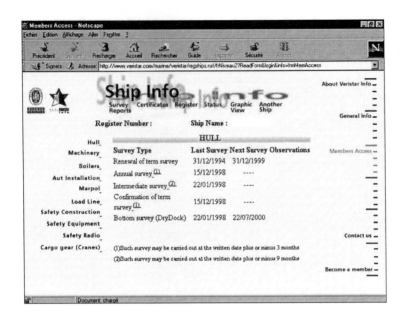

Figure 9: On-line ship information

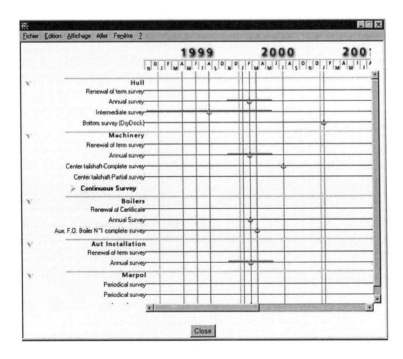

Figure 10: Ship visit planning

5.3. Vessel's equipment and installations

For the 21st century, a new concept of proactive classification is appearing, based on continual risk analysis of the owner's planned maintenance system. The first application concerns the machinery throughout their entire life-cycle.

The procedures respond to current requests for risk-based, maintenance-centred certification and effective life-cycle-cost management. The analysis covers the engine room, and also the impact of all shipboard installations on vessel safety.

To assess the risk, the system uses the details of the vessel's technical description, the intended employment and maintenance procedures provided by the owner, and the information from the Classification Society, manufacturer's advice, publicly available data sources.

During ship operations, data are collected in order to audit the performance of the vessel and its maintenance, which are evaluated through risk analysis tools and readjusted according to the findings. The procedures complement ISM code requirements where appropriate.

A measure for severity of failure effects produced as result of an unwanted event is introduced by means of a Significant Index $\{\sigma\}$, which associated with the Expected Life Failure Frequency $\{\varepsilon\}$ provides the Risk Index $\{\mathbf{R}\}$, measure of the expected loss:

$$\mathbf{R} = \sigma \cdot \varepsilon$$

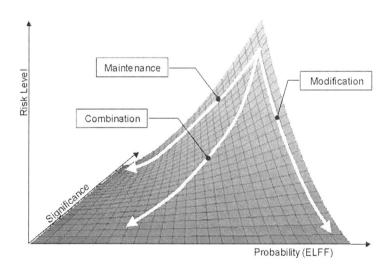

Figure 11: Risk evolution versus ε and σ

The analysis starts by performing a functional dissection of shipboard installations which provides the basis of the system ship database. Then a initial analysis is performed using the owner copy of his planned maintenance system with technical justifications for the various running times.

This is reviewed and submitted to risk analysis, which is discussed and agreed with the owner before implementation of the database.

The owner should have in place a computerised planned maintenance system. This form the basis for control of items for survey and inspection. The system should have controlled access and each entry should be individually signed. A back up system must be installed and kept up-date and there should be a facility to highlight items that are overdue for maintenance.

Annually a risk analysis is performed to review any changes in the operating parameters of the ship and her machinery and any proposals for revision of the planned maintenance system. The review takes place in conjunction with the annual survey and auditing of machinery and performance monitoring.

In addition to annual verifications, during the performance monitoring in the owner's office, the planned maintenance is reviewed for any specific problems that have occurred.

6. Next challenge

This extension of the IT use in shipbuilding, shipping and classification is surely not the end of a period of progress, but the beginning of new times, the information society.

The maritime world does not escape to this general change in the world economy, and the future will be only ensured by improving the on-going mutation.

The success of this mutation will be the result of the efficiency of the methods and tools in allowing access and exchange of the information between the various actors in real time.

But the actors are numerous and so they will be obliged to organise and standardise the data architectures and exchanges between shipyards, equipment manufacturers, Classification Societies, owners, national and international authorities, etc...

This question has been yet perfectly identified by the "politicians" as the G7 minister conference launched 11 pilot projects, one of them dealing with Maritime Information Systems (MARIS).

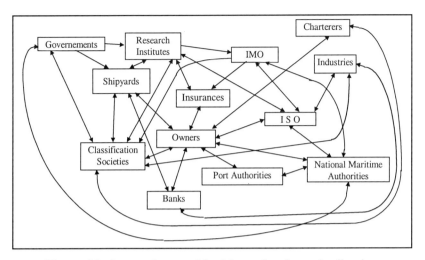

Figure 12: A complex world with needs of standardisation

MARIS is composed by 4 chapters: MARTRANS (Multimodal logistic and transport), SAFEMAR (Safety and Environmental protection), MARSOURCE (Marine resources for the future), MARVEL (Intelligent production systems).

In parallel, with the target of rigorous IT component standard and exchange protocol, within ISO framework, a project name STEP is under progress. This project deals with ship general arrangement, line drawings, ship structure, piping systems, engine and equipments.

Multiple Criteria Genetic Algorithms : A Catamaran Design Study

Pratyush Sen and David Todd

Department of Marine Technology and Engineering Design Centre
Armstrong Building, University of Newcastle, Newcastle-upon-Tyne, UK
pratyush.sen@ncl.ac.uk, d.s.todd@ncl.ac.uk

Abstract

This chapter describes the philosophy and architecture of a multi-objective design tool developed in the ESPRIT IV project called FRONTIER. The paper explains the important concepts that lie behind the tool and demonstrates its use by tackling a multiple criteria trimaran design problem. The system is shown to be able to perform an effective search of the design space and allow the user to efficiently arrive at a single chosen solution to a complex multi-variable design problem.

1 Introduction

Decision making in design consists largely of generation of alternatives and choice over those generated alternatives. As each design option typically has a range of performance attributes the evaluation of the worth of a design is usually one based on multiple criteria evaluations. In other words, designs that are good with respect to some attributes would often be less attractive in terms of other attributes and some form of priority ordering over attributes is necessary in order to rank the competing designs. This priority ordering reflects the value system of the designer in the context in which he finds himself, and is really a mechanism for handling the inherent conflicts in design.

As value systems are necessarily specific to individuals or groups of individuals (e.g. a design team, or an operator) the above approach personalises the choice of the optimal solution. This is quite different from classical optimisation, where a mono-criterion paradigm implies that the formulation of the problem leads directly to the solution in terms of the most favourable value for the criterion. In the absence of any conflict between design performance criteria this could be a rational approach, but general design problems often involve a conflict resolution process as implied above and the analytical and synthesis tools in design must allow for this.

Within the above context decision problems in design may be categorised to fall into two broad classes. These are problems of

(i) Selection : This implies choice of an alternative, over prioritised attributes, given a collection of candidate solutions, and
(ii) Synthesis : This implies synthesis of a design solution or solutions on the basis of prioritised objectives, where an objective can be thought of as an attribute with direction (i.e. cost is an attribute, minimum cost is an objective.)

It can thus be argued that one approach to design could be represented as a multiple criteria synthesis process, to assemble a set of candidate designs, associated with a multiple criteria selection procedure to choose an acceptably efficient design from the set. There is today a large body of techniques (Sen and Yang, 1998) dealing with these classes of problems, with associated opportunities, limitations and data requirements.

The rest of this chapter deals with an approach that was taken by the EU funded project FRONTIER and an example design of a catamaran for seakeeping, that combines FRONTIER's multiple criteria selection procedure with user supplied design routines.

1.1 The Aim of Project FRONTIER

Project FRONTIER is about the design of an "Open System for Collaborative Design Optimisation Using Pareto Frontiers". It was designed to be a multi-partnered collaborative design environment for product optimisation based on multiple objectives. A Pareto frontier is defined by all solutions that are efficient or non-dominated; where non-dominance in turn is defined by reference to solutions where performance enhancement with respect to one objective is only possible at the expense of another. Since all such solutions are inherently superior in at least one performance aspect when compared to another solution, it is obviously true to say that such solutions are non-dominated. This can be examined conveniently for the bi-criteria problem below.

The best solutions in terms of criterion 1 and 2 (both maximising, without loss of generality) are A and B respectively. Hence, the ideal solution that combines the best values of the two criteria would obviously be O. But the physical constraints in a problem do not allow the search for a solution to go beyond the surface defined by AB. Furthermore, any solution X within the feasible region will be dominated by other feasible solutions, represented in this example by the shaded wedge. This will always be the case unless X lies on the surface AB. Thus all non-dominated solutions must lie on this surface. This is termed the Pareto surface or Pareto frontier.

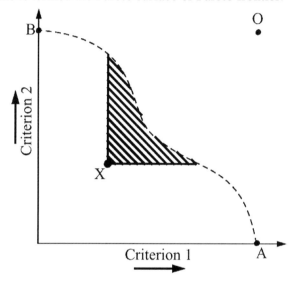

Figure 1 - Dominance

The design problem in a multiple criteria context thus becomes a task in which solutions on the Pareto frontier AB have to be found and the "best" solution selected in terms of the designer's priorities. As will be seen in the following, the philosophy of FRONTIER is to do precisely that.

2 The FRONTIER System

In software terms the FRONTIER system is a general perpose design tool which enables the designer to search for optimal designs over a number of criteria (e.g. cost, efficiency,...) within a given design space. The designs generated during optimisation form the trade-off surface (Pareto Frontier) which is then passed into a selection tool which is used in selecting a single design which best suits the designer's aspirations.

The system is made up of a number of distinct parts which are integrated to form the complete FRONTIER system (Figure 2):

1. GUI - Graphical User Interface, includes visualisation and setup tools.
2. Optimization Tools - Several methods used to perform single/multiple objective optimisation.
3. Distributed Processing Architecture - Manages processes on several machines.
4. Decision Making Tools - Aids designer in selection of 'best' design.
5. Problem Models - Provided by the user to perform search on.

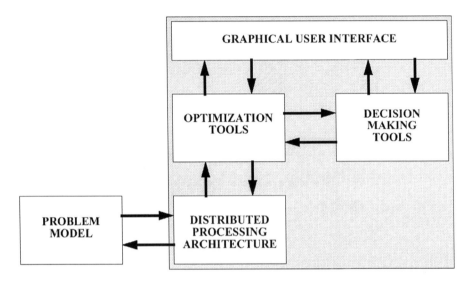

Figure 2 - The FRONTIER System

2.1 GUI

The user interface uses a browser type front end. This allows the system to be implemented using a combination of HTML (Used in web pages) and Java/JavaScript. Such an architecture was chosen because of its portability across systems and as such FRONTIER had been tested successfully on Unix, Linux, SGI, and HP operating systems.

2.2 Optimisation Tools

The system uses an evolutionary technique called the Genetic Algorithm (GA). The GA is a computational technique which evolves solutions from a population of individuals via a process of natural selection and random mating and mutation. The technique was first developed by Holland (1962) but has only come into prominence in the last 10 years due to the increases in available desktop computing power. Goldberg (1989) outlines the simple GA as shown in Figure 3.

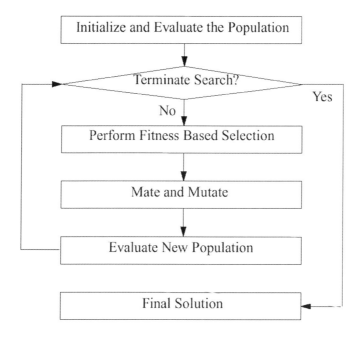

Figure 3 - The simple genetic algorithm

The FRONTIER system uses a GA for carrying out single and multiple objective search. The single objective search method can be used if the simple weights of the various objectives are known in advance or after a set of utility curves (see section 2.4) have been generated. The multiple objective search method used in FRONTIER is an enhanced version of the simple GA, called the Multiple Objective Genetic Algorithm (MOGA). The MOGA randomly generates a population of individuals. Each individual represents one possible design. The individuals can be assessed on several criteria which can be specified based on the problem objectives. These criteria are maintained separately at all times, allowing simultaneous optimisation of all criteria during the search. However, instead of finding a single near-optimal solution, as in the use of normal GA, the MOGA finds a set of solutions which define the trade-off surface between these search criteria. These solutions form the Pareto Set or Efficient Boundary. In a multiple criteria problem one would ideally like to obtain a solution which performs well on all criteria. Due to the nature of such problems, system limitations and constraints in the real world prevent us from doing so. Hence the generation of a Pareto frontier, the set of solutions where any attempted improvement in one criteria will lead to sacrifice in another, provides a useful insight into the trade-offs involved. The system works by initially generating a random set of solutions and evaluating them on all criteria. The solutions are arranged on a grid which is joined end to end and top to bottom to form a toroid shape. Crossover then occurs between solutions which are close to each other on the grid. The idea of crossover is that two designs (parents) can be combined together to form another two solutions (children) which are better than their parents. If this is the case the parents are replaced by the children. As the search progresses from generation to generation the population slowly converges towards the trade-off surface. Eventually progress slows leaving an approximation of the surface defined by a set of Pareto optimal solutions This is shown visually in Figure 4. The MOGA is specially designed to be as efficient as possible and reduce the number of calls to the user evaluation routines. This is done to permit the use of computationally intensive analysis such as CFD and FE modelling within user evaluations without making the optimisation times prohibitive. Another benefit of using the FRONTIER system is derived from its distributed nature, this is outlined in section 2.3. A more detailed technical explanation of the mechanics of the MOGA is available in Poloni (1997).

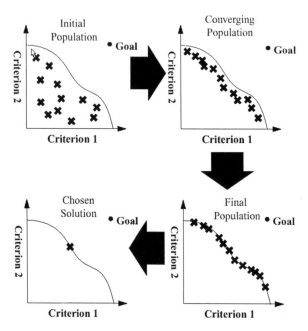

Figure 4 - Multiobjective Search

The system also includes local search tools based on hill climbing algorithms which will perform a limited search from a given starting design. This is used when a good design has been identified but some fine tuning is necessary.

2.3 Distributed Processing Architecture

The industrial partners in project FRONTIER were interested in applying CFD abd FE tools within design. The level of complexity and numerical intensity of such modelling methods led to an increase in the time required to perform the analysis. When using methods such as the Genetic Algorithm many calls to such functions may be required. This results in very long processing times. Additionally there may be a requirement to run different processes on different machines.

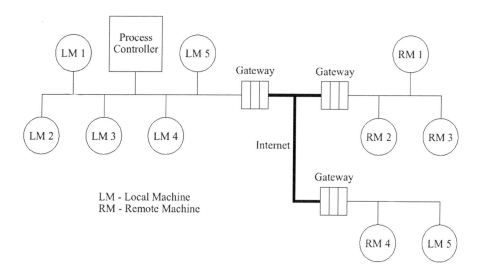

Figure 5 – Distributed Processing Architecture

One of the strengths of FRONTIER as an optimisation tool is the ability to manage the assignment of processing tasks across multiple machines. The system used in FRONTIER is called the FRONTIER Virtual Machine (FVM) where the interaction between the processes appears transparent (Figure 5). The FVM is constructed as follows. A central controller is first chosen to assign tasks to a set of pre-defined hosts. These hosts can either be at the same geographical location as the controller or at remote sites anywhere in the world. The controller can use any combination of hosts to perform processing and will handle the messages being sent from the machines. The setup process is very simple to perform. On each machine a piece of software called the wrapper is executed which enables the machine to send and receive messages. On the controlling machine the FVM is set up by adding the host names of each machine one by one. The controller contacts the machine and confirms if the wrapper is running. If it is the machine will send a response to the controller and it will be enabled for running processes. Once all the machines have been set up the optimisation process can start. The controller is initialised and then begins to aportion evaluation tasks to each machine in the FVM. The machines will perform their tasks and when each machine completes they return the results to the controller and the controller assigns another task. This process is repeated until the search is terminated by the user or all calculations in the MOGA are complete.

2.4 Decision Making Tools

After the MOGA optimisation the decision making software takes a sub-set of the generated designs, ranks them in preference order based on a set of pairwise comparisons, and then derives a set of utility functions to describe the preferences.

The software performs this as follows. Firstly the user examines a sub-set of solutions pairwise and expresses preferences in terms of these. The system then tries to fit a set of utility functions which describe these preferences. A marginal utility function is fitted for each of the criteria in question. These marginal utility functions are then combined to form a single measure of a design's worth. If it is unable to fit a set of utility functions it means that the preferences are inconsistent. In this case the user is informed which comparison is the most inaccurate and he can modify his judgements accordingly by, for example, simply reversing the inconsistent preference statement. After this swap the program is run again. This process is repeated until a consistent set of relationships is identified. At this point a set of consistent utility functions have been found, one for each of the evaluation criteria. The resulting functions can then be used to rank any number of designs, not just the ones used in the comparison set.

Utility functions describe the significance of a metric or criterion to the person judging that metric. A simple example of this is that if someone earns 5000 ECU and is given a 1000 ECU pay rise it is more important to him than someone earning 20000 ECU having the same rise. T increase in utility due to the pay rise is usually more significant for the lower pay. This is shown in Figure 6.

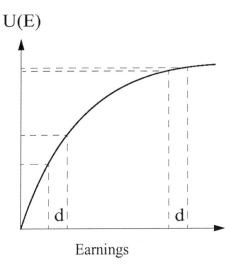

Figure 6 - Utility

The total utility for various competing options is based on a weighted (or non-weighted) summation of the marginal utility functions for all of the criteria involved in a given problem. This total utility value can be used to rank all the available options in preference order. The total utility of a design is calculated as shown in Figure 7.

Here three utility functions exist for Speed, Efficiency and Price respectively. For a design d with attribute values d_{speed}, $d_{eff.}$ and d_{price} its utility with respect to the three attributes can be obtained on the basis of the three marginal utility functions, translating from the attribute to the utility axis. This is done for all the attributes, and the individual utilities are summed to give the total utility as shown in Figure 7. The utility curves are usually normalised such that the total utility of an ideal solution will be 1 and that of the worst possible solution will be 0.

2.5 *Problem Model*

The final component of the FRONTIER system is the problem model. This model is totally user defined and is treated as a 'black box' by the optimisers. The model input is given in terms of a set of design variables and constraints that completely describe the system and the output from the model should be the objective values for that particular set of parameters.

The evaluation may be performed using a single piece of modelling software or a linked collection of tools. The FRONTIER system allows the user to define the evaluation process logic in terms of scripts and also allows the user to define the format for input and output files to allow for resonably easy integration. A simple example would illustrate how the FRONTIER framework could be used in association with user software to conduct multiple criteria design.

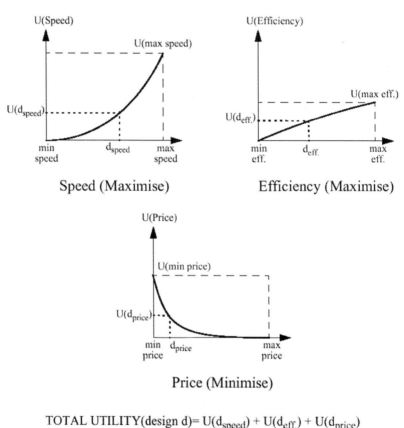

TOTAL UTILITY(design d)= $U(d_{speed}) + U(d_{eff.}) + U(d_{price})$

Figure 7 - Total Utility

3 Multiple Criteria Catamaran Design for Seakeeping

There is often a need for engineering systems to operate over a range of different conditions with variable likelihoods associated with such conditions. This gives rise to the problem of achieving robust designs that perform reasonably well over those conditions. The aim of this example application is to present an optimisation methodology for robust design of catamarans from a seakeeping point of view, using scenario decomposition and Taguchi's robust design approach in a multiple criteria context.

The aim of robust design is to minimise the influence of uncertain or uncontrollable parameters by minimising the variability in the response or performance of a design while keeping its mean response at some target value. This can be done by maximising the signal-to-noise ratio.

In the seakeeping analysis of catamarans where historical data on which to base a new design is relatively scarce it is possible to profitably employ a scenarios based analysis. In this approach the signal-to-noise based formulation of Taguchi can be generalised simply by considering a range of operating scenarios with associated probabilities. In the case in question this uncertainty can be taken to be the directionality of the wave heading, for example. If a collection of S scenarios is used to represent all possible headings of interest then Taguchi's formulation for a single criterion can be written as

$$S/N(x) = -\log_{10}\left[\sum_{s=1}^{S}(f(x/z^s)-T)^2 \times p_s\right]$$

where p_s = probability associated with scenarios s.

z^s = values of uncertain parameters in scenario s.
T = target value of attribute.

Hence for K criteria the above formulation can be generalised to the following :

$$\underset{x}{Max}\{S/N_k(x) = -\log_{10}\left[\sum_{s=1}^{S}(f_k(x/z^s)-T_k)^2 \times p_s\right], k=1,2,..K\}$$

This multiple criteria formulation can be used to derive a Pareto optimal set of non-dominated solutions.

The principal aim here is to minimise certain motion characteristics of a catamaran for different wave headings, ranging between 90° (beam seas) and 180° (head seas), and to do this by choosing appropriate dimensions and hull form. This is done by modifying a parent hull form. The parent demihull has the dimensions shown in Table 1 where L_p, B_p, T_p, H_{sp} represent the length, breadth, draught and separation distance of demi-hulls respectively for the parent form. The parameters LCB_p and LCF_p represent the longitudinal position of the centre of buoyancy and centre of floatation (centroid of waterplane) with respect to the after end of the craft, and CW_{p_p} is a measure of the area of the waterplane. The variables ∇ and C_b represent the underwater volume of the demi-hull and its block coefficient.

Parameter	Parent Value	Parameter	Parent Value
L_p	104.00 (m)	LCB_p	45.408 (m)
B_p	9.00 (m)	LCF_p	43.306 (m)
T_p	4.50 (m)	Cwp_p	0.758
Hs_p	31.00 (m)	CB	0.397
∇	1672.55 (m^3)	Speed	40.0 Knots

Table 1 – The Parent Demihull Characteristics

The seakeeping analysis uses linear strip theory and is fully described in Hearn et al (1994). The design development scheme consists of generation of variant demi-hulls through a systematic variation of some primary and secondary design variables. In this example application a set of variant designs is produced by small changes in the parent form. Four performance criteria are considered. These are the basic responses of heave amplitude, roll amplitude, pitch amplitude and the compound response-relative bow motion. The last criterion is a measure combining the three basic responses, and allows the compound motions of the catamaran to be assessed, especially in oblique wave headings.

The six design variables $x = (x_1, x_2, ...x_6) = (L, B/T, H_s, C_{WP}, LCB, LCF)$ as defined in Table 7.1 are considered in two groups. The primary design variables are length (L), breadth to draught ratio (B/T) and the separation between the demihulls of the catamaran (Hs). The remaining three variables are referred to as secondary variables. The parameter z is evaluated over nine wave headings between 180° (head seas) and 90° (beam seas). In this example all headings are considered equally likely, so $p_s = 1/9$. The robust optimisation strategy thus becomes:

$$\underset{x}{Max}\{S/N_k(x) = -\log_{10}\left[\sum_{s=1}^{S}(f_k(x/z^s) - T_k)^2 \times \frac{1}{9}\right], k = 1,2,3,4\}$$

4 Results

The non-dominated or Pareto optimal solutions are obtained by creating variant designs through a simple perturbation of the three primary design variables. This could have been done using the MOGA optimiser of FRONTIER or equivalent in the following manner. The design variations for the three primary variables are as follows:

L   : 1 ± 0.1 in steps of 0.05 (i.e. $\pm 10\%$ variation in steps of $\pm 5\%$)
B/T : 1 ± 0.1 in steps of 0.05
H_S : 1 ± 0.1 in steps of 0.05

Initially the FVM could be set up to use three machines to reduce processing time. More processors could be used. The set up screen from FRONTIER is shown in Figure 8. The user may add and remove hosts to the list and also create groupings of machines for easier management. The controller itself can also act as a processing element and is called 'localhost'.

The optimisation phase could then be initiated and the system left to generate and optimise designs. During this procedure the processes can be monitored and each machine has a state indicator demostrating what phase of the evaluation process it is in. Following completion of search design tables (Table 2) and graphs (Figure 9) can be generated. Figure 9 shows the trade-off between roll and pitch. An emerging Pareto frontier towards the upper right hand corner of the figure is clearly discearnible.

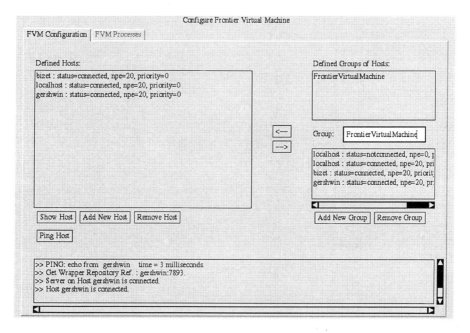

Figure 8 – Setting up the FRONTIER Virtual Machine

	Parameters			Criteria			
	ΔL%	ΔB/T%	ΔHs%	Heave(dB)	Pitch(dB)	Roll(dB)	RBM(dB)
1	-5.0000	-10.0000	-10.0000	6.9372	15.3381	2.4447	6.3923
2	5.0000	10.0000	10.0000	6.8438	19.1872	2.5865	6.8327
3	0.0000	10.0000	10.0000	6.1819	7.9100	-0.3776	8.5016
4	5.0000	5.0000	10.0000	6.9329	16.7476	7.4053	6.4656
5	0.0000	5.0000	10.0000	6.1645	7.8047	5.5222	10.0961
6	10.0000	0.0000	10.0000	6.8808	13.0745	10.8571	5.2839
7	5.0000	0.0000	10.0000	6.9001	11.8422	8.1982	5.0751
8	-5.0000	-5.0000	0.0000	6.9762	13.4082	5.4809	4.9013
9	-10.0000	-5.0000	0.0000	7.2764	11.1131	4.7353	4.3594
10	0.0000	-5.0000	-10.0000	6.1508	7.6588	8.3186	9.8139
11	-10.0000	-5.0000	-10.0000	7.2764	11.1131	3.8911	4.9367
12	-5.0000	-5.0000	-10.0000	6.9762	13.4082	4.7291	5.6957
13	-10.0000	-10.0000	-10.0000	7.2411	12.9420	3.6884	5.7528
14	10.0000	10.0000	10.0000	6.8514	17.9598	6.9071	6.1825
15	10.0000	5.0000	10.0000	6.8908	15.8289	9.1926	5.9075
16	-10.0000	-5.0000	10.0000	7.2764	11.1131	5.0582	3.7533
17	10.0000	-5.0000	10.0000	6.6281	9.9164	11.4248	3.8082
18	10.0000	-10.0000	0.0000	7.2411	12.9420	3.9183	5.2209

Table 2 – The Non-dominated solution set

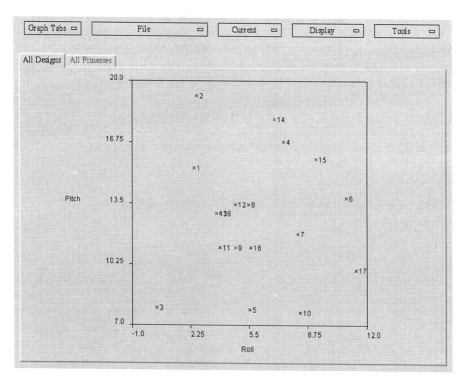

Figure 9 – Output Designs plotted on Pitch and Roll axes.

The results show that beneficial motion characteristics can be obtained for both positive and negative changes in design variables. However, some of the detailed results are worth noting. For heave response the best solutions

326

are (9,11,16). These results indicate that a reduction in L and B/T is beneficial, irrespective of changes in H_S. Thus the value of H_S can, within reason, be chosen on the basis of other considerations. The best solution for pitch (2,14) indicate increases in all three primary design variables. In roll the two best solutions (6,17) have the maximum permissible increases in L and H_S with either no or negative increase in B/T. The principal point of interest is that conflicting changes in design can produce comparable signal-to-noise ratios.

Design's Rank:

Rank	Design No.	Rank Value
1	2	0.999382
2	14	0.92495
3	4	0.847703
4	15	0.782076
5	1	0.752088
6	12	0.610883
7	8	0.583954
8	13	0.578669
9	6	0.577406
10	18	0.565806
11	7	0.481061
12	11	0.421317
13	9	0.370967
14	16	0.254337
15	3	0.218906
16	5	0.211067
17	10	0.200195
18	17	0.181579

Figure 10- The Final Ranking of Designs

These designs were then passed directly into the FRONTIER decision making tool. To identify the overall best solution pairwise comparisons can be made in order to derive a set of utility functions.

Thus, if Alternative 2 is preferred to 9
       Alternative 4 is preferred to 3
       Alternative 14 is preferred to 11

and   Alternative 15 is preferred to 16

then the ranking (Figure 10) and utility curves (Figure 11) obtained and are illustrated on the following page.

It is obvious that to be in harmony with the above pairwise comparisons pitch is the most important criterion, and solutions with good pitch characteristics therefore come out on top. Since the sum of the individual utility values based on the marginal utility functions of Figure 11 constitute a single composite performance criterion, it would be possible to use this to carry out a single criterion based search to find the overall "best" solution that currently may not even be in the list of 18 candidate designs shown in Table 2 and Figure 10.

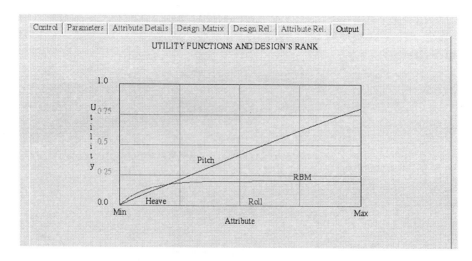

Figure 11 – The Generated Utility Functions

5 Conclusions

This contribution explains and demonstrates a Multi-Disciplinary Optimisation tool which wa recently developed within the EU funded project FRONTIER. The capabilities of the system make it suitable for performing initial and detailed engineering design and allow the user to efficiently investigate design spaces within a multiple criteria context, balancing competing design requirements.

Acknowledgements

FRONTIER was developed for a European Commission funded project within the ESPRIT IV framework. FRONTIER Consortium Partners : University of Bergen (Norway), University of Newcastle (UK), University of Trieste (Italy), British Aerospace (UK), Calortecnica (Italy), Daimler-Chrysler Aerospace (Germany), DERA (UK), Zanussi (Italy). More information can be found on the web site: http://frontier.ii.uib.no/ .

References

D.E. GOLDBERG, (1989), "Genetic Algorithms in Search Optimization and Machine Learning", Addison-Wesley, ISBN 0-201157-67-5

G.E. HEARN , P.N.H. WRIGHT and W. HILLS, (1994), "Seakeeping for Design: The Demands of Multihulls in Comparison to Monohulls", *Proceedings of International Conference on Computer Applications in Shipbuilding 94*, Vol.2, pp11.125-11.144.

J.H. HOLLAND (1962), "Outline for a Logical Theory of Adaptive Systems", *Joint Association of Computing Machinery*, Vol.9, pp297-314.

C. POLONI , M. FEARON and D. NG, (1996), "Parallelisation of Genetic Algorithm for Aerodynamic Design Optimisation", *Adaptive Computing in Engineering Design and Control 96*, I. C. Parmee (Ed), ISBN 0-905227-61-1 University of Plymouth, UK, pp59-64.

P. SEN and J.B.YANG, (1998), "Multiple Criteria Decision Support in Engineering Design", Springer-Verlag, London , ISBN 3-540199-32-2.

AUTOMATIC FAIRING AND SHAPE-PRESERVING METHODOLOGIES

P.D. Kaklis[1] and H. Nowacki[2]

[1] Ship-Design Lab, Dept. of Naval Architecture and Marine Engineering, National Technical Univ. of Athens, 9 Heroon Polytechneiou, Zografou 157 73 Athens, kaklis@deslab.ntua.gr

[2] Institut fuer Schiffs- und Meerestechnik, Fachgebiet Schiffsentwurf, Technische Univ. Berlin, Sekr. SG 10, Salzufer 17-19, 10587 Berlin, Horst.Nowacki@ism.tu-berlin.de

Abstract

The availability of robust and efficient geometric kernels is of major importance for the satisfactory performance of any CAD/CAM system. This paper focuses on the issues of *fairness* and *shape-preservation,* that play an important role in the process of creating high quality, from both the functional and aesthetic points of view, free-form curves and surfaces. More specifically, the paper provides the CAD/CAM practitioner and software developer an overview of the outcomes of the Human Capital and Mobility Network FAIRSHAPE (project: ERBCHRX-94-0522, duration: 1994-1997), devoted on the development of automatic methodologies for creating fair and/or shape-preserving curves/surfaces in the context of interpolation or approximation.

1. Fairing and Shape Preservation

Computer Aided Design (**CAD**) has nowadays become an indispensable part of the industrial system. Computer Aided Geometric Design (**CAGD**), which constitutes the geometric kernel of CAD, is of major importance for the satisfactory performance of any CAD system.

One of the every-day tasks, that a modern CAD system should be able to accomplish efficiently and robustly, is the generation of a *fair (visually pleasing)* curve, that interpolates or approximates, within a designer-specified tolerance, a set of 2D or 3D points. Even when a very flexible curve representation scheme, like *B*-splines, is used, it is quite possible that, for some data sets, the resulting curve is not fair enough. In this case, some processing *(fairing)* of the geometry of the curve is required, in order to reach an acceptable curve. Clearly, the notions of *fair (curve/surface)* and *fairing (process)* admit of various interpretations, which stems from the diversity of CAD environments in which fairing is to materialized. Nevertheless, and without attempting to give a universal definition, we may legitimately assert that:

1. ***Fairness*** *is a geometrical and/or functional property of a shape (curve/surface) or shape segment, that is usually quantified by measures based on integrals of shape characteristics, e.g., minimum strain energy or minimum integral of curvature squared, and*

2. ***Fairing*** *is the process of improving the fairness measure in face of given equality and inequality constraints.*

Far more difficult is the task of generating a fair surface from a given set of scattered 3D data points or a network of curves with regular (e.g., quadrilateral) or irregular (e.g., quadrilateral mixed with triangular) topology. It is rarely sufficient to design composite surfaces, that satisfy only interpolation and boundary smoothness conditions. Within individual surface patches, flat spots, regions of excessive curvature or unwanted undulations often mar the appearance of a surface that otherwise fits well to its neighbors. Practical application abound for this technology in the design of the outer skin of automobiles, the design of ship hulls and the design for aircraft.

An obvious approach towards curve-fairing is interactive (real time) fairing; here, an expert user identifies the control points that need to be modified, introduces appropriate corrections and plots the new curve and the corresponding curvature plot. This process is repeated until a curve of acceptable fairness is obtained. Interactive fairing of curves as well as surfaces is cost-inefficient, for it makes extensive use of human resources (where cost continuously increases) and minimal use of computer power (where cost continuously decreases).

Generally speaking, the situations in which fairing is necessary lie in a spectrum, at one end of which is shape design, while at the other one is:

Shape preservation, *i.e., preservation of the positivity, monotonicity, convexity and other intrinsic shape characteristics of the curve/surface from* *which the given data set has been obtained via a manual, interactive or automatic measuring technique.*

At this latter end, a CAD system should possess automatic methods capable for generating curves and surfaces that preserve the shape of the underlying data (data points or curve networks) to be interpolated or approximated. In other words, automatic shape-preserving methodologies permit a CAD system to represent the geometry of an object to be manufactured with far greater accuracy than usual. Recalling that the modern trend in manufacturing is to move quality assurance from quality control of the product to quality control of the production process, one can legitimately expect that a CAD system, endowed with shape-preservation methodologies, will definitely improve the performance of the associated **Computer Aided Manufacturing (CAM)** system.

2. Methodologies, Algorithms and Comparative Studies

This section can be used as a navigation tool in the contemporary scientific literature on automatic algorithms for fairing and shape-preservation with emphasis on shape-preserving interpolation or approximation, alternative fairness metrics and fairing processes as well as industrial applications that rely on the use of such techniques.

(i) Shape-Preserving Interpolation and Approximation for Curves and Surfaces

- *Shape preserving interpolation by planar curves; see Goodman (1996).* This review paper discusses alternative requirements for shape preserving interpolation by planar curves. How these may be satisfied is then illustrated for four different schemes employing C^2/G^2 polynomial/rational polynomial splines.

- *Co-convexity preserving curve interpolation; see Carnicer and Floater (1996a).* This work proposes an algorithm for constructing C^1 co-convexity preserving interpolants, that is to say, functions which are convex where the data is convex and concave in regions where the data is concave. The interpolants can be chosen to consist of cubic and parabolic pieces. The main tool is the numerical computation of C^2 convexity preserving interpolation to convex data arising from the minimization of certain functionals.

- *Shape-preserving interpolation in R^3; see Kaklis and Karavelas (1997).* This paper develops and tests a simple automatic algorithm for constructing curvature- and torsion-continuous interpolants in R^3, which are shape-preserving in a sense that takes into account the convexity, torsion, coplanarity and collinearity information contained in the polygonal line connecting the interpolation points. The algorithm exploits the asymptotic properties of a family of C^2-continuous polynomial splines of non-uniform degree, which tend to the above-mentioned polygonal line, as the segment degrees tend to infinity. The performance of the algorithm is tested for a three-dimensional data set, containing coplanar and collinear groups of points as well.

- *Local schemes for constructing G^2-continuous shape preserving polynomial sextic splines interpolating planar and spatial data; see Asaturyan et al. (1998a, 1998b).* The first method is a local scheme for interpolation of two-dimensional data that constructs shape-preserving parametric curves with fairness characteristics. The curve is constructed from piecewise polynomials of degree six and exhibits geometric continuity of order two. The second scheme is an automatic algorithm for constructing shape-preserving interpolants in R^3, which conform with the convexity and torsion information contained in the polygonal line that connects the given interpolation points. The resulting curve is curvature and torsion continuous, obtained via piecewise polynomials of degree six.

- *Rational shape-preserving interpolation in R^3; see Goodman and Ong (1996).* This work firstly discusses requirements and alternative criteria for spatial shape-preserving interpolation. Then, it proposes two local schemes using rational cubics. Both schemes ensure continuity of tangent directions and magnitude of curvatures, while the second one gives curves with continuous osculating planes.

- *Abstract schemes for constrained interpolation; see Costantini and Sampoli (1998).* The proposed techniques describe how a method similar to that of alternating projections can be used to obtain viable algorithms for a general and abstract formulation of constrained curve construction problems.

- *Shape-preserving approximation of curves; see Juettler (1997a).* This method generalizes an algorithm of Dierckx to the case of planar parametric curves. Using a reference curve it generates linear sufficient conditions for the convexity of the approximant. This leads to a quadratic programming problem which can be solved exactly, e.g., with an active set strategy.

- *Discrete linear conditions ensuring the local convexity of parametric tensor-product Bezier surfaces; see Juettler (1997d).* This work provides a method for the construction of linear sufficient convexity conditions for polynomial tensor-product spline functions. As the main new feature of this construction, the obtained conditions are *asymptotically necessary:* increasing the number of linear inequalities in a suitable manner will adapt them to any finite set of convex spline surfaces. Based on such linear constraints, the problem of least-squares approximation of scattered data by convex spline surfaces takes the form of a quadratic programming problem.

- *Discrete convexity criteria for tensor-product parametric B-spline surfaces; see Koras and Kaklis (1999).* This paper provides four alternative sets of discrete conditions, which ensure that a patch of a parametric tensor-product B-spline surface is locally convex. These conditions are at most of degree six with respect to the control points of the surface. Their weakness is analytically investigated and graphically illustrated for a bicubic *B*-spline surface of industrial interest.

- *Shape-preserving interpolating skinning surfaces; see Juettler (1997c).* In this work, a sequence of given contour curves is interpolated by a surface composed of tensor-product *B*-spline patches. The interpolation scheme preserves the signs of the sectional curvature of the contours. Based on an appropriate linearization of the shape constraints, this task is formulated as a quadratic problem which is then handled with the aid of an active set strategy.

- *Convexity-preserving curve and surface fitting; see Juettler (1997b, 1998a, 1998b).* This bunch of methods is based on the use of linearized convexity conditions for the construction and modification of parametric spline curve and surfaces. With the help of a so-called reference curve/surface it is possible to find data-dependent systems of linear inequalities for the control points, which imply the desired convexity properties. As a consequence, several problems of shape-preserving curve or surface construction and modification can be formulated as optimization problems with linear constraints.

- *Convexity preserving interpolation of scattered data; see Carnicer and Floater (1996b).* All convex interpolants to convex bivariate Hermite scattered data are bounded above and below by two piecewise linear functions u and l, respectively. This work discusses numerical algorithms for constructing u and l and how, in certain cases, they form the basis for constructing a C^1 convex interpolant using Powell-Sabin elements.

(ii) **Fairness Metrics and Fairing Algorithms**

- *Convexity-preserving fairing; see Pigounakis and Kaklis (1996).* This work proposes a two-stage automatic algorithm for fairing C^2-continuous cubic parametric *B*-splines under convexity, tolerance and end constraints. The first stage is a global procedure, yielding a C^2 *B*-spline which satisfies the local-convexity, local-tolerance and end constraints imposed by the designer. The second stage is a local fine-fairing procedure employing an iterative knot-removal knot-reinsertion technique, which adopts the curvature-slope discontinuity as the fairness measure of a C^2 spline. This procedure preserves the convexity and the end properties of the output of the first stage and, moreover, it embodies a global tolerance constraint. The performance of the algorithm is discussed for four data sets: a circular point-set, a station from a model of a semi-planning craft, the hub of a turbine blade and the midship section of a *full-body* ship.

- *Numerical experimentation with the Roulier-Rando fairness metrics; see Gerostathis et al. (1999).* The Roulier-Rando fairness metrics attempt to quantify the difference between a surface and a perfectly fair primitive shape, e.g., sphere, cylinder, plane, that the surface should locally resemble. In this work, the afore-mentioned metrics are firstly expressed for arbitrarily parameterized surfaces. Next, the authors' numerical experience with an implementation of the metrics is presented and illustrated by means of an example of academic and one example of industrial interest.

- *Removing shape failures from tensor-product B-spline surfaces; see Kaklis and Koras (1997). The p*aper studies the effect caused, on the local shape of a tensor-product *B*-spline surface, by the movement of a subset of its control net. We then propose two discrete approaches for removing shape failures from such surfaces, without altering them more than is needed. The second approach is a simple quadratic-programming method, that is suitable for restoring the shape of almost shape-preserving tensor-product *B*-spline surfaces. The performance of the proposed method is tested and discussed for three industrial data sets, originating from the automotive industry (part of the roof of a car, part of a car motor-hood and part of a car's fender).

- *Comparative study of alternative curve-fairing techniques; see Nowacki et al. (1996).* In this work, results are compared for different choices of a fairness criterion applied to a variety of data sets. The improvements achievable by going from integer to rational cubic B-spline curves are examined in particular. Fairness quality can be raised both by lessening the constraints as well as increasing the freedoms in curve representation.

- *Analysis and visualization of curve properties; see Westgaard and Heimann (1998).* This work gives an overview of different measures and techniques for investigating the local properties of a curve. These measures are based on curve derivatives, the Frenet frame, curvature and torsion, as well as their derivatives. Two promising geometric measures are introduced, namely variation of curvature and variation of torsion, allowing to reveal curve deficiencies that are not detectable form the curvature and torsion distributions. To judge the quality of a curve, good intuitive visualization techniques are needed. In this connection, appropriate visualization techniques are developed that enable showing the geometric properties *close* to the curve.

- *Higher-order fairness measures for surface interpolation; see Nowacki et al. (1998).* This work is a comparative study that describes the experiences gained in applying different (up to the fourth) orders of fairness measures to two specific test cases, a single-patch car hood and a multiple-patch mesh interpolating a ship surface. A modular fairing toolkit, the GoTools software, was developed and tested in which the fairness measures and constraints can be systematically varied without changing any other assumptions. The article investigates the effect of different fairness measures upon the characteristics of the resulting shapes.

- *Fair surface reconstruction from point clouds; see Dietz (1998a).* The method attempts to reconstruct fair B-spline surfaces from scattered data points. The points are assumed to have arbitrary boundaries and varying densities; additionally normal vector information may be given. The basic idea of the presented algorithm is to obtain a smooth approximation surface by simulating the deep-drawing process of a metal sheet. The only prerequisite is a distance and an angle tolerance, all other quantities being automatically computed during the iterative algorithm. This includes the parameterization of the points, the appropriate degree of smoothing as well as the necessary number of patches. The well known thin plate energy is utilized and supplied with a local support to yield better results. The whole reconstruction algorithm is largely linear and stable.

- *Energy-based fairing techniques for curves and surfaces; see Hadenfeld (1996).* These methods are based on a local iterative scheme for fairing polynomial or rational B-spline Bezier curves and surfaces. Changing one control point in every step and using a quadratic fairness functional, the main advantage is that we can determine an exact solution of this new control point and that we can simply fulfill a given distant tolerance constraint.

(iii) Applications

- *Parameterizing wing surfaces using Partial Differential Equations; see Bloor and Wilson (1996).* A method is presented for generating three-dimensional surface data given two-dimensional section data. The application on which this paper concentrates is that of producing wing surfaces through a set of airfoil sections. It is an extension of a new method for the parameterization of complex three-dimensional shapes, called the **PDE** (Partial Differential Equation) Method. The method views surface generation as a boundary-value problem, and produces surfaces as the solutions of elliptic partial differential equations of fourth order.

- *Aerodynamic design of a wing-body combination; see Sevant et al. (1998).* This work deals with the design of a wing-body combination with maximized lift. Most emphasis is placed upon the design of the wing-body fairing which connects the body and the wing. The fairing is created using the PDE method. The boundary-value-problem approach adopted by this method ensures inherent continuity (to any required degree) between adjacent surface patches and, also, enables complex surfaces to be parameterized using a small number of shape parameters. To obtain maximum lift, an aerodynamic analysis method is coupled with a method for numerical *minimization*. This approach to aerodynamic design, known as direct numerical optimization, has the major drawback of potentially prohibitive computational costs. However, the succinct parameterization afforded by the PDE method yields substantial reductions in these costs. Results are presented which illustrate the success of this design approach in achieving a wing-body combination with maximized lift.

- *Creation of fair B-spline fillets; see Dietz (1998b).* This method handles the problem of fair filling holes in CAD models with trimmed tensor product *B*-spline surfaces. The boundaries of the holes may be n-sided or even arbitrary. Besides the boundaries themselves, tangential information is given either by normal vectors along the boundaries or via strip of sampled points surrounding the hole. The surface fillet to be computed has to satisfy prescribed distance tolerances and angle tolerances at the boundaries. The basic idea of the method is to simulate the deforming process of a metal sheet. This is done by means of an iterative algorithm utilizing thin plate energy minimization, least squares techniques and parameter correction. In a final step, the overlapping parts of the *B*-spline surface are trimmed away at the boundaries of the hole.

- *Fair filleting between curves and surfaces; see Ginnis (1998).* This method enables the interactive construction of a non-circular C^2-continuous fillet between two given intersecting curves. The basic requirement is a smooth and visually pleasing curvature distribution. The algorithm was developed in close contact with DaimlerChrysler designers. An extension to surface filleting is also included.

- *Interpolation and approximation with developable surfaces; see Hoschek and Schneider (1997).* Developable surfaces, i.e., ruled surfaces with zero Gaussian curvature, can be described with the help of dual splines in R^3. The developable surfaces are envelopes of a one parameter set of planes. This work proposes algorithms for interpolation and approximation of lines, points and planes with developable surfaces and discusses applications as feeder and blankholder constructions.

- *Ship-lines fairing; see Pigounakis et al. (1996).* Three-dimensional curves are playing an increasing role in ship-hull modeling and many other areas of CAD. The problem of evaluating and improving the fairness of such a curve is considered in this work and three solutions (algorithms) are proposed representing all major methodologies currently pursued by CAD researchers: local fairing by knot removal, and local/global fairing based on ``energy" minimization. The performance of the algorithms is studied for both cubic and quintic B-splines using realistic test-cases. Finally, a comparison with existing techniques is presented and some visualization tools for spatial-curve fairing are briefly discussed.

- *Comparing two fairing methods in the context of Tribon Initial Design; see Ives-Smith (1996).* A comparative study of two methods for the automatic fairing of *B*-spline curves is made. The methods discussed are the Eck-Hadenfeld algorithm and the Pigounakis-Sapidis-Kaklis method. By using existing datastores from the Tribon Initial Design module LINES, tests were carried out to evaluate the effectiveness of the two algorithms.

3. A (still ongoing) **Benchmarking Experiment**

According to the approved Work Programme of FAIRSHAPE, the Steering Committee of the project has decided to undertake and materialise a Benchmarking Experiment, aiming to establish a state-of-the-art evaluation of the quality of fairness, achievable by current curve and surface fairing and shape-preserving methodologies in the context of alternative fairness measures and geometric constraints.

Since such an initiative should not be limited within FAIRSHAPE, the scope and the participation rules were distributed by e-mail, in early spring '97, to an extensive list of European researchers that are active in the area of CAGD. As a result of this, rather limited, publicity, two of the eventually received contributions originated from research groups not belonging to the network. Overall, the current Benchmark Collection comprises eight contributions, stemming from six universities and two industries. A representative sample from this collection will appear in a volume under preparation by Applegarth et al. (1999). The material in this book is organised in three major chapters, focusing on:

Shape-Preserving Interpolation, presenting two contributions from benchmarking with the three-dimensional *chair* point-set (see Fig. 1).

Fairing, presenting three contributions from benchmarking with the *chine3* curve from a fast boat (see Figs. 2) and four contributions from benchmarking with a patch from the *hood* of a car-model (see Fig.3).

Constrained Approximation, presenting three contributions from benchmarking with measurements from the surface of a *lens* (see Fig. 4) and two contributions from benchmarking with a set of *waterlines* near the fore part of a ship (see Fig. 5).

Each benchmark problem is documented with a description of the input data, in text and graphics format, and the associated constraints, e.g., shape constraints, prescribed boundary tangents or fixed tolerances with respect to the control points of a curve/surface. Next, the documentation includes the contribution of each participant, structured as follows:

- the name and address of the scientists that have been involved in the experiment,
- a very brief description of the adopted technique, usually pointing to the pertinent reference(s) of the scientific literature, and
- the values of the ensuing list of *fairness functionals*, that measure the fairness of the resulting fair curve/surface.

Curve fairness functionals: Let $Q(u)$, u in $I[u_1,u_N]$, be a sufficiently smooth parametric curve in the two/three-dimensional affine space E^2/E^3, with s, • and • denoting its arc length, curvature and torsion, respectively. The functionals, adopted for measuring the fairness of a curve, have as follows:

L_{2j} = integral, over I, of the squared norm of the j-th parametric derivative of $Q(u)$, j=1,2,3,

$L_{2\bullet}$ = integral, over I, of the square of the curvature • of $Q(u)$,

$L_{2\bullet'}$ = integral, over I, of the square of the derivative of • with respect to the arc length s of $Q(u)$,

$L_{2\bullet}$ = integral, over I, of the square of the torsion • of $Q(u)$,

max_• = maximum, over I, of the absolute of the curvature • ,

#mono_• = number of monotonic segments, over I, in the curvature distribution • ,

max_• = maximum, over I, of the absolute of the torsion • ,

#sign_• = number of sign changes, over I, in the torsion distribution • .

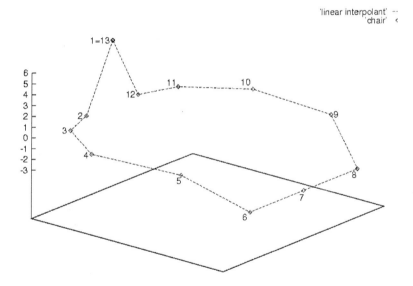

Figure 1. Benchmarking in the area of **Shape-Preserving Interpolation:** the *chair* data set, **provider:** NTUA, **basic constraint:** smooth interpolant imitating the shape of the polygonal interpolant.

Surface fairness functionals: Let s(u,v), (u,v) in • =I[u_1,u_N]x I[v_1,v_M], be a sufficiently smooth parametric surface in the three-dimensional affine space E^3, with • $_i$, i=1,2, denoting its principal curvatures. The functionals, adopted for measuring the fairness of a surface, have as follows:

L_{22} = thin plate energy of $s(u,v)$,

L_{23} = integral, over • , of the sum of squared norms of the parametric partial derivatives of $s(u,v)$ with respect to uuv and uvv,

$L_{2\cdot 1,2}$ = integral, over • , of the sum of the squared principal curvatures of $s(u,v)$,

$max|•_{1+2}|$ = maximum, over • , of the sum of the absolute values of the principal curvatures of $s(u,v)$,

$maxK$ = maximum, over • , of the absolute of the Gaussian curvature • =•$_1$•$_2$ of $s(u,v)$,

$maxH$ = maximum, over • , of the absolute of the mean curvature $H=0.5(•_{1+}•_2)$ of $s(u,v)$.

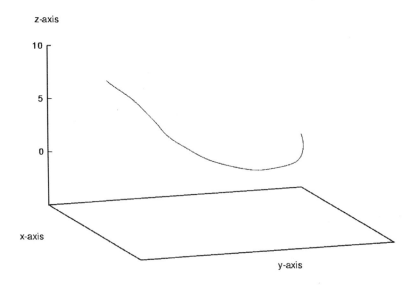

Figure 2a: Benchmarking in the area of **Fairing:** the *chine3* curve, **provider:** NTUA, **basic constraint:** improve the curvature and torsion distributions of the curve at a maximum deviation of 20 mm from the above initial curve.

The documentation concludes with graphical information, usually containing curvature and torsion plots (see, e.g., Figs. 2b,c), for curves, and Gaussian-, mean-curvature as well as isophote distributions (see, e.g., Fig. 3) for surfaces.

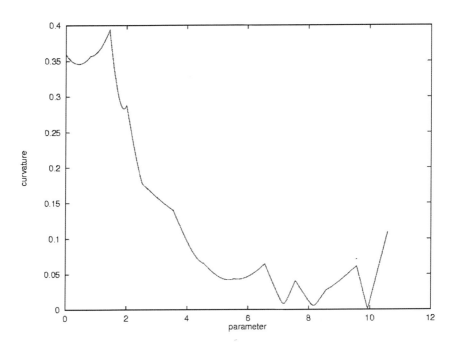

Figure 2b. The curvature distribution of the initial *chine3* curve.

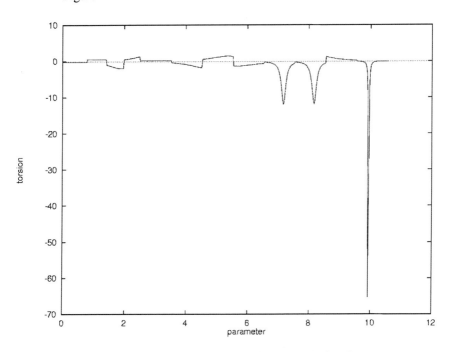

Figure 2c. The torsion distribution of the initial *chine3* curve

Note that, by anonymous ftp at the ftp-site of SDL-NTUA (ftp.deslab.naval.ntua.gr), the perspective benchmarker can have access to the FINAL ANNOUNCEMENT of the Benchmarking Experiment, containing the GENERAL RULES OF THE BENCHMARK as well as all necessary information for downloading the required data and software or uploading her/his own benchmark contribution to the proper ftp-site.

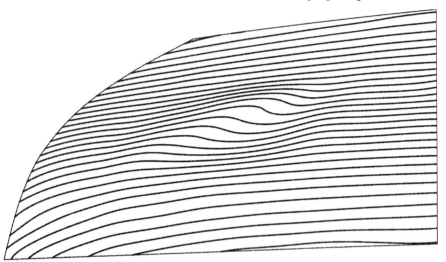

Figure 3. Benchmarking in the area of **Fairing:** the h*ood* patch, **provider:** Daimler Chrysler AG, **basic constraint:** improve the above isophote distribution of the patch at a maximum deviation of 1mm from the initial surface.

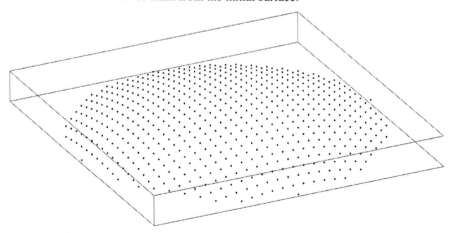

Figure 4. Benchmarking in the area of **Shape-Constrained Approximation:** the l*ens* data set, **provider:** University of Erlangen-Nuernberg, **basic constraint:** approximate the given point-set by a convex *B*-Spline patch at a maximum deviation of 0.005 mm.

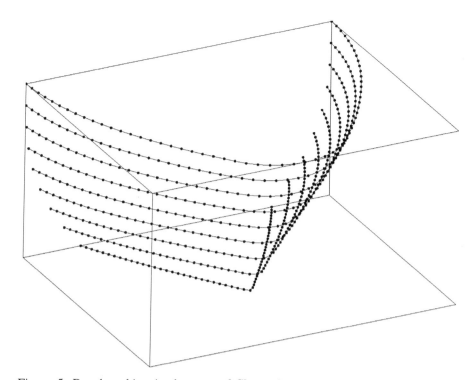

Figure 5. Benchmarking in the area of **Shape-Constrained Approximation**: the *watelines* data set, **provider:** KCS UK Ltd., **basic constraint:** constant-sign Gaussian curvature.

Ackowledgements

The authors would like to thank their partners in the FAIRSHAPE consortium (DaimlerChrysler AG, TU Darmstadt, Univ. Florence, Univ. Zaragoza, Univ. Leeds, Kockums Computer Systems UK Ltd., Univ. Dundee) for their contribution into materializing the strategic and technical aims of the project. In this connection, the financial support of the European Commission (Directorate General XII) is gratefully appreciated. On this occasion, the first of the authors would like to express his gratitude to Professor J. Hoschek (TU Darmstadt) for strengthening with his authority the initiative for establishing an HCM network on fairing and shape-preservation.

References

I. APPLEGARTH, P.D. KAKLIS and S. WAHL, (1999), *Benchmark Tests on the Generation of Fair Shapes subject to Constraints,* Teubner Stuttgart (to appear).

S. ASATURYAN, P. COSTANTINI and C. MANNI, (1998a), "G^2 Shape-Preserving Parametric Planar Curve Interpolation", in H. Nowacki and P.D. Kaklis (eds.): *Creating Fair and Shape-Preserving Curves and Surfaces,* Teubner Stuttgart, pp. 89-98.S.

ASATURYAN, P. COSTANTINI and C. MANNI, (1998b), "Shape-Preserving Interpolating Curves in R^3", in H. Nowacki and P.D. Kaklis (eds.): *Creating Fair and Shape-Preserving Curves and Surfaces,* Teubner Stuttgart, pp. 99-108.

M.I.G. BLOOR and M.J. WILSON, (1996), "Parametrizing Wing Surfaces using Partial Differential Equations", in J. Hoschek and P.D. Kaklis (eds.): *Advanced Course on Fairshape,* Teubner Stuttgart, pp. 161-173.

J. CARNICER and M.S. FLOATER, (1996a), "Co-convexity Preserving Curve Interpolation", in J. Hoschek and P.D. Kaklis (eds.): *Advanced Course on Fairshape,* Teubner Stuttgart, pp. 17-28.

J. CARNICER and M.S. FLOATER, (1996b), "Algorithms for Convexity Preserving Interpolation of Scattered Data", in J. Hoschek and P.D. Kaklis (eds.): *Advanced Course on Fairshape,* Teubner Stuttgart, pp. 171-184.

COSTANTINI and M.L. SAMPOLI, (1998), "Abstract Schemes and the Construction of Constrained Interpolating Curves", in H. Nowacki and P.D. Kaklis (eds.): *Creating Fair and Shape-Preserving Curves and Surfaces,* Teubner Stuttgart, pp. 121-130.

U. DIETZ, (1998a), "Fair Surface Reconstruction from Point Clouds", in M. Daehlen, T. Lyche and L.L. Schumaker (eds.): *Mathematical Methods for Curves and Surfaces,* Vanderbilt University Press, Nashville, pp. 1-8.

U. DIETZ, (1998b), "Creation of Fair *B*-spline Surface Fillets", in H. Nowacki and P.D. Kaklis (eds.): Creating Fair and Shape-Preserving Curves and Surfaces", Teubner Stuttgart, pp. 251-260.

T.P. GEROSTATHIS, K.G. KORAS and P.D. KAKLIS, (1999), "Numerical Experimentation with the Roulier-Rando Fairness Metrics", *Mathematical Engineering in Industry,* vol. 7, No. 2, pp. 195-210.

A. GINNIS, (1998), "Fair Fillet between Curves and its Extension to Surfaces", in H. Nowacki and P.D. Kaklis (eds.): *Creating Fair and Shape-Preserving Curves and Surfaces,* Teubner Stuttgart, pp. 2601-270.

T.N.T. GOODMAN, (1996), "Shape Preserving Interpolation by Planar Curves", in J. Hoschek and P.D. Kaklis (eds.): *Advanced Course on Fairshape,* Teubner Stuttgart, pp. 29-38.

T.N.T. GOODMAN and B.-H. ONG, (1996), "Shape Preserving Interpolation by Curves in Three Dimensions", in J. Hoschek and P.D. Kaklis (eds.): *Advanced Course on Fairshape,* Teubner Stuttgart, pp. 39-46.

J. HADENFELD, (1996), "Fairing of B-spline Curves and Surfaces", in J. Hoschek and P.D. Kaklis (eds.): *Advanced Course on Fairshape,* Teubner Stuttgart, pp. 59-75.

J. HOSCHEK and M. SCHNEIDER, (1997), "Interpolation and Approximation with developable Surfaces", in A. Le Mehaute, Ch. Rabut and L.L. Schumaker (eds.): *Curves and Surfaces with Applications in CAGD,* Vandebilt University Press, Nashville, pp. 185-202.

B. JUETTLER, (1997a), "Shape Preserving Least-Squares Approximation by Polynomial Parametric Spline Curves", *Computer Aided Geometric Design,* vol. 14, pp. 731-747.

B. JUETTLER, (1997b), "Surface Fitting Using Convex Tensor Product Splines", *Journal of Computational and Applied Mathematics,* vol. 84, pp. 23-44.

B. JUETTLER, (1997c), "Sectional Curvature Preserving Interpolation of Contour Lines", in A. Le Mehaute, C. Rabut und L.L. Schumaker (eds.): *Curves and Surfaces with Applications in CAGD,* Vanderbilt University Press, Nashville, pp. 203-210.

JUETTLER, (1997d), "Linear Convexity Conditions for Parametric Tensor-Product Bezier Surface Patches", in T.N.T. Goodman and R. Martin (eds.): *The Mathematics of Surfaces VII,* Information Geometers, Winchester, pp. 189-208.

B. JUETTLER, (1998a), "Convex Surface Fitting with Tensor-Product Bezier Surfaces", in M. Daehlen, T. Lyche and L.L. Schumaker (eds.): *Mathematical Methods for Curves and Surfaces IV,* Vanderbilt University Press, Nashville, pp. 263-270.

B. JUETTLER, (1998b) "Construction and Modification of Convex Parametric Spline Curves and Surfaces", in H. Nowacki and P.D. Kaklis (eds.): *Creating Fair and Shape-Preserving Curves and Surfaces,* Teubner Stuttgart, pp. 219-230.

A. IVES-SMITH, (1996), "A Comparative Study of two Curve Fairing Methods in Tribon Initial Design", in J. Hoschek and P.D. Kaklis (eds.): *Advanced Course on Fairshape,* Teubner Stuttgart, pp. 47-56.

P.D. KAKLIS and M.I. KARAVELAS, (1997), "Shape preserving Interpolation in R^3", *IMA Journal of Numerical Analysis,* vol. 17, No. 3, pp. 373-419.

P.D. KAKLIS and G.D. KORAS, (1997), "A Quadratic Programming Approach for Removing Shape Failures from Tensor Product B-spline Surfaces", *Computing Supplement,* vol. 13, No. 2, pp. 177-188.

G.D. KORAS and P.D. KAKLIS, (1999), "Convexity Conditions for Parametric Tensor-Product B-spline Surfaces", *Advances in Computational Mathematics,* vol. 10, No. 3-4, pp. 291-309.

H. NOWACKI, J. HEIMANN, E. MELISSARATOS AND S.-H. ZIMMERMANN, (1996), "Experiences in Curve Fairing", in J. Hoschek and P.D. Kaklis (eds.): *Advanced Course on FAIRSHAPE,* Teubner Stuttgart, pp. 9-16.

H. NOWACKI, G. WESTGAARD and J. HEIMANN, (1998), "Creation of Fair Surfaces Based on Higher Order Fairness Measures with Interpolation Constraints", in H. Nowacki and P.D. Kaklis (eds.): *Creating Fair and Shape-Preserving Curves and Surfaces,* Teubner Stuttgart, pp. 141-162.

K.G. PIGOUNAKIS and P.D. KAKLIS, (1996a), "Convexity-Preserving Fairing", *CAD,* vol. 28, No. 12, pp. 981-994.

K.G. PIGOUNAKIS, N.S. SAPIDIS and P.D. KAKLIS, (1996), "Fairing Spatial B-spline Curves", *Journal of Ship Research,* vol. 40, No. 4, pp. 351-367.

N.E. SEVANT, M.I.G. BLOOR and M.J. WILSON, (1998), "Aerodynamic Design of a Wing-Body Combination", in H. Nowacki and P. Kaklis (eds.): *Creating Fair and Shape-Preserving Curves and Surfaces,* Teubner Stuttgart, pp. 271-280.

G. WESTGAARD and J. HEIMANN, (1998), "Analysis and Visualisation of Geometric Curve Properties", in M. Daehlen, T. Lyche and L.L. Schumaker (eds.): *Mathematical Methods for Curves and Surfaces IV,* Vanderbilt University Press, Nashville.

VARIATIONAL PRINCIPLES FOR SURFACE GENERATION AND MODIFICATION WITH THE FUNCTIONAL OF THE CLAMPED PLATE

Alexa Nawotki

Department of Computer Science, University of Kaiserslautern, P.O. Box 3049, 67653 Kaiserslautern, Germany
nawotki@informatik.uni-kl.de

Abstract

Variational design is a frequently used method in CAD for the construction of smooth curves and surfaces. The objects are computed so that they minimise a special functional. This proceeding is based on the Hamiltonian Principle, a basic mechanical law. One possible choice is the functional of the clamped plate. The full physical derivation of this functional makes clear that it expresses in fact the stored energy in a surface. This functional naturally extends to a physically-based modification of surfaces as follows: It includes two parameters, which describe the material behaviour. They can be utilised as modification tools, if existence and uniqueness of the solution is still guaranteed, what in fact can be shown. The solution is computed with the Finite Element Method. An implementation was done with bicubic Bézier-functions on a rectangular grid. Finally, some figures show typical results of this approach.

1 Introduction

Variational design is a very popular method for the construction of high-quality curves and surfaces. For example, it can be utilised for the construction of smooth and streamlined ship hulls. Roughly speaking it delivers curves respectively surfaces from some boundary information. More exact a function is computed, which minimises a functional under some boundary conditions. How is this proceeding justified, and how can the solution be computed?

The physical and the mathematical answers to the first question are different at first glance, but they are just different views of the same thing: In physical terms, the minimisation is justified by the 'Hamiltonian Principle', and the functional must describe the energy stored in the object. The mathematical answer is determined by the demand that the related minimisation problem has to be uniquely solvable and that the given boundary information is sufficient for the computation of the solution.

If the functional and the boundary conditions are chosen following the described mathematical requests, existence and uniqueness can be shown, but very rarely the problem can be solved analytically, i.e. exactly. Different proceedings for the approximation of the solution are possible. Again, a glance at the theoretical background is very useful. It makes the possibilities and the consequences of this choice foreseeable. The surroundings, i.e. input format, aim of the computation, further applications, permissible costs, etc. are crucial for this decision.

Finally, one example is given that the background information gives new possibilities in the design process. Looking at the derivation of the functional that describes the energy stored in a thin, elastic, isotropic plate it is quite natural to ask what happens, if the material parameters in this functional are modified. It is demonstrated that this values can be used as intuitive modelling tools and all necessary technical steps are sketched.

2 Basics on Variational Design

Variational design determines a curve or surface so that it minimises a functional. The foundation of this proceeding is given in theoretical mechanics, namely by the

Hamiltonian Principle: *Let a mechanical system be described by functions q_i, i=1,...,n, where n is the number of degrees of freedom. The system between a fixed starting state $q_i(t_0)$ at starting time t_0 and a fixed final state $q_i(t_1)$ at final time t_1 moves in such a way that the functions $q_i(t)$ make the integral*

$$J = \int_{t_0}^{t_1} L(q_i(t), \dot{q}(t)) \, dt = \int_{t_0}^{t_1} \left(T(q_i(t), \dot{q}(t)) - U(q_i(t), \dot{q}(t)) \right) dt \tag{1}$$

stationary, compared with all functions $\tilde{q}_i(t)$, which fulfil equal boundary conditions.

T *is the kinetic energy,* U *the potential energy, and* L=T-U *the Lagrange function.*

For stationary problems, i.e. T=0, the Lagrange function coincides with the (negative) potential energy, and the functional J expresses an energy.

An almost equivalent formulation of the Hamiltonian principle is given by the system of Euler equations:

$$\frac{d}{dt}\left(\frac{\partial L}{\partial \dot{q}_i}\right) - \frac{\partial L}{\partial q_i} = 0, \quad i = 1,\ldots,n \tag{2}$$

'Almost equivalent' denotes that a solution of (2) solves (1), and vice versa, if the solution of (1) is sufficiently smooth for the required differentiations, it solves (2). Thus, the Euler equations are a little bit stricter than the Hamiltonian formulation.

It is necessary in both cases to have initial and/or boundary conditions for the computation of a solution.

One frequent choice for (2) is the biharmonic differential equation $\Delta^2 u = 0$. This equation has several advantages: The solution is a minimal surface, it is possible (and necessary) to include the function values and the first derivatives on the boundary in the computation, and these both boundary values are blended in a specific way: Let Ω be a bounded domain with piecewise smooth boundary, n the outer normal vector, Δ the Laplace operator $\partial^2/\partial x_i^2$, and G Green's function, i.e. it holds

$$\Delta^2 G = 0 \quad \text{in } \Omega/\{p\},$$
$$G = 0, \quad \text{and} \quad \frac{\partial G}{\partial n} = 0 \quad \text{on } \partial\Omega. \tag{3}$$

Then the following blending rule is valid for all $p \in \Omega$:

$$u(p) = \int_{\Omega} \left(u\Big|_{\partial\Omega} \frac{\partial(\Delta G)}{\partial n} - \Delta G \left(\frac{\partial u}{\partial n}\right)\Big|_{\partial\Omega} \right) ds. \tag{4}$$

It is not obvious at first glance, why the biharmonic differential equation is of the Euler type (2), but this can be recognised by the corresponding variational formulation:

$$J(\varsigma) = \frac{h^3}{24} \int \frac{E}{1-v^2} \left(\left(\frac{\partial^2 \varsigma}{\partial x^2} + \frac{\partial^2 \varsigma}{\partial y^2}\right)^2 - 2(1-v)\left(\frac{\partial^2 \varsigma}{\partial x^2}\frac{\partial^2 \varsigma}{\partial y^2} - \left(\frac{\partial^2 \eta}{\partial x \partial y}\right)^2\right) \right) dxdy \tag{5}$$

This functional expresses the strain energy of a thin, isotropic[1], clamped plate. h denotes the thickness of the plate, ς the deformation from the equilibrium state, and E and v are material constants. The next section includes the derivation of this functional from basic physical laws.

3 The Deduction of the Functional of the Clamped Plate

First the strain and the stress tensor are derived (3.1, 3.2). From those follows the expression of the internal energy of a surface element (3.3), and finally the energy of a thin, elastic, isotropic, clamped plate (3.4). (The functional can also be derived from a differential-geometrical background, see Nawotki and Hagen (1998a).)

---

[1] The material is homogeneous and without preferred direction.

3.1 The Strain Tensor

An elastic body changes its form and its volume, if outer forces effects it and it cannot switch over to translation and rotation. This behaviour is worded in formulas now:

Let the deformation vector u_i denotes the difference between the shifted co-ordinate $\bar{x}_i$ and the original co-ordinate x_i. Then the squared distance of two infinitesimal neighboured points changes from

$$dl^2 := \sum_i dx_i^2 \quad \text{to} \quad d\bar{l}^2 := \sum_i d\bar{x}_i^2 = \sum_i (dx_i + du_i)^2 \qquad (6)$$

by a deformation.

The last expression reformulates with the total differential $du_i = \bullet \ _j \partial u_i / \partial x_j \cdot dx_j$ as

$$\begin{aligned}
d\bar{l}^2 &= \sum_{i=1}^{3} \left(dx_i + \sum_{j=1}^{3} \frac{\partial u_i}{\partial x_j} dx_j \right)^2 \\
&= \sum_{i=1}^{3} \left(dx_i^2 + 2 \sum_{j=1}^{3} \frac{\partial u_i}{\partial x_j} dx_j dx_i + \left(\sum_{j=1}^{3} \frac{\partial u_i}{\partial x_j} dx_j \right)^2 \right) \\
&= \sum_{i=1}^{3} dx_i^2 + \sum_{i,j=1}^{3} \left(\frac{\partial u_i}{\partial x_j} dx_i dx_j + \frac{\partial u_i}{\partial x_j} dx_j dx_i \right) + \sum_{i,j,k=1}^{3} \frac{\partial u_i}{\partial x_j} \frac{\partial u_i}{\partial x_k} dx_j dx_k \\
&= dl^2 + 2 \sum_{i,j=1}^{3} u'_{ij} dx_i dx_j,
\end{aligned} \qquad (7)$$

with

$$u'_{ij} := \frac{1}{2} \left(\frac{\partial u_i}{\partial x_j} + \frac{\partial u_j}{\partial x_i} + \sum_{i=1}^{3} \frac{\partial u_k}{\partial x_i} \frac{\partial u_k}{\partial x_j} \right). \qquad (8)$$

The non-linear term can be neglected for small deformation, and thus the 'strain tensor' can be defined as

$$u_{ij} := \frac{1}{2} \left(\frac{\partial u_i}{\partial x_j} + \frac{\partial u_j}{\partial x_i} \right). \qquad (9)$$

Now all required information concerning the strain tensor is collected, and the examination of the next tensor can be started.

3.2 The Stress Tensor

In an elastic body two different types of forces exist and must hold up: volume-forces $\int_V \underline{F} dV$ and surface-forces $\int_{\partial V} \underline{P} df$. It is well-known from the Gaussian integral theorem that this is possible for continuous F_i if a '*stress tensor*' σ_{ij} exists with

$$F_i = \sum_{j=1}^{3} \frac{\partial \sigma_{ij}}{\partial x_j}. \tag{10}$$

From that follows for every component i

$$\int_{\partial V} P_i df = \int_V F_i dV = \int_V \sum_{j=1}^{3} \frac{\partial \sigma_{ij}}{\partial x_j} dV = \int_{\partial V} \sum_{j=1}^{3} \sigma_{ij} n_j df, \tag{11}$$

if $\underline{n}=(n_1, n_2, n_3)^T$ symbolises the outer normal. (11) holds for arbitrary volumes, and that yields

$$P_i = \sum_{j=1}^{3} \sigma_{ij} n_j. \tag{12}$$

The strain tensor is obviously symmetric, and the same is true for the stress tensor: If equation (10) is put in the definition of the angular momentum

$$M_{ij} = \int (F_i x_j - F_j x_i) dV, \tag{13}$$

it follows with the relation $\partial x_i / \partial x_j = \delta_{ij}$ and the Gaussian theorem

$$\begin{aligned} M_{ij} &= \int_V \left(\sum_{k=1}^{3} \frac{\partial \sigma_{ik}}{\partial x_k} x_j - \sum_{k=1}^{3} \frac{\partial \sigma_{jk}}{\partial x_k} x_i \right) dV \\ &= \int_V \sum_{k=1}^{3} \frac{\partial}{\partial x_k} (\sigma_{ik} x_j - \sigma_{jk} x_i) dV - \int_V (\sigma_{ij} - \sigma_{ji}) dV \\ &= \int_{\partial V} \sum_{k=1}^{3} (\sigma_{ik} x_j - \sigma_{jk} x_i) n_k df - \int_V (\sigma_{ij} - \sigma_{ji}) dV. \end{aligned} \tag{14}$$

The angular momentum has to be compensated by surface forces, i.e. it must be possible to reformulate the right hand side as a pure surface integral. That holds for all volumes and thus the volume-integral must vanish for all volumes. Therefore holds $\sigma_{ij}=\sigma_{ji}$. This is the desired symmetry relation, which is necessary in the derivation of the deformation energy.

3.3 The Internal Energy

The internal energy of a surface-element $d\underline{f}=\underline{n}\cdot df$ is the product of the force $\underline{P}df$ and the caused deformation $d\underline{u}$. Using relation (12) it can be written as

$$A_{df} = \underline{P}df\,d\underline{u} = \sum_{i=1}^{3} P_i du_i df = \sum_{i,j=1}^{3} \sigma_{ij} n_j du_i df. \qquad (15)$$

The Taylor theorem delivers together with (10), the relations $\partial(n_j df)/\partial x_j = 0$, $dx_i n_j df = \delta_{ij}\,dV$, and the denotation $O(.)$ for the Landau-symbol

$$A_{df}(x+dx) - A_{df}(x) = \sum_{k=1}^{3} \frac{\partial}{\partial x_k}\left(\sum_{i,j=1}^{3} \sigma_{ij} du_i n_j df\right) dx_k + \ddot{I}(dx^2)$$

$$= \sum_{i,j=1}^{3} \frac{\partial}{\partial x_j}\left(\sigma_{ij} du_i\right) dV + \ddot{I}(dx^2)$$

$$= \left(\sum_{i=1}^{3} F_i du_i + \sum_{i,j=1}^{3} \sigma_{ij} d\frac{\partial u_i}{\partial x_j}\right) dV + \ddot{I}(dx^2). \qquad (16)$$

The first term corresponds to the outer force, but the second is more interesting: It must be compensated inside the body. Thus the internal energy per volume dW is in linear accuracy

$$dW = \sum_{i=1}^{3} \sigma_{ii} d\frac{\partial u_i}{\partial x_i} + \sum_{\substack{i,j=1 \\ i<j}}^{3} \sigma_{ij} d\left(\frac{\partial u_i}{\partial x_j} + \frac{\partial u_j}{\partial x_i}\right)$$

$$= \sum_{i=1}^{3} \sigma_{ii} du_{ii} + 2\sum_{\substack{i,j=1 \\ i<j}}^{3} \sigma_{ij} du_{ij}$$

$$= \sum_{i,j=1}^{3} \sigma_{ij} du_{ij}. \qquad (17)$$

In the last step the symmetry relation of the stress tensor was used. Equation (17) implies the important formula

$$\frac{\partial W}{\partial u_{ij}} = \sigma_{ij}. \qquad (18)$$

Now we use the Taylor theorem for expanding the internal energy in terms of the strain tensor

$$W = W_0 + \sum_{i,j=1}^{3} \frac{\partial W}{\partial u_{ij}}(0) u_{ij} + \sum_{i,j,k,l=1}^{3} \frac{\partial^2 W}{\partial u_{ij} \partial u_{kl}}(0) u_{ij} u_{kl} + \ddot{I}(u^3). \qquad (19)$$

Only the inner forces are under examination, i.e. $\sigma_{ij}=0$, and therefore the linear term vanishes. Now, a simplification is used, namely only the quadratic terms with indices ii and ij are kept:

$$W = W_0 + \frac{1}{2}\sum_{i,j=1}^{3}\frac{\partial^2 W}{\partial u_{ii}\partial u_{jj}}(0)u_{ii}u_{jj} + \frac{1}{2}\sum_{i,j=1}^{3}\frac{\partial^2 W}{\partial u_{ij}^2}(0)u_{ij}^2. \tag{20}$$

For an isotropic body, the '*Lamé-coefficients*' are defined for arbitrary $i \neq j$, $i, j \in \{1, 2, 3\}$ by

$$\text{const.} = \frac{\partial^2 W}{\partial u_{ii}\partial u_{jj}}(0) =: \lambda,$$

$$\text{const.} = \frac{\partial^2 W}{\partial u_{ij}^2}(0) =: 2\mu. \tag{21}$$

This yields

$$W - W_0 = \frac{\lambda}{2}\left(\sum_{i=1}^{3}u_{ii}\right)^2 + \mu\sum_{i,j=1}^{3}u_{ij}^2. \tag{22}$$

Differentiating (22) according to u_{ij}, it follows for the stress tensor

$$\sigma_{ij} = \lambda\delta_{ij}\sum_{k=1}^{3}u_{kk} + 2\mu\, u_{ij} \quad \text{for} \quad i,j=1,\ldots,3. \tag{23}$$

Vice versa, the strain tensor depends on the stress tensor. Summing up the diagonal elements of σ_{ij}

$$\sum_{i=1}^{3}\sigma_{ii} = \sum_{i=1}^{3}\left(\lambda\delta_{ii}\sum_{j=1}^{3}u_{jj} + 2\mu\, u_{ii}\right)$$

$$= \sum_{i=1}^{3}\left(\lambda\sum_{j=1}^{3}u_{jj} + 2\mu\, u_{ii}\right)$$

$$= (3\lambda + 2\mu)\sum_{i=1}^{3}u_{ii} \tag{24}$$

yields with equation (23)

$$\sigma_{ij} = \delta_{ij}\frac{\lambda}{3\lambda+2\mu}\sum_{k=1}^{3}\sigma_{kk} + 2\mu\, u_{ij}. \tag{25}$$

A simple reformulation gives

$$u_{ij} = \frac{1}{2\mu}\sigma_{ij} - \delta_{ij}\frac{\lambda}{(3\lambda+2\mu)2\mu}\sum_{k=1}^{3}\sigma_{kk} \quad \text{for} \quad i,j=1,\ldots,3. \tag{26}$$

Now, the desired energy expression can be derived.

3.4 The Energy of the Clamped Plate

Compression and stretching are holding up in a neutral zone, which lies in the middle of a stressed plate. There a co-ordinate system is put up. The displacements from this plane depend only on x and y, approximately, and they are denoted • (x, y)=u_z.

The following assumptions are necessary and in linear accuracy admissible: The displacements in the xy-plane are neglectable, $u_x(x,y,z=0)=0=u_y(x,y,z=0)$. The surface-forces should vanish, too. The normal is approximately the normed z-axis, yielding $0=P_i =• _{iz}$. From (26) and these assumptions follows

$$0 = \acute{o}_{xz} = 2ì\, u_{xz},$$
$$0 = \acute{o}_{yz} = 2ì\, u_{yz},$$
$$0 = \acute{o}_{zz} = \ddot{e}(u_{xx} + u_{yy} + \frac{2ì + \ddot{e}}{\ddot{e}} u_{zz}). \tag{27}$$

The two first equations together with the definition of the strain tensor (9) lead to

$$\frac{\partial u_x}{\partial z} = -\frac{\partial u_z}{\partial x} = -\frac{\partial \varsigma}{\partial x},$$
$$\frac{\partial u_y}{\partial z} = -\frac{\partial u_z}{\partial y} = -\frac{\partial \varsigma}{\partial y}. \tag{28}$$

Integration with respect to z (from 0 to z) delivers

$$u_x = -z \frac{\partial \varsigma}{\partial x} \quad \text{and} \quad u_y = -z \frac{\partial \varsigma}{\partial y}. \tag{29}$$

It follows by differentiation, the equations (27), (29), and the definition (9)

$$u_{xx} = -z \frac{\partial^2 \varsigma}{\partial x^2},$$
$$u_{yy} = -z \frac{\partial^2 \varsigma}{\partial y^2},$$
$$u_{zz} = \frac{\ddot{e} z}{2ì + \ddot{e}} \left(\frac{\partial^2 \varsigma}{\partial x^2} + \frac{\partial^2 \varsigma}{\partial y^2} \right),$$
$$u_{xy} = \frac{1}{2} \left(\frac{\partial u_x}{\partial y} + \frac{\partial u_y}{\partial x} \right) = -z \frac{\partial^2 \varsigma}{\partial x \partial y},$$
$$u_{xz} = 0 = u_{xz}. \tag{30}$$

The desired functional for a thin, isotropic, homogeneous plate • is obtained by substituting these terms into the formula of the inner energy per volume

(22) and integrate with respect to z form –h/2 to h/2 (h is the thickness of the plate). The result is

$$J = \frac{h^3}{6} \int\int_\Omega \left(\frac{\ddot{e}+\dot{i}}{\ddot{e}+2\dot{i}} (\varsigma_{xx}+\varsigma_{yy})^2 - (\varsigma_{xx}\varsigma_{yy} - \varsigma_{xy}^2) \right) dxdy. \quad (31)$$

The Lamé-coefficients • and • are theoretical quantities without physical meaning. The next section describes two experimentally ascertained parameters, which can be used instead.

4 The Material Parameters

One material parameter is the modulus of elasticity or Young's modulus, E. It can be measured as the factor of proportionality between the strain • l_i/l_i and the stress P_i, i.e.

$$P_i =: E \frac{\ddot{A} l_i}{l_i}. \quad (32)$$

That is Hook's law, i.e. a linear relation between stress and strain is assumed. Additionally pressure is expected to shorten a body, and tension to make it longer that means, E > 0.

The second quantity, which is necessary to describe the behaviour of a stressed body, depicts that an object may change its size not only parallel (l), but also orthogonal (b) to the force direction. It is called *Poisson's ratio*, and is defined as

$$í := -\frac{\ddot{A}b/b}{\ddot{A}l/l}. \quad (33)$$

An extension in one direction causes a shortening in the other and vice versa, thus the minus sign guarantees that • is positive.

It is possible to compute an upper bound for • . Look at a rectangular box with width b and length l under tension. For small deformations hold

$$\begin{aligned} \ddot{A}V &= (b+\ddot{A}b)^2(l+\ddot{A}l) - b^2 l = \\ &= b^2 \ddot{A}l + 2bl\ddot{A}l + 2b\ddot{A}b\Delta l + \ddot{A}b^2 l + \ddot{A}b^2 \ddot{A}l = \\ &\approx b^2 \ddot{A}l + 2bl\ddot{A}l. \end{aligned} \quad (34)$$

This yields to

$$\frac{\ddot{A}V}{V} \approx \frac{b^2 \ddot{A}l + 2bl\ddot{A}b}{b^2 l} = \frac{\ddot{A}l}{l} + 2\frac{\ddot{A}b}{b} = \frac{\ddot{A}l}{l}(1-2í). \quad (35)$$

Assuming that under tension the volume of a body does not get smaller, i.e., $0 \leq \Delta V/V$, it follows $0 \leq \nu \leq \frac{1}{2}$.

The following table shows typical sizes of the material. It proves that both constants are independent from each other.

E	ν	material
10^6 N/m²	-	caoutchouc
$1.6 \cdot 10^{10}$ N/m²	0.44	lead
$7.5 \cdot 10^{10}$ N/m²	0.17	glass
$21 \cdot 10^{10}$ N/m²	0.28	steel
$52.8 \cdot 10^{10}$ N/m²	0.26	iridium

The connection to the theoretical coefficients can be established by an example: Let the examined body be a cube and its faces define a Cartesian coordinate system. A force operates parallel to the z-axis, i.e. $p = \sigma_{zz}$, and all other tensor coefficients vanishes. From equation (26) follows

$$u_{xx} = -\frac{\lambda}{(3\lambda + 2\mu)2\mu} p = u_{yy},$$

$$u_{zz} = \frac{\lambda + \mu}{(3\lambda + 2\mu)\mu} p, \qquad (36)$$

and the mixed coefficients are zero.

For infinitesimal deformations hold $\sigma \cdot l_i/l_i \to u_{ii}$. Thus this situation is represented with the new material parameters from the definitions (32) and (33) as $p = \sigma_{zz} = E u_{zz}$, and $u_{xx} = u_{yy} = -\nu u_{zz}$. After some lengthy computations this yields

$$E = \frac{(3\lambda + 2\mu)\mu}{\lambda + \mu}, \qquad \nu = \frac{\lambda}{2(\lambda + \mu)},$$

$$\lambda = \frac{E\nu}{(1 - 2\nu)(1 + \nu)}, \qquad \mu = \frac{E}{2(1 + \nu)}. \qquad (37)$$

If the Lamé-coefficients in (31) are replaced by these parameters, one gets the function of the clamped plate formulated as in (5).

In the standard case the material parameters are constant everywhere. By making these values location-dependent, a new modelling tool is constructed. But before this approach can be tested, it must be shown that an unique solution exists, even if the material parameters vary over the space of definition. This modification of the functional of the clamped plate is called 'polytropic' from now on.

5 The Existence and Uniqueness of the Solution

Let Ω be a non-empty, open, and bounded subset of $\Re^n$. Then

$$\|v\|_m := \sqrt{\sum_{|á|=m} \int_{\Omega} \left(\partial^á v\right)^2 dx} \tag{38}$$

is a norm, and

$$|v|_m := \sqrt{\sum_{|á|=m} \int_{\Omega} \left(\partial^á v\right)^2 dx} \tag{39}$$

a semi-norm. The closure of C_0^∞ respectively the norm $\| \cdot \|_m$ is a Hilbert space, the so-called Sobolev space of order m, $H_0^m(\cdot)$.

The limitation of Ω, which is trivial for most application, is theoretically essential. For example, it allows the following statement to be checked easily (just partial integration):

Lemma. *Let Ω be a bounded, non-empty, open subset of $\Re^n$. For all $v \in H_0^2(\Omega)$,*

$$|v|_2 = \|Äv\|_{L^2(\Omega)} |Äv|_0. \tag{40}$$

Now, the existence and uniqueness of the solution of the polytropic functional of the clamped plate can be shown using the following theorem.

Lax-Milgram Theorem. *Let H be a Hilbert-space and a: H x H $\to \Re$ an H-elliptic bilinear form (i.e. $a(\cdot,\cdot)$ is continuous and $a(v, v) \geq C \cdot \|v\|$ for a positive constant C). The variational problem*

$$J(v) = \frac{1}{2} a(v, v) - l(v) \to \min_{\{v \in H\}} \tag{41}$$

has exactly one solution for every $l \in H^*$.

Thus it must be shown that the bilinear form $a(\cdot,\cdot)$, which belong to the polytropic functional of the clamped plate, is continuous and $H_0^2(\Omega)$-elliptic.

Corollary. *Let $0 \leq v(x) < 1$, $E(x) \cdot h^3/(24(1-v^2(x))) > 0$ be continuous and real-valued functions on $\Re^n$, and Ω a bounded, open, non-empty subset of $\Re^n$. Then the bilinear form*

$$a(u, v) = \int_{\Omega} \frac{E(x)h^3}{24\left(1-í^2(x)\right)} \left(í(x) Äu Äv + (1-í(x)) \sum_{i,j=1}^{n} u_{ij} v_{ij} \right) dx \tag{42}$$

is continuous and $H_0^2(\Omega)$-elliptic in $H_0^2(\Omega)$.

Proof: It is sufficient to establish the statements for $u, v \in C_0^\infty(\Omega)$, because this set is dense in $H_0^2(\Omega)$. In the following let x_i denote a point in Ω and C_i a positive constant.

- *Continuity:* First the triangle-inequality is used for the separation of the fraction. Then the Mean Value Theorem for integrals, which holds for positive, continuous functions, allows to move this term in front of the integral.

$$|a(u,v)| = \left| \int_{Ù} \frac{E(x)h^3}{24(1-í^2(x))} \left(í(x)Äu\,Äv + (1-í(x))\sum_{i,j=1}^{n} u_{ij}v_{ij} \right) dx \right|$$

$$\leq \int_{Ù} \left| \frac{E(x)h^3}{24(1-í^2(x))} \right| \cdot \left| í(x)Äu Äv + (1-í(x))\sum_{i,j=1}^{n} u_{ij}v_{ij} \right| dx$$

$$= \left| \frac{E(x_1)h^3}{24(1-í^2(x_1))} \right| \int_{Ù} \left| í(x)Äu Äv + (1-í(x))\sum_{i,j=1}^{n} u_{ij}v_{ij} \right| dx \quad (43)$$

The first term in brackets is cut short as C_1.

Then the arguments are repeated. The remaining terms which contain material parameters are separated using the triangle inequality, and the Mean Value Theorem for integrals is utilised to move these terms in front of the integrals:

$$|a(u,v)| \leq C_1 \int_{Ù} \left(í(x)|Äu|\cdot|Äv| + (1-í(x))\sum_{i,j=1}^{n} |u_{ij}|\cdot|v_{ij}| \right) dx$$

$$= C_1 \left(í(x_2)\int_{Ù} |Äu|\cdot|Äv|dx + (1-í(x_3))\int_{Ù} \sum_{i,j=1}^{n} |u_{ij}|\cdot|v_{ij}| \right) dx \quad (44)$$

With the inequality of Cauchy-Schwarz this relation can be rewritten using the $L^2(\Omega)$-norm. Here the absolute values can be neglected, because inside the norm appear real-valued squared functions, only.

$$|a(u,v)| \leq C_2 \|Äu\|_{L^2(\Omega)} \|Äv\|_{L^2(\Omega)} + C_3 \sum_{i,j=1}^{n} \|u_{ij}\|_{L^2(\Omega)} \|v_{ij}\|_{L^2(\Omega)} \quad (45)$$

For the first term the lemma from above is used and the second is estimated with the semi-norm.

$$|a(u,v)| \leq C_2 |u|_2 |v|_2 + C_3 n^2 |u|_2 |v|_2$$

$$\leq C_4 \|u\|_2 \|v\|_2 \quad (46)$$

Therefore, $a(.,.)$ is continuous.

- *Ellipticity:* Since $\partial^i v \in H_0^1(\Omega)$, constants $F_i > 0$ follow by the Poincaré-Friedrich inequality such that

$$\sqrt{\sum_{j=1}^{n} \|\partial^j \partial^i v\|_{L^2(\Omega)}^2} = |\partial^i v|_1 \geq F_i \|\partial^i v\|_{L^2(\Omega)}. \quad (47)$$

For $F:=\min_{\{i=1,\ldots,n\}}\{F_i^2\}$. Then the above estimate and Poincaré-Friedrich yield

$$|v|_2^2 = \sqrt{\sum_{i=1}^n \sum_{j=1}^n \|\partial^j(\partial^i v)\|_{L^2(\Omega)}^2} \geq \sum_{i=1}^n F_i^2 \|\partial^i v\|_{L^2(\Omega)}^2 \geq F \sum_{i=1}^n \|\partial^i v\|_{L^2(\Omega)}^2$$
$$= F|v|_1^2 \geq G\|v\|_{L^2(\Omega)}^2 \tag{48}$$

for some constant G>0. Altogether, the result is a positive constant H with

$$|v|_2^2 = \frac{1}{3}\left(|v|_2^2 + |v|_2^2 + |v|_2^2\right) \geq \frac{1}{3}\sum_{i,j=1}^n \|\partial^{ij} v\|_{L^2(\Omega)}^2 + \frac{1}{3}F\sum_{i=1}^n \|\partial^i v\|_{L^2(\Omega)}^2 + \frac{1}{3}G\|v\|_{L^2(\Omega)}^2$$
$$\geq H\|v\|_2^2. \tag{49}$$

The Mean Value Theorem for integrals for the material terms again, yields

$$a(v,v) = \frac{E(x_4)h^3}{24(1-\hat{\imath}^2(x_4))}\left(\hat{\imath}(x_5)\int_{\hat{U}} (\ddot{A}v)^2 dx + (1-\hat{\imath}(x_6))\int_{\hat{U}} \sum_{i,j=1}^n v_{ij}^2 dx\right) =$$
$$= C_5 \|\ddot{A}v\|_{L^2(\Omega)}^2 + C_6 |v|_2^2. \tag{50}$$

With the lemma and (48) follows that

$$a(v,v) = C_5 |v|_2^2 + C_6 |v|_2^2 \geq C_7 \|v\|_2^2. \tag{51}$$

This completes the proof.

Now we know that it is admissible to use the material parameters as forming tools for the surface, because of the above Corollary for n=2. The practical realisation verifies that the elongation due to internal stress can be raised making the material locally softer or weakened by making it stiffer. The next section describes the technical proceeding.

6 Computation of the Solution

In the last section it turned out that the fitting solution space for this problem is the Sobolev-space $H_0^2(\bullet)$. This space is complete, but unfortunately infinitely dimensional. Thus only an approximate solution can be computed, for example with the Finite Element Method (6.1). An unusual choice of the base functions (6.2) modifies the construction of the elementary (6.3) and the stiffness matrix (6.4).

6.1 The Finite Element Method

First, the infinite dimensional space $H_0^2(\bullet)$ is restricted to a finite dimensional subspace S_h. Then the problem is solved in this smaller space. (The Lax-Milgram Theorem guarantees existence and uniqueness in the subspace too, as long as it is complete.)

For the approximate solution w_h of the variational problem must hold

$$a(v, w_h) = l(v) \quad \text{for all} \quad v \in S_h. \tag{52}$$

Let $\{\bullet_1, \ldots, \bullet_N\}$ be a base of S_h. Because of the linearity of $a(.,.)$ the last equation is equivalent to the system

$$a(\ddot{O}_i, w_h) = l(\ddot{O}_i) \quad \text{for all} \quad i = 1, \ldots, N. \tag{53}$$

If the approximate solution is written in this base as well, i.e.

$$w_h = \sum_{j=1}^{N} z_j \ddot{O}_j \quad \text{for some} \quad z_j \in \Re, \tag{54}$$

it follows

$$\sum_{i=1}^{N} a(\ddot{O}_i, \ddot{O}_j) z_j = l(\ddot{O}_i) \quad \text{for all} \quad i = 1, \ldots, N. \tag{55}$$

That is, expressed as a matrix

$$Az = c \quad \text{with}$$
$$A_{ij} := a(\ddot{O}_i, \ddot{O}_j) \quad \text{for} \quad i, j = 1, \ldots, N,$$
$$z^T := (z_1, \ldots, z_N), \quad \text{and} \quad c^T := \bigl(l(\ddot{O}_1), \ldots, l(\ddot{O}_N)\bigr). \tag{56}$$

A is called the *stiffness matrix*, and the proceeding *'Ritz method'*. The problem has been reduced to a finite, quadratic system of linear equations. If this system is invertible, it is uniquely solvable, and the approximate solution can be computed with standard numerical methods.

A particular kind of the Ritz method is the Finite Element Method. It is marked by the special choice of the base functions $\bullet_i$ of the solving subspace S_h: First the domain of definition is divided up in many pieces, which can easily transformed onto one element only, in two dimensions usually squares or triangles. Next, the restriction of the base on every element has to be a polynomial (this makes the computations simple), the support of it must be included in 'few' elements (that guarantees a thin matrix) and the base functions must be included in the theoretical solving space.

Let T_h denotes the triangulation, then the stiffness matrix can be divided up according to

$$A_{ij} = a(\ddot{O}_i, \ddot{O}_j) = \sum_{T \in T_h} a(\ddot{O}_i|_T, \ddot{O}_j|_T) =: \sum_{T \in T_h} A_{ij}(T). \quad (57)$$

If T' denotes the model element, then $A_{ij}(T')$ is called the *'elementary matrix'*. Only this matrix must be computed. Then the result is mapped from T' onto every other element and all the matrices are added up to the stiffness matrix A. Now, which triangulation, and which base functions should be used for the solution of the functional of the polytropic, clamped plate?

6.2 The Choice of the Base Functions

The base functions must lie in the solving space $H_0^2(\bullet)$, and they should be polynomials on every element of the triangulation. It is possible to use C^1-splines, or splines of higher continuity, for treating the functional of the clamped plate (5): C^1-splines are C^∞-continuous everywhere except at the knots/boundaries. There the limits from left and right hand side have finite differences only. These finite values appear on a set of measure zero, and thus they do not influence the result of the integration. Thus, C^1-splines are included in the closure of C_0^∞ respectively the norm $\bullet .\bullet_2$, i.e. they are included in $H_0^2(\bullet)$.

The higher the established continuity, the higher is the required degree of the polynomials and the computation costs raise with the degree too. Thus C^1-continuity is chosen. Triangles can be used as elements, but then polynomials of degree five are necessary to ensure C^1-continuity. If a rectangular grid is chosen, bicubic polynomials are sufficient for the desired smoothness.

Depart from the standard proceeding, Bézier-functions are used as base in the Finite Element approach, because a conversion of the solution to a CAD/CAM-representation would be necessary otherwise. That changes the construction of the matrices slightly. First of all, the matrix for one rectangle must be computed.

6.3 The Elementary Matrix

The starting point is a simplification of the bilinear form in (42). The factor $h^3/24$ is neglected, because it is a global factor and never influences the minimisation. The material parameters shall serve as forming tools, but unfortunately they are in rational form. Therefore the ratios $E/(1-\bullet^2)$ and $E/(1+\bullet)$ are simplified by deducing them as geometric series and stopping with the quadratic term. This is admissible, because v is small. The functions $E(x, y)$ and $\bullet(x, y)$ are supposed to change linearly, thus a bilinear approach is used for both parameters.

Let $Ö_i, i = 1,\ldots,K$ be the base function of the Finite Element space and $u_h = \sum Ö_j z_j$ the approximate solution according to the grid with index h. Putting u_h in formula (42) with simplified material parameters and minimising the energy varying the coefficient z_k delivers

$$0 = 2\sum_{i=1}^{K} z_i \int_{T'} E(x,y) \left(\left(\frac{\partial^2 Ö_i}{\partial x^2} \frac{\partial^2 Ö_k}{\partial x^2} + \frac{\partial^2 Ö_i}{\partial y^2} \frac{\partial^2 Ö_k}{\partial y^2} + 2 \frac{\partial^2 Ö_i}{\partial x \partial y} \frac{\partial^2 Ö_k}{\partial x \partial y} \right) + \right.$$
$$\left. E(x,y) í(x,y) \left(\frac{\partial^2 Ö_i}{\partial y^2} \frac{\partial^2 Ö_k}{\partial x^2} + \frac{\partial^2 Ö_i}{\partial x^2} \frac{\partial^2 Ö_k}{\partial y^2} - 2 \frac{\partial^2 Ö_i}{\partial x \partial y} \frac{\partial^2 Ö_k}{\partial x \partial y} \right) \right) dxdy. \quad (58)$$

If the material parameters $E(x, y)$ and $•(x, y)$ are polynomial functions, the following integrals must be solved

$$\iint x^n y^m \left(\frac{\partial}{\partial x}\right)^i \left(\frac{\partial}{\partial y}\right)^j Ö_p(x,y) \left(\frac{\partial}{\partial x}\right)^k \left(\frac{\partial}{\partial y}\right)^l Ö_q(x,y) \, dxdy \quad (59)$$

with $i+j=2$, $k+l=2$, $i, j, k, l \in \{0, 1, 2\}$, $p, q \in \{1,\ldots,K\}$, and $n, m \in \{0, 1, 2\}$.

Bézier-functions are used as base $•_i$, and thus the derivatives of a Bernstein-polynomial

$$B_i^n = \binom{n}{i}(1-t)^{n-i} t^i \quad (60)$$

are required. They can be expressed as differences of Bernstein-polynomials B_j^{n-1}. Thus (59) can be computed using the easy to verify equation

$$\int_0^1 B_i^n(t) B_j^m(t) t^k \, dt = \frac{1}{n+m+k+1} \frac{\binom{n}{i}\binom{m}{j}}{\binom{n+m+k}{i+j+k}}. \quad (61)$$

In the main, some binomial coefficients (with not higher faculties than 8!) must be computed and combined for the computation of the elementary matrix.

These calculations must be done for every grid element and then all contributions are summed up to the global stiffness matrix.

6.4 The Stiffness Matrix

The boundary values reduce the size of the stiffness matrix, because every value fixes a coefficient z_j, which must not be minimised any longer and must be erased with the corresponding row/column from the linear system of equations.

The establishment of the required continuity is slightly different from the standard case, where monomial base functions are used. C^0-continuity demands that the first coefficients of the new element coincides with the last coefficient of the old one. Thus both accompanying rows/columns are added and replaced by their sum. C^1-continuity requires that the next coefficient of the new element is a linear combination of the both last of the old one. Therefore the row/column belonging to the new element coefficient are erased and (with the appropriate scaling factor) added to the both others.

Altogether this yields a linear system of equations of size 4·number of elements, and the system is sparse with band-structure. The next section describes the result of these computations.

7 Physically Based Modification of Surfaces

Local different sizes of the modulus of elasticity E and of Poisson's ratio • simulates a plate consisting of distinct materials. The idea is to modify the surface by changing the material parameter in the functional. The effect of the internal stress is raised by the parameters of soft material or weakened by the parameters of a stiffer one. So the appearance of the face can be modelled illustrative and simple, without loosing the minimisation property and the connection to 'real' shapes.

The following figures show the influences of some modifications. All figures are zoomed to that size, which fits best in the picture-frame. If a parameter value is not mentioned, it is 1 [unit] for E respectively 0.25 for • . The first two figures show the result of a global change of Poisson's ratio. The global rising of • from 0.25 to 10 makes the material softer and therefore the deepening is increased.

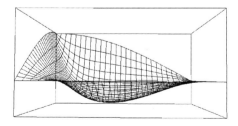
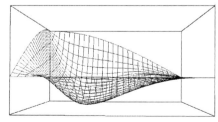

Figure 1: starting face   Figure 2: • =10

The second pair shows the result, if the natural limit of a material constant is exceeded. (It should be mentioned that this boundary exists as well from physical considerations (compare section 4) as from the existence and uniqueness proof. There was required that for the material parameters hold $0 \leq v < 1$ and $E > 0$ (compare section 5)).

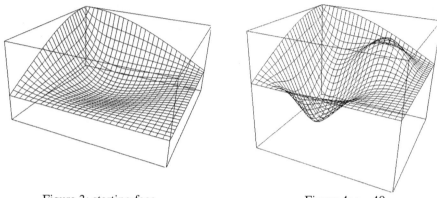

Figure 3: starting face   Figure 4: • =40

Figure 4 shows the surface for • =40, which is very much larger than both bounds and out of every mechanical meaning. But this seems so only, because the absolute size is just of relative expressiveness. The one-to-one correspondence to the real material parameters was lost by the simplification of the fraction terms (see 6.3).

If E is raised, no modification of the face appears at all. The factor does not influence the minimisation, because it can be cancelled out in the computation from the very beginning. (Of course, the physics behind is different; varying forces are necessary to produce the same boundary conditions for different material parameters).

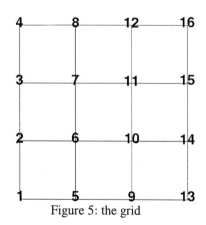

Figure 5: the grid

In the last examples the parameters are manipulated at the knots of an equidistant grid with 3x3 elements. The knots are ordered from bottom to top and from left to right, as sketched in figure 5.

Again, the original surface is the one in figure 3.

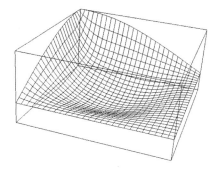 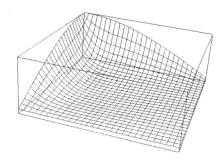

Figure 6: $E_7=10$ Figure 7: $E_6=E_7=10$, $E_{10}=E_{11}=100$

The last two figures show the differences between the starting face and the modified surfaces. Local changes causes local deformations. It can be seen that the maximal change is at the place, where the material parameter was modified, but other points may move, too (note that the z-axis in the last two pictures is scaled with the factor 10).

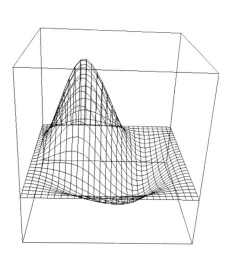 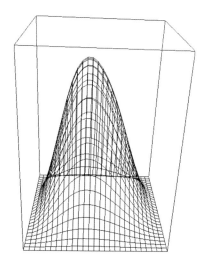

Figure 8: $E_7=10$ Figure 9: $E_6=E_7=10$, $E_{10}=E_{11}=100$

References

H. HAGEN, S. HEINZ and A. NAWOTKI, (1997), "Variational Design with Boundary Conditions and Parameter Optimized Surface Fitting", *Geometric Modeling: Theory and Practice*, Strasser, Klein and Rau (Eds.), Springer, pp. 3-13.

H. HAGEN and A. NAWOTKI, (1998), "Variational Design and Parameter Optimized Surface Fitting", *Geometric Modelling, Computing Supplement 13*, G. Farin, H. Bieri, G. Brunett, and t. DeRose, Springer, pp. 121-134.

A. NAWOTKI, (1995), "Konstruktion von Bézierflächen aus der Plattengleichung mit variablen Materialparametern", University of Kaiserslautern, master thesis.

A. NAWOTKI and H. HAGEN, (1998a), "Physically Based Modeling", *Creating Fair and Shape Preserving Curves and Surfaces*, H. Nowacki and P. Kaklis, Teubner, pp. 133-139.

A. NAWOTKI and H. HAGEN, (1998), "Simulation-Based Modeling", *Approximation Theory IX, Volume II, Computational Aspects*, C. Chui and L. Schumaker (Eds), Nashville, pp. 243-250.

A. NAWOTKI and H. HAGEN, (1998), "Surface Generation in a Simulation Based Modelling Process", *Automotive Mechatronics Design and Engineering*, D. Roller (Ed), pp. 443-449.